Collins

CAPE® REVISION GUIDE
ACCOUNTING

Carl Herrera & Lystra Stephens-James

Collins

HarperCollins Publishers Ltd
The News Building
1 London Bridge Street
London SE1 9GF

First edition 2015

10 9 8 7 6 5

© HarperCollins *Publishers* Limited 2015

ISBN 978-0-00-811605-7

www.collins.co.uk/caribbeanschools

A catalogue record for this book is available from the British Library.

Typeset by QBS
Printed by CPI Group (UK) Ltd, Croydon CR0 4YY

Authors: Lystra Stephens-James and Carl Herrera
Publisher: Elaine Higgleton
Commissioning Editor: Tom Hardy
Managing Editor: Sarah Thomas
Copy Editor: Sylvia Worth
Proofreaders: Carol Osborne and Stephen York

Acknowledgements
p1: Michael Utech/Getty Images, p10: Nednapa Sopasuntorn/Shutterstock, p24: StockLite/Shutterstock, p32: Peeter Viisimaa/iStockphoto, p36: PzAxe/Shutterstock, p48: Michaeljung/Shutterstock, p60: Iofoto/Shutterstock, p75: Monkey Business Images/Shutterstock, p85: Potstock/Shutterstock, p96: Casper1774 Studio/Shutterstock, p107: Thomas Coex/Staff/Getty Images, p110: DCPhoto/Alamy, p115: istidesign/Shutterstock, p121: Enviromantic/iStockphoto, p128: Gallo Images - Flamingo Photography/Getty Images, p138: Monkey Business Images/Shutterstock, p147: Blend Images/Shutterstock, p156: ArtistAllen/iStockphoto, p164: Jose Luis Pelaez Inc/Getty Images, p171: Patrick Hertzog/AFP/Getty Images, p179: Romakoma/Shutterstock, p187: From2015/iStockphoto, p194: JGI/Tom Grill/Getty Images, p206: Andrey Popov/Shutterstock, p219: Charts and BG/Shutterstock, p232: Bao Feifei/Xinhua Press/Corbis

Contents

Preface iv

Guidelines for revision iv

Key content areas of accounting v

Unit 1: Financial accounting
Module 1: Accounting theory, recording and control systems

    1. Accounting fundamentals 1

    2. Recording financial information 10

    3. Accounting and administrative controls systems 24

Module 2: Preparation of financial statements

    4. Forms of business organisations 32

    5. Preparation and presentation of statement of
comprehensive income (income statement) and
statement of retained earnings 36

    6. Preparation of financial statements 48

    7. Accounting for partnerships 60

Module 3: Financial reporting and interpretation

    8. Preparation of cash flow statement (indirect method only) 75

    9. Financial statement analysis: ratios 85

    10. Notes, disclosures and post balance sheet events, receivership and liquidation 96

Unit 2: Cost and management accounting
Module 1: Costing principles

    11. Introduction to cost and management accounting 107

    12. Manufacturing accounts preparation 110

    13. Cost classification and cost curves 115

    14. Elements of cost: materials 121

    15. Elements of cost: labour 128

    16. Elements of cost: overheads 138

    17. Decision-making 147

Module 2: Costing systems

    18. Traditional costing vs. Activity based costing 156

    19. Job costing 164

    20. Process costing 171

    21. Service sector costing 179

    22. Marginal costing vs. Absorption costing techniques 187

Module 3: Planning and decision-making

    23. Budgeting 194

    24. Standard costing and variances 206

    25. Cost volume profit (CVP) analysis 219

    26. Capital budgeting techniques in investment decision-making 232

    Answers for multiple choice questions 248

    Index 250

Preface

The first edition of the CAPE Accounting Revision Guide is produced for students preparing to sit the Caribbean Examinations Council (CXC) accounting examinations.

This guide reviews the content of both Units 1 and 2 of the syllabus. Each chapter begins with a preview of the material covered in that chapter. In addition, we feature 'Key points to note' and there are 'Test your knowledge' exercises within each major section of the chapters. As an additional feature, multiple choice questions are included at the end of each chapter, with answers supplied in a separate section at the end of this Revision Guide.

We wish to express our heartfelt thanks to our colleague and dear friend, Mr Rainer Ali for editing our manuscript. In addition, we thank our families and friends for the support which allowed us to complete this Revision Guide.

Carl Herrera
Lystra B. Stephens-James

Guidelines for revision

Revision strategy

There are many different ways of learning and so this Revision Guide offers you a number of tools to help you through. The following suggestions may be helpful:

- Believe in yourself. This is important. Yes, it is a challenge. But **you can succeed**.
- Remember the reason why you are doing it.
- Plan ahead. Make your plan work by developing a detailed study plan.
- Use the latest syllabus for guidance on the structure of the examination, the number of papers, the length of each paper, marks allocated to each question and the structure of the School Based Assessment.
- You need to grasp the details of the syllabus. Retain everything because this will help you to better understand. Make sure you understand the Key Content areas of each module. These are listed below.
- Read the online school reports.
- If you find parts of your course content are challenging, try and master these sections.
- Work in groups with your peers. Try 'teaching' key concepts and processes to a friend.
- Get help from your teachers.
- Take notes. Use your own notes as a guide. Draw mind maps. Also give yourself cues to identify concepts and processes.
- Keep reviewing your work. This will ensure that you have grasped all of the essentials.

Cues

For practical questions:

1. State the technique or formula you plan to use.
2. Ensure you use the information from the question in applying the relevant technique or formula.
3. If required, interpret the outcome of the calculation or technique.

Key content areas of accounting

These listings are the key content areas in CAPE Accounting. They are all explained in the chapters of the Revision Guide. It is important that you understand each of them.

UNIT 1. Module 1: Accounting theory, recording and control systems

1. The nature and scope of financial accounting
2. Accounting methods
3. Accounting standards
4. Conceptual Framework of Accounting
5. Recording financial information
6. Accounting and administrative control systems
7. Technology and financial accounting

UNIT 1. Module 2: Preparation of financial statements

1. Forms of business organisations
2. Advantages and disadvantages of the various business organisations
3. Statement of comprehensive income (income statement) preparation
4. Statement of changes in equity
5. Statement of financial position (balance sheet) preparation
6. Preparation of financial statements from incomplete records
7. Income and expenditure accounts
8. Accounting for changes in partnerships
9. Incorporation of an unincorporated business
10. Accounting for changes in corporations
11. Corporation tax

UNIT 1. Module 3: Financial reporting and interpretation

1. Disclosure requirements relating to social and ethical issues in financial reporting
2. Inflation and accounting
3. Contingencies and events after the end of the reporting period
4. Published financial statement
5. Preparation of statements of cash flow (indirect method only)
6. Ratio analysis
7. Limitations of financial statements
8. Analysis of performance
9. Liquidation and receivership

UNIT 2. Module 1: Costing principles

1. Introduction to cost and management accounting
2. Cost and management accounting vs Financial accounting
3. Manufacturing accounts
4. Labour costs
5. Remuneration
6. Cost classification
7. Cost curves
8. Material control
9. Inventory or stock valuation methods
10. Economic order quantity
11. Overhead costs
12. Principles and methods of calculating costs

UNIT 2. Module 2: Costing systems

1. Costing systems
2. Job costing
3. Activity-based costing
4. Process costing
5. The application of costing systems to the services industry
6. Marginal costing and absorption costing
7. Income statements

UNIT 2. Module 3: Planning and decision-making

1. Budgeting
2. Master budget
3. Standard costing
4. Variance analysis
5. Cost volume profit analysis
6. Capital budgeting techniques
7. Investment decision-making

In the Examination Room

Remember the following points as you walk into the Examination Room.

1. Have a positive attitude. Relax. Remain calm and confident.
2. Work with your calculators.
3. Read ALL instructions carefully.
4. Be sure that you know EXACTLY what the question is asking.
5. Make a plan for answering each question.
6. Make sure you use the correct principle or technique that directly relates to the question asked.
7. Manage your time wisely. Allocate time for each question.
8. Answer ALL the questions.
9. Review your answers before you hand in the answer booklet to the invigilator. Ensure that you:
   a. Number the responses (including the sections) in your answer booklet as they are numbered in the question paper.
   b. Secure your answer sheets.

Chapter 1

Accounting fundamentals

Objectives

At the end of this chapter you will be able to:

- describe the nature, scope and limitations of financial accounting
- describe the steps of the accounting cycle
- discuss accounting methods for recording financial information
- justify the use of standards in accounting
- discuss why the IFRS for SMEs was developed
- discuss the conceptual framework of accounting.

The development of accounting

Recording and communicating economic events occurred through the ages in narrative form in many of the early civilisations. In 1494, Luco Pacioli, an Italian, described the double entry system of debit (Dr) and credit (Cr) to be recorded in journals and ledgers. That system has remained basically the same today. 'Financial accounting deals with recording, summarising and communicating economic events of entities based on established principles, standards and legislation.' (Caribbean Examination Council, 2012, p. 1) These established principles, standards and legislation (unique to each jurisdiction) are referred to as Generally Accepted Accounting Principles (GAAP).

Significance of accounting information

The focus of financial accounting is to report to external users a summary of past economic events of the recently concluded financial period, reflecting the entity's financial performance and financial position. This should be done in a timely manner to allow the users to make effective economic decisions. These reports are called general purpose financial statements.

Limitations of accounting information

The limitations of accounting information are as follows:

1. Assumptions, subjective judgements and estimates are required in the measurement and reporting of business activity.
2. Non-financial events or factors may contribute to the entity's success but cannot be measured monetarily; for example, good working employees or suitable distribution location.
3. Reports are based on historic cost and not the fair market value (current value).

Users and their needs

Users' needs for financial reporting are set out in Table 1.1.

Table 1.1 Users and their needs for financial reporting

User	Need for financial reporting to
Shareholders	• Assess management's stewardship • Determine distributable profits and dividends
Potential investors	• Determine whether to make equity investments
Trade unions/ Employees	• Assess the company's ability to pay employees for effective negotiation
Banks and other financial lending agencies	• Assess the security of money lent or to be lent to the company
Government	• Determine tax to be levied on the company • Determine taxation policies • Include in the country's national income statistics
Securities Exchange Commission	• Regulate activities of enterprises
Financial analysts	• Analyse the company in relation to other companies
Trade creditors	• Assess the company's ability to pay its short-term obligations
Managers	• Assess their own stewardship and for planning ahead

The accounting cycle is illustrated in Figure 1.1.

Figure 1.1. The accounting cycle

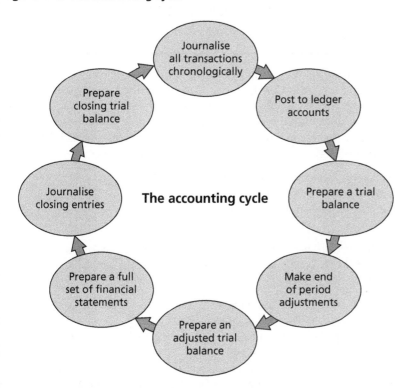

Accrual vs Cash basis accounting

Cash basis accounting is a method in which revenue is recorded when cash is received, and expenses are recorded when cash payments are made. Accrual basis accounting is a method in which revenue is recorded when it is earned and expenses are recorded when they are incurred rather than when cash is received or disbursed. Accrual basis accounting is required in the preparation of general purpose financial statements as it takes into account all the economic activity of the entity that *has occurred* during the financial period under review. This gives a true and fair view of the entity's performance, allowing for greater ability to predict future cash flows.

Use of standards in preparation of financial statements

Accounting standards are guidelines of best accounting practice in the treatment of accounting information and for financial reporting. They are not rules. The IASB (International Accounting Standards Board) is the standard-setting body of the IASC (International Accounting Standards Committee), an independently run private-sector organisation. The IASB consists of 14 members, of which 3 may be part-time. The IASB consists of representatives from four basic groups:

1. preparers of general purpose financial statements
2. users of general purpose financial statements
3. the auditing profession
4. academia.

The IASB is responsible for the approval of IFRSs (International Financial Reporting Standards) and related documents. The standard-setting process called 'Due Process' is as follows:

1. The IASB sets up a steering committee.
2. The steering committee identifies issues.
3. The steering committee studies national and regional requirements and practice in relation to the issues.
4. The steering committee prepares and presents a Point Outline to IASB.
5. The Point Outline is converted to an Exposure Draft and sent out to member organisations for discussion/ feedback.
6. After comments are received and revisions are approved by the IASB, the revised Exposure Draft is adopted and issued as an IFRS.

Small and medium-sized entities (SMEs) make up more than 95 per cent of the world's companies.[1] As a result, there has always been a dire need for standards for SMEs financial reporting. The *International Financial Reporting Standard for Small and Medium-sized Entities (IFRS for SMEs)* was developed giving consideration to, complying with and borrowing from current IASs and IFRSs and is in line with the IASB's *Conceptual Framework of Accounting*. As the development of this standard had gone through **due process**, on 09 July 2009 the IASB issued the IFRS for SMEs.[2] Most businesses in the Caribbean are SMEs and jurisdictions have adopted the IFRS for SMEs as part of their GAAP.
Issuing the IFRS for SMEs:

1. makes it simpler for SMEs to comply with the requirements of the one standard than adhering to the full set of IFRSs and IASs and many national GAAPs requirements
2. reduces the cost associated with meeting the requirements of the full set of IFRSs and IASs
3. simply meets the needs and capabilities of SMEs.

Member institutes of the Institute of Chartered Accountants of the Caribbean (ICAC), incorporated on 28 October 1988 with headquarters in Jamaica, are listed below:

- Bahamas Institute of Chartered Accountants
- Institute of Chartered Accountants of Barbados
- Institute of Chartered Accountants of the Eastern Caribbean
  - St. Kitts Nevis Branch
  - St. Lucia Branch

---

[1] IASB's website: http://www.ifrs.org
[2] Deloitte website: www.iasplus.com

- Antigua/ Barbuda Branch
- Dominica Branch
- Grenada Branch
- Montserrat Branch
  - St. Vincent and the Grenadines Branch
- Institute of Chartered Accountants of Guyana
- Institute of Chartered Accountants of Jamaica
- Institute of Chartered Accountants of Trinidad and Tobago

Test Your Knowledge

1.	What comprises GAAP in any jurisdiction?	[3 marks]
2.	Name five institute members of ICAC.	[5 marks]
3.	What are the steps involved in the IASB's **due process**?	[6 marks]
4.	Explain the difference between cash basis and accrual basis accounting.	[4 marks]
5.	List four users of financial statements and explain their needs for financial statements.	[12 marks]
6.	Who makes up the IASB?	[8 marks]
7.	Why do SMEs need the IFRS?	[5 marks]
8.	List the steps in the accounting cycle	[4 marks]

The Conceptual Framework of accounting

The fundamental reason why general purpose financial statements are produced worldwide is to satisfy the requirements of external users, as they make economic decisions.

The *Conceptual Framework*, also known as the *Framework for the Preparation and Presentation of Financial Statements*, is an outline developed first by the Americans and adopted by the IASB. The purpose of the Conceptual Framework is to:

a. assist the IASB in development of future International Accounting Standards (IASs) and IFRSs

b. promote harmonisation of regulations, accounting standards and procedures, and, as a result, reduce the number of alternative accounting treatments permitted by IASs

c. assist national standard-setting bodies in developing national standards

d. assist preparers of financial statements in dealing with topics for which no IAS currently exists

e. assist auditors in arriving at an opinion as to whether financial statements conform to IASs.

With the above purposes in mind, the *Conceptual Framework* analyses accounting information or policies by sifting them through the following levels.

Level I: the objectives

The objectives seek to identify the goals and purpose of the particular accounting information or policy. An objective is considered useful only if it provides information that is:

a. useful in credit and investment decisions

b. useful or helpful in assessing future cash flows

c. about enterprise resources, claims on resources, use of resources and change in resources.

Level II: qualitative characteristics

These are the attributes of accounting information that makes it useful to all users.

a. Relevance: if it has the ability to influence the user's decisions, thereby making a difference. Relevant information must possess the following attributes:

    1. Predictive value: it can be used to help project future outcomes of the entity.

    2. Feedback or confirmatory value: it confirms or corrects information on past expectations.

    3. Be timely: it is given to the user in a time that can help in making a reliable decision.

    4. Materiality: if the economic decisions of the user are affected by the omission or misstatement of it, then it is material.

b. Reliability: the information is free of error and bias, is complete and is the faithful representation of the situation. This is usually determined by an independent external auditor and reflected in that Auditor's Report. It is defined by the following characteristics:

    1. Completeness: the information must be complete within the boundaries of materiality and cost. Omission may result in misleading information.

    2. Faithful representation: the information must be factual in relation to transactions and other events.

3. Neutrality: the information must not favour one user or group of users over another and there must be no bias.
4. Substance over form: transactions should be recorded according to their substance rather than their legal form.
5. Prudence: on making judgements on transactions and events, assets and income must not be overstated and liabilities and expenses understated.

c. Comparability: users must be able to compare the financial statements of a company over a period of time to identify trends. Users must also be able to compare financial statements of different companies. Companies must disclose what accounting policies they employed for comparability.

d. Consistency: similar items such as, for example, inventory valuation and depreciation of fixed assets must be treated in the same way in the accounting period and from one period to the next. If there is a change in accounting method or policy, then the company must **disclose** it with justification by way of **notes to the financial statements**.

e. Understandability: financial reporting provided to users must not be so complex that a user with a reasonable knowledge of business and economic activities and accounting, and a willingness to study the information with reasonable diligence, would not be able to understand it.

Elements of financial statements

The entity's full set of financial statements, consisting of statement of financial position (balance sheet), statement of comprehensive income (income statement), statement of changes in equity, statement of cash flows and notes to financial statements is a reflection of the effects of its transactions and other events. The effects of these transactions and other events are grouped into broad categories called *elements*, which are listed in Table 1.2.

Table 1.2: List of elements of financial statements

Assets	Liabilities	Equity	Investment by owners (Net assets)
Distribution to owners	Comprehensive income	Revenues	Expenses
Gains	Losses		

Level III: Recognition, measurement and disclosure principles

Assumptions

The following assumptions are made:

a. Economic, separate or business entity concept: the activities of the owner and the company are separate and must be so reflected in the accounts.

b. Going concern: the business will continue for the foreseeable future. As a result, financial statements are prepared and presented in that way. If the business will not continue for the foreseeable future then it must be recorded at liquidation value (selling price less cost of disposal).

c. Monetary unit: this is also known as *unit of measure* or *money measurement* concept. This states that financial statements should be prepared in one stable monetary unit and that non-monetary items may not be recorded.

d. Objectivity: financial statements must be free from bias.

e. Periodicity: this is also known as the *time period assumption*, which states that financial information is needed by users periodically; therefore financial statements are prepared and presented in artificial time periods.

Principles

The principles of the framework include the following:

a. Historic cost concept: all transactions are recorded at cost at the time they occur.
b. Revenue recognition: revenue should be recognised when there is an inflow of net assets from a sale of goods or services.
c. Matching: the expenses that were incurred in the period are matched against the revenue of the same period.
d. Accruals: the effects of transactions and other events are recognised when they occur, rather than when cash or cash equivalent is received or paid, and they are reported in the financial statements for the period to which they relate.
e. Duality: every transaction must be entered twice – once as a debit (Dr) and once as a credit (Cr).
f. Separate valuation: where two transactions occur such as buying from and selling to a supplier with no agreement to set-off the amounts, the debtor and creditor must be shown separately.
g. Full disclosure: circumstances and situations that make a difference to the users of financial statements should be disclosed. This can be done by data in the financial statements or by way of notes to the financial statements.

Constraints

These allow for flexibility in applying the guidelines of the framework without reducing its usefulness.

a. Cost-benefit to the company. Will the benefits of including certain information in the financial statements outweigh the costs, or vice versa?
b. Materiality: the information is material if it influences the decision of the user; if not it is considered immaterial and can be summarised.
c. Industry practice: the peculiar nature of some industries and business concerns sometimes requires departure from basic accounting theory.
d. Conservatism (prudence): when in doubt, choose the solution that will be least likely to overstate assets and income and understate expenses and liabilities.

Test Your Knowledge

1. What are the purposes of the *Conceptual Framework of Accounting*?
   [10 marks]

2. Explain the qualitative characteristics of relevance and comparability.
   [8 marks]

3. What are the five sub-characteristics of reliability? **[5 marks]**

4. Explain the sub-characteristics of substance over form, completeness and prudence. **[9 marks]**

5. Explain three constraints of the IASB's Conceptual Framework. **[6 marks]**

6. Define any three assumptions of the Conceptual Framework. **[6 marks]**

7. Discussion question: in a case where an accountant wants to include an item in the financial statements, how must he or she be guided by the IASB's Conceptual Framework? **[20 marks]**

MULTIPLE CHOICE QUESTIONS

1. Which of the following persons described the double entry system?

   (A) Price Coopers

   (B) Bob Gopee

   (C) Adam Smith

   (D) Luco Pacioli.

2. Generally Accepted Accounting Principles (GAAP) are described as:

   (A) established principles, standards and legislation for use in financial accounting

   (B) guidelines that managers use to make short-term decisions

   (C) policies established as code of conduct in a business

   (D) benchmarks for allocating costs.

3. Which of the following users of accounting information determines taxation policies?

   (A) Trade Unions

   (B) Shareholders

   (C) Government

   (D) Securities Exchange Commission.

4. Which of the following agencies is responsible for the approval of accounting standards?

   (A) International Accounting Standards Board (IASB)

   (B) International Accounting Standards Committee (IASC)

   (C) International Chartered Accountants of Trinidad and Tobago (ICATT)

   (D) International Chartered Accountants of Jamaica (ICAJ).

5. The IASB is responsible for the approval of International Financial Reporting Standards (IFRS) for SMEs related documents. Which of the following is step/stage number 5 in the standard-setting process?

   (A) setting up of steering committee

   (B) adoption of Exposure Draft and issue of IFRS for SMEs

   (C) steering committee prepares and presents a Point Outline

   (D) Point Outline converted to an Exposure Draft.

6. The purpose of the Conceptual Framework is to:

   I   promote harmonisation of regulations

   II   assist preparers of financial statements

   III assist IASB in developing future IASs and IFRSs.

   (A) I and II

   (B) II and III

   (C) II and III

   (D) I, II and III

Chapter 2

Recording financial information

Every transaction in accounting can be recorded using a general journal. Accounting software is mainly centred on the use of general journals to record transactions and make adjusting entries in the financial statements. This chapter focuses on the use of general journals to record transactions and for adjusting entries.

Recording transactions

Example

a. 1 June 2015: a sole trader, Najja Celestine, started a business called Basketball Gamers with $8 000 cash.

General Journal

Date	Details	Debit	Credit
2015			
01 June	Cash	8 000	
	Capital		8 000
	Owner's initial investment		

b. 2 June, 2015: deposited $6 000 cash into the bank.

General Journal

Date	Details	Debit	Credit
2015			
02 June	Bank	6 000	
	Cash		6 000
	Deposited $6 000 into the bank		

c. 5 June 2015: purchased a photocopier on credit for office use from Fax Us Ltd.

General Journal

Date	Details	Debit	Credit
2015			
05 June	Office equipment (or photocopier)	6 000	
	Fax Us Ltd		6 000
	Purchased photocopier from Fax Us Ltd		

d. 9 June, 2015: purchased goods for resale from J. Morgan, paying $1 500 cash.

General Journal

Date	Details	Debit	Credit
2015			
09 June	Purchases	1 500	
	Cash		1 500
	Purchased goods for resale		

Objectives

At the end of this chapter you will be able to understand and use journals in the double-entry system of accounting as it relates to entries:

- expenses
- revenues
- assets
- adjusting entries (adjustments)
- capital and reserves
- and liabilities.

Don't forget

Cash includes cash, bank, marketable securities, fixed deposits and other short-term investments

Adjusting entries

Inventories

Recording beginning and ending inventory as adjustments to the accounts

Example

John Swimmers has a business called Splash-a-lot and at 01 April 2014 beginning inventory was $4 000 and at 31 March 2015 ending inventory was $5 000.

Required

Record the general journals to close off beginning inventory to the income statement and closing inventory.

Solution

General Journal

Date	Details	Debit	Credit
2015			
31 March	Income statement	4 000	
	Inventory		4 000
	To close off beginning inventory account		

General Journal

Date	Details	Debit	Credit
2015			
31 March	Inventory	5 000	
	Income statement		5 000
	To record closing inventory		

Accounting for consumables such as office supplies and small tools

Example

G. Chambers Company Ltd started the year 2015 with an office supplies inventory of $7 600 and at the end of the year had $3 300 of office supplies inventory.

Required

Record the general journal to show the office supplies expense for 2015.

Solution

Working:

Office supplies expense = Opening inventory − Closing inventory
= $7 600 − $3 300
= $4 300

General Journal

Date	Details	Debit	Credit
2015			
31 Dec	Office supplies expense	4 300	
	Office supplies inventory		4 300
	To expense office supplies used during 2015		

Closing off an expense account

Expenses include losses and those expenses that arise in the course of ordinary activities of an entity. (IFRS for SMEs Section 2.26)

Example

The trial balance as at 31 December 2015 indicates that the rent expense for the year was $18 000.

Required

Close off the rent expense account.

Solution

General Journal

Date	Details	Debit	Credit
2015			
31 December	Income statement	18 000	
	Rent expense		18 000
	To close off rent expense account		

Closing off a revenue account

Revenue or Income includes gains that arise in the course of ordinary activities of an entity. (IFRS for SMEs Section 2.25)

Example

Bel Bell company sells cell phones on behalf of Digicel Ltd. Its revenue is generated from the commission on the sale of the cell phones. Its total commission revenue for the year 2015 was $405 000.

Required

Close off the revenue account.

Solution

General Journal

Date	Details	Debit	Credit
2015			
December 2015	Commission revenue	405 000	
	Income statement		405 000
	To close off the commission revenue account		

Recording depreciation calculated for the period

Example

The cost of machinery at the end of the year 2015 was $76 000 and the allowance for depreciation as at 01 January 2015 was $16 000.

Required

Calculate depreciation for the year using the reducing balance method at 10 per cent per annum and show the relevant journal entry for this adjustment.

Solution

Reducing balance method formula:
Net book value* × Given percentage
*Fixed asset at cost − Accumulated depreciation

Working:

Depreciation for the year: ($76 000 − $16 000) × 10 %

$60 000 × 10 %

$6 000

General Journal

Date	Details	Debit	Credit
2015			
31 December	Income statement	6 000	
	Allowance for depreciation		6 000
	Depreciation for machinery for 2015		

Test Your Knowledge

Prepare journals for the following transactions:

1. 01 January 2017, Jacob Tours started business with the owner, Mrs Jacob, investing $40 000 of her own funds which was deposited into the business's bank account. **[3 marks]**

2. 16 May 2015, Marley Bob bought goods on credit from Jamaica Emporium for $15 000. Record the information in the books of Jamaica Emporium. **[3 marks]**

3. Dangriga Company's financial year ended on 30 September 2018. The merchandise inventory information was as follows:

    a. Beginning inventory: $16 000

    b. Ending inventory: $19 000

    Record the closing entries at the end of the period for both beginning and ending inventory for Dangriga Company. **[6 marks]**

4. Cockscomb Advertising Agency office supplies were $54 000 at the beginning of 2015 and $26 000 at the end of the year. Record the journal to expense the office supplies. **[5 marks]**

5. Conaree Restaurants supplied the following information for year ended 31 December 2014:

    Kitchen equipment at cost $360 000

    Accumulated depreciation at 31 December 2013 $210 000

    Record the journal for the annual depreciation for the firm if the firm uses:

    a. Straight line depreciation method at 10 per cent.

    b. Reducing balance depreciation method at 10 per cent. **[8 marks]**

Deferrals (prepayments) and accruals (amounts owing, outstanding or due)

Expenses

Example

Max Enterprises paid $15 000 for the year for rent in 2015. The monthly rent is $1 000.

Required

a. Prepare a statement showing how much rent was incurred in 2015 and whether there is a prepayment or accrual at the end of the accounting period.

b. Prepare the necessary journal to close off the rent expense account.

Solution

a. Rent expense paid $15 000

   Rent for 2015 ($1000 × 12 months)   ($12 000)

   Rent expense prepaid $ 3 000

b. General Journal

Date	Details	Debit	Credit
2015			
December	Income statement	12 000	
	Prepaid rent expense	3 000	
	Rent expense		15 000
	To close off the rent expense account and record prepayment		

Test Your Knowledge

1. Flava Ltd pays its employees a total of $15 000 per month in wages. For the year 2015 the business paid $210 000 in wages.

   a. Prepare a statement showing the total wages for 2015 and whether there is a prepayment or accrual at the end of the accounting period.   **[3 marks]**

   b. Prepare the necessary journal to close off the wages expense account.   **[4 marks]**

Example

Max Enterprises paid $15 000 for 2015 in rent expenses. The monthly rent is $1 500.

Required

a. Prepare a statement showing how much rent was incurred in 2015 and whether there is a prepayment or accrual at the end of the accounting period.

b. Prepare the necessary journal to close off the rent expense account.

Solution

a. Rent expenses paid $15 000

   Rent for 2015 ($1 500 × 12 months)   ($18 000)

   Rent expense accrued   ($ 3 000)

b. General Journal

Date	Details	Debit	Credit
2015			
31 December	Income statement	18 000	
	Rent expense		15 000
	Accrued rent expense		3 000
	To close off rent expense account and to record accrual		

Test Your Knowledge

2. Flava Ltd pays it employees a total of $20 000 per month as wages. For the year 2015 the business paid $210 000 in wages.

    a. Prepare a statement showing the total wages for 2015 and whether there is a prepayment or accrual at the end of the accounting period.   **[3 marks]**

    b. Prepare the necessary journal to close off the wages expense account.   **[4 marks]**

Revenue

Example

Max Enterprises collects commission for the sale of cell phones. The monthly revenue is $2 000. For the year 2015, $30 000 was received.

Required

a. Prepare a statement showing the total commission revenue for 2015 and whether there is a prepayment or accrual at the end of the accounting period.

b. Prepare the necessary journal to close off the commission revenue account.

Solution

a. Commission revenue received $30 000

    Commission revenue for the period ($2 000 × 12 months)   ($24 000)

    Commission revenue accrued $ 6 000

b. General Journal

Date	Details	Debit	Credit
2015			
31 December	Commission revenue	30 000	
	Income statement		24 000
	Commission revenue prepaid		6 000
	To close off the commission revenue account and record prepayment		

Test Your Knowledge

Boysie Roh Ltd collects revenue for subletting part of its building to Barber Cuts for $1500 per month. The business collected $21 000 from Barber Cuts in 2015.

a. Prepare a statement showing rent revenue for 2015 and whether there is a prepayment or accrual at the end of the accounting period. **[3 marks]**

b. Prepare the necessary journal to close off the rent revenue account. **[4 marks]**

Example

Max Enterprises collects commission for the sale of cell phones. The monthly revenue is $3 000. For the year 2015 $30 000 was received.

Required

a. Prepare a statement showing the total commission revenue for 2015 and whether there is a prepayment or accrual at the end of the accounting period.

b. Prepare the necessary journal to close off the commission revenue account.

Solution

a.
Commission revenue received	$30 000
Commission revenue for the period ($ 3 000 × 12 months)	($36 000)
Commission revenue prepaid	($ 6 000)

b. General Journal

Date	Details	Debit	Credit
2015			
31 December	Commission revenue	30 000	
	Accrued commission revenue	6 000	
	Income statement		36 000
	To close off the commission revenue account and record accrual		

Test Your Knowledge

Boysie Roh Ltd collects revenue for subletting part of its building to Barber Cuts for $2400 per month. The business collected $21 000 from Barber Cuts in 2015.

a. Prepare a statement showing how much rent revenue was for 2015 and whether there is a prepayment or accrual at the end of the accounting period. **[3 marks]**

b. Prepare the necessary journal to close off the rent revenue account. **[4 marks]**

Recording equity

Equity is the residual interest in the assets of an entity after deducting all its liabilities. (IFRS for SMEs 2009 Section 2.15 (c))

Issue of common stock (ordinary shares)

There are three basic types of issue of shares:

1. General issue of shares. This is an issue (sale) of shares to the general public of a public limited company, or to new shareholders of a limited company. A general issue can be at par, at a value above par (i.e. premium) and no-par value.
   a. At par value

Example

McMillan Ltd issues 20 000 shares of common stock at par value $2.00 per share on 04 February 2015.

Required

Record the journal for this transaction.

Solution

General Journal

Date	Details	Debit	Credit
2015			
04 February	Cash	40 000	
	Common stock		40 000
	Issue of 20 000 shares at par $2.00		

b. At a value above par

Example

Harvey Ltd issues 20 000 shares of common stock at $5.00 each that have a par value of $2.00 per share on 05 June 2015.

Required

Record the journal for this transaction.

Solution

General Journal

Date	Details	Debit	Credit
2015			
05 June	Cash	100 000	
	Common stock		40 000
	Paid-in capital in excess of par (share premium)		60 000
	Issue of 20 000 shares at $5.00 each with par $2.00		

c. At no-par value

Example

Wilson Ltd issues 6000 shares of common stock at no-par value on 09 March 2015. The market price per share was $6.00.

Required

Record the journal for this transaction.

Solution

General Journal

Date	Details	Debit	Credit
2015			
04 February	Cash	36 000	
	Common stock		36 000
	Issue of 6000 shares at no-par value		

Test Your Knowledge

K. Gooding Ltd is seeking to issue 10 000 shares of common stock on 01 May 2015. Record the journal for the following options:

a. Shares issued at par $3.00. **[3 marks]**

b. Shares issued at market value of $5.00 with par value $3.00 per share. **[4 marks]**

c. Shares issued at no-par value with a market value of $4.00 per share. **[4 marks]**

2. Rights issue. This is an issue of shares to current shareholders. The value of the share is usually above par but discounted to the market value of the share. The shareholders are in no way duty-bound to purchase these shares.

Example

Timothy Ltd issues 20 000 shares of common stock to its existing shareholders with par value $4.00 per share and market value of $6.00 on 04 February 2015. The company is offering a 10 per cent discount on the market value to its current shareholders. The issue was fully subscribed.

Required

Record the journal for this transaction.

Solution

General Journal

Date	Details	Debit	Credit
2015			
04 February	Cash (20 000 shares @ $6.00 × 90%)	108 000	
	Common stock (20 000 shares @ par $4.00)		80 000
	Paid-in capital in excess of par (108 000 – 80 000)		28 000
	To record rights issue		

3. Bonus issue. This is a gift of shares to current shareholders, usually given to them in place of cash dividend.

Example

Williams Ltd has 20 000 shares of common stock at par value $2.00 per share outstanding at 31 December 2015. The company gave a bonus issue of one for every five stocks held on 31 December 2015 as dividends for 2015.

Required

Record the journal for this bonus issue.

Solution

General Journal

Date	Details	Debit	Credit
2015			
31 December	Retained earnings (20 000 shares ÷ 5) × $2.00	8 000	
	Common stock		8 000
	To record a bonus issue		

Don't forget

A company can redeem shares known as **Treasury Stock**. It is deducted from equity.

Test Your Knowledge

Khaleeq Ltd has an authorised share capital of 45 000 shares on 01 August 2015. The firm issued 15 000 shares of common stock on 01 August 2015 at market value of $7.00 with a par value of par $5.00. On 01 August 2016 the firm issues a rights issue of one for every three held at $6.00 per share. On 01 August 2017 the firm made a bonus issue of one for every two held. Record the journal for these three transactions. **[11 marks]**

Reserves

Capital reserves are gains or profits made on such transactions as:

- revaluation of non-current assets (revaluation reserve)
- issue of shares (share premium or paid-in capital in excess of par).

Revenue reserves are the setting aside of profits from the normal operations of business (undistributed profits). It can be specific such as a:

- currency fluctuation reserve
- education and training reserve.

Or general such as:

- general reserve
- retained profits (retained earnings).

Key point

Reserves form part of the equity section.

Recording assets

An asset is a resource controlled by the entity as a result of past events and from which future economic benefits are expected to flow to the entity (IFRS for SMEs 2009 Section 2.15 (a)).

Investments

Example

Sale of a short-term investment with a book value of $4 000 for $3 500 on 06 May 2015.

Required

Record the journal for the sale of the investment.

Solution

General Journal

Date	Details	Debit	Credit
2015			
06 May	Cash	3 500	
	Income Statement: Loss on sale of short-term investment	500	
	Short-term investment		4 000
	Sale of short-term investment		

Example

Jack Company decided to sell its investment in WITCO of 3 000 shares (long-term investment) with a book value of $12 000 for $20 000 on 01 September 2015.

Required

Record the journal for this transaction.

Solution

General Journal

Date	Details	Debit	Credit
2015			
01 September	Cash	20 000	
	Long-term investment		12 000
	Income statement: Gain on sale of long-term investment		8 000
	Sale of long-term investment in WITCO shares		

Basket purchase

This involves the purchase of a group of non-current assets at a special price (called basket price) for the group below that of the sum of the individual value of the assets. The value of each asset is prorated based on its value in relation to the value of the basket price.

Example

Ward Co. purchased a group of non-current assets from DVAK Ltd with a cheque for $600 000 on 01 April 2015. The fair market values of the assets were as follows:

Land	350 000
Plant	150 000
Furniture and fixtures	225 000
Machinery	200 000
Motor vehicle	75 000

Required

Prepare the journal for this transaction.

Solution

Working:

Details	Fair market value	Prorating basket price calculation	Prorated price of asset
Land	350 000	350000 ÷ 1000000 × 600000	210 000
Plant	150 000	150000 ÷ 1000000 × 600000	90 000
Furniture and Fixtures	225 000	225000 ÷ 1000000 × 600000	135 000
Machinery	200 000	200000 ÷ 1000000 × 600000	120 000
Motor Vehicles	75 000	75000 ÷ 1000000 × 600000	45 000
Total	1 000 000		600 000

General Journal

Date	Details	Debit	Credit
2015			
01 April	Land	210 000	
	Plant	90 000	
	Furniture and fittings	135 000	
	Machinery	120 000	
	Motor vehicles	45 000	
	Cash		600 000
	To record basket purchase		

Test Your Knowledge

Woodpecker Co. purchased a group of non-current asset from Bentwood Ltd with a cheque for $500 000 on 01 October 2015. The fair market values of the assets were as follows:

Land	200 000
Plant	160 000
Furniture and fixtures	300 000
Machinery	65 000
Motor vehicle	75 000

Prepare the journal for this transaction.   **[12 marks]**

Recording liabilities

A liability is a present obligation of the entity arising from past events, the settlement of which is expected to result in an outflow from the entity of resources embodying economic benefits. (IFRS for SMEs 2009 Section 2.15 (b))

Examples of non-current (long-term) liabilities include a loan/note payable from a financial institution for more than one year, a mortgage or debenture bonds.

Example
Penco Company received proceeds of a 10 per cent note payable for $175 000 from Belmont Bank Ltd on 01 March 2015 payable in 10 years.

Required

Prepare the necessary journal.

Solution

General Journal |

Date	Details	Debit	Credit
2015			
01 March	Bank	175 000	
	10% note payable (Belmont Bank Ltd)		175 000
	Proceeds from note payable		

Instalment/payment on loan

Example
On 31 December 2015, the end of the financial period for Penco Company, the interest on the 10 per cent note payable for 175 000 is to be recorded in the financial statements of the company.

Required

Record the journal to accrue for the outstanding interest expense.

Solution

Working:

Accrued interest: 175 000 × 10% × 10 months = $14 583

General Journal |

Date	Details	Debit	Credit
2015			
31 December	Income statement	14 583	
	Accrued interest		14 583
	To record accrued interest for 10 months ending 31 December 2015		

Test Your Knowledge

Bayfords Hotels took a $5 000 000, 8 per cent, 10-year loan from Basseterre Bank on 01 June 2015. At the end of its financial period, 31 December 2015, the transaction was not recorded. Prepare the journals to record:

a.   The receipt of the loan   [5 marks]

b.   The accrued interest at the end of the period.   [5 marks]

MULTIPLE CHOICE QUESTIONS

1. A chamber of solicitors provide legal services to a customer for $10 000. The customer pays $8 000 and agrees to pay the balance in 2 weeks. How should this transaction be recorded?

(A) Dr Cash $8 000

   Cr Service Revenue $8 000

(B) Dr Service Revenue $8 000

   Cr Cash $8 000

(C) Dr Cash $8 000

   Dr Service Revenue $2 000

   Cr Accounts Receivable $10 000

(D) Dr Cash $8 000

   Dr Accounts Receivable $2 000

   Cr Service Revenue $10 000

2. Cash includes:

   I   bank

   II   marketable securities

   III   long-term investments.

(A) I

(B) I and II

(C) I and III

(D) II and III

3. The correct journal entry to close off the beginning inventory is:

(A) Dr Inventory   Cr Income Statement

(B) Dr Income Statement   Cr Inventory

(C) Dr Purchases   Cr Inventory

(D) Dr Inventory   Cr Purchases

4. John issues 30 000 shares of common stock at par value at $5.00 per share. The journal for recording the transaction is:

(A) Dr Cash $150 000

   Cr Common Stock $150 000

(B) Dr Common Stock $150 000

   Cr Cash $150 000

(C) Dr Cash $150 000   Cr Sales $150 000

(D) Dr Sales $150 000   Cr Cash $150 000

The following information refers to questions 5 and 6. Dyann issues 10 000 shares of common stock to its shareholders with a par value of $3.00 per share and a market value of $5.00. Dyann's company is offering a 5 per cent discount to its current shareholders.

5. The type of issue of shares is a:

(A) Bonus issue

(B) Local issue

(C) Rights issue

(D) General issue

6. The journal entry to record the fully subscribed issue is:

(A) Dr Cash $47 500

   Cr Common Stock $30 000

   Cr Paid-in capital in excess of par $17 500

(B) Dr Paid-in capital in excess of par $17 500

   Dr Common Stock $30 000

   Cr Cash $47 500

(C) Dr Cash $47 500

   Cr Capital $47 500

(D) Dr Capital $47 500

   Cr Cash $47 500

7. A Bonus issue is:

   I   a gift of shares

   II   a debt received

   II   dividends proposed.

(A) I

(B) II

(C) I and II

(D) I and III

Chapter 3

Accounting and administrative controls systems

Internal control systems

Categories

Internal control systems are the whole system of controls put in place by management. They are divided into two categories:

1. accounting controls, and
2. administrative controls.

Objectives

The major objectives of internal control, as espoused by the Institute of Internal Auditors, are to:

- ensure the accurate and reliable recording and reporting of financial information
- promote compliance with management's policies and procedures
- safeguard the assets of the organisation from wastage, theft and fraud
- encourage the efficient use of the organisation's resources
- promote the accomplishment of the organisation's goals and objectives.

Principles of internal control systems

For the internal control system to be effective, it must possess the following six principles.
They are:

1. Establishment of responsibility (proper authorisation):
   In applying this principle, employees selected by management must be competent, reliable and ethical. The organisation must offer suitable salaries to attract employees that meet these criteria. There must also be a clear assignment of responsibility and authority to every employee.
2. Segregation of duties:
   There must be the segregation (separation) of duties within the organisation in an attempt to limit fraud, theft and wastage of resources, thereby safeguarding the assets of the organisation. Segregation of duties should occur in two areas.
   a. Separation of accounting from the other functional areas of the business; production, marketing, human resources and research and development. Cash is the 'life blood' of any organisation and accounting departments provide independent information for management in all areas.
   b. Separation of custody of assets from the maintenance of the accounting records. For example, the person who collects inventory when delivered to the organisation must not be the person who maintains the receipt and disbursement of the inventory. Or the person who prepares the purchase order must not be the person who receives the goods and maintains inventory balances. Accountants must not handle cash and cashiers must not have access to accounting records.
3. Independent internal verification:
   This is mainly for the purpose of validation and is done by employees of the organisation such as managers, immediate supervisors, internal auditors and external auditors.
   a. Managers and supervisors, on a day-to-day basis, check work done by subordinates to ensure company policies and procedures are followed and that the organisation's goals and objectives are being met.
   b. Internal auditors are employees of the organisation and usually fall under the Finance Department but report directly to the Audit Committee of the Board of Directors. Their main responsibility is to ensure that employees comply with policies and procedures. They do this by doing regular or spot (surprise) checks on employees anywhere in the organisation.

These checks need not be of an accounting nature but in relation to any functional area of business. Therefore, internal auditors need not possess accounting qualifications but the technical skills in the area they are auditing.

   c. External auditors are independent to the company and are hired to express an opinion as to whether the financial statements agree with General Accepted Accounting Principles (GAAP) of the jurisdiction. Both types of auditors do not only identify errors but make helpful suggestions for improvement to the organisation's systems.

4. Documents procedures or documentation:

All documents used in the organisation in relation to the use of its assets such as cash, inventory or any other resource should be pre-numbered. This will make it a lot easier to account for gaps and to clearly assign responsibility for the missing documents. It is also useful for recording the documents, as the numbers can serve as references.

5. Physical, mechanical and electronic controls:

With the advances in technology there is a dwindling difference between these three groups. This is why they are grouped together. They include such things as:

   a. Physical walls and fences at the workplace.

   b. Locks on gates, doors, drawers and having safes to restrict access by unauthorised personnel.

   c. Security guards, fireproof cabinets and vaults, and safety deposit boxes.

   d. Cameras for monitoring the movement of customers and employees.

   e. Sensors attached to products to deter theft. The sensor usually sounds an alarm if it is removed by an unauthorised person.

   f. Various levels of access via passwords into offices and using computer software, including smart cards for different levels of employees.

   g. Point of sale terminals for use by credit and debit cards to reduce the amount of cash held on the organisation's premises, minimising losses should cash be stolen.

6. Other controls include the following:

   a. Fidelity bond (insurance): this is an insurance policy taken out by the company against the theft of cash by the organisation's employees which allows for reimbursement of any losses.

   b. Job rotation: allowing employees to function in other areas of the organisation from time to time.

   c. Mandatory vacation: demand that employees take annual vacation leave.

Job rotation and mandatory vacation are administrative controls by management to ensure employees do not have complete control over any aspect of the organisation and to discourage collusion.

Test Your Knowledge

1. Which principle of internal controls encourages mandatory vacation and a fidelity bond? **[1 mark]**

2. List three objectives of internal controls. **[3 marks]**

3. Explain the internal control principle of establishment of responsibility. **[5 marks]**

4. Identify and explain five areas of the internal control principles of physical, mechanical and electronic controls. **[10 marks]**

Table 3.1 Application of the six principles of internal controls in an organisation

Internal control principle	Cash collection	Accounts receivable	Accounts payable	Inventory	EDP Environment
Establishing responsibility	Employee must be able to prepare a receipt or work the relevant cash register. Integrity required. Lines of authority must be clear.	Must be able to update the relevant records with accuracy. Basic accounting knowledge required. Lines of authority must be clear.	Must be able to update the relevant records with accuracy. Basic accounting knowledge required. Lines of authority must be clear.	Must be able to update the relevant records with accuracy. Basic willingness to be trained in the system of recording required. Lines of authority must be clear.	Must have basic computer literacy skills or be qualified to operate the relevant software. Lines of authority must be clear.
Segregation of duties	Cashiers with responsibility for cash collection must not be responsible for updating customer records. Persons entering data must not have authority to alter records or reconcile cash with receipts.	Responsibility for receipts of cash and cheques from customers and updating accounts receivable records. One employee must not be responsible for both.	Responsibility for cash disbursements to creditors and verifying or changing data in payable records; these must not be handled by one employee. The duties must be separate.	The employee who requests the inventory must not be the same person who maintains custody of the inventory.	The person with the responsibility to alter data must not be the same employee who enters the data.
Independent internal verification	A supervisor should be responsible for verifying receipts against cash collected. A bank reconciliation should be done periodically (as often as possible) to verify deposits to the bank match with the bank statement.	The work of employees who make entries to update records can be checked by a supervisor or internal auditor to ensure balances are accurate.	The work of employees who make entries to update records can be checked by a supervisor or internal auditor to ensure balances are accurate. A bank reconciliation should be done periodically to verify payments to suppliers match with the bank statement.	Regular or 'spot' checks can be done to verify inventory balances by supervisors and / or internal auditors.	Verification of the data is done by a supervisor at a terminal away from where data is entered. An integrated system allows for work done by any employee to be seen in real time and a notice (via email) can be sent to the employee to make the necessary adjustments.
Document procedures	All receipts must be pre-numbered.	All invoices must be pre-numbered.	All cheques must be pre-numbered.	All requisition forms and purchase orders must be pre-numbered and done in duplicate or triplicate to ensure that all relevant departments have a copy.	Entering data on forms provided by the software that generates numbers in a key field automatically, which can also be printed. This eliminates the duplication of numbers and allows for copies to be made of them.

Table 3.1 continued

Internal control principle	Cash collection	Accounts receivable	Accounts payable	Inventory	EDP Environment
Physical, mechanical, and electronic controls	Use of debit and credit card machines to avoid the need to access cash. Cash registers that open only when the total of the items is entered and have locks on them. Cashiers collect funds from behind secure glass. Cash and goods are handed through a turntable to avoid any external access. Cameras focused on cashiers and customers at the cash register. Security guards on the compound.	Sales invoices for debtors are secured in a locked drawer or cabinet. Paid invoices of debtors are stamped 'payment received', dated and filed away in a fireproof cabinet.	Purchase invoices from suppliers are secured in a locked drawer or cabinet. Paid invoices of creditors are stamped 'paid' and filed away in a fireproof cabinet.	All inventories are stored in a locked room with clearly stated restricted access. The lock can be a physical one to open with a key or electronically. Cameras are set up at the stores area to discourage or track unauthorised access.	Smart buildings that restrict access to employees of certain levels by scanning employee identification cards to enter doors. Vaults to store cash overnight. Restricted access to company's software by use of passwords. Data entry can be traced to an employee by means of an employee unique entry code.
Other controls	Fidelity bond for employees that handle cash.	Employee rotated or sent on mandatory vacation to ensure accuracy of records.	Employee rotated or sent on mandatory vacation to ensure accuracy of records.	Employee rotated or sent on mandatory vacation to ensure accuracy of records.	Employee rotated or sent on mandatory vacation to ensure accuracy of records.

Test Your Knowledge

1. Janet Morgan Pharmacy collects cash over the counter from customers and stores it in an unlocked drawer. All employees that interface with customers collect cash and go to the drawer to store it and provide change. The items sold are recorded in a book that is also kept in the same drawer where the cash is stored. Using the principles of internal control, what can be put in place to correct this situation?   **[10 marks]**

2. How would documents be recorded in an EDP environment?   **[3 marks]**

3. What safeguards can be put in place for collection of cash at a gas station?   **[10 marks]**

4. Julio Sammy, a medical doctor wants to institute internal controls:

    a. What system can he put in place to store the inventory of drugs?   **[6 marks]**

    b. Cash is collected by his secretary who also updates the customer records and deposits cash in the local bank. What is the weakness in internal controls and what can be done to correct this?   **[6 marks]**

Table 3.2 Internal and external auditors compared

	Internal auditor	External auditor
Appointment	Hired by management	Appointed and approved by the majority of shareholders (common stockholders) at the Annual General Meeting (AGM)
Report to whom	They report to the Audit Committee of the Board Of Directors (BOD) or directly to the BOD	To the shareholders at the AGM
Relationship with the organisation	Employee	Independent of the firm they are auditing
Role	Examine the efficiency and effectiveness of policies and procedures implemented by management and the adherence to them guided by internal controls	Their operations are to examine the financial statements of the organisation they audit and express an opinion on its true and fair view
Type of report	Formal letter detailing concerns and suggestions for corrections	Standard report on the financial statements expressing its true and fair view in all material respects and to sign audited financial statements of the business
How often are audits done	As required by management (weekly, monthly or in an ad hoc manner)	Annually
Qualifications	Suited to the required job, as internal audits can be for any functional area of business (finance, production, marketing, human resources or research and development)	Accounting and auditing qualification required. Only qualified accountants are allowed to sign audited reports on the financial statement of a business

Table 3.3 Technology and financial accounting

	Manual accounting systems	Computers in accounting	Computerised accounting systems
How is information recorded	Written by hand on designated business documents and in accounting books	Written by hand on business documents and entered into a spreadsheet, database or document writer program on computers	The transaction is either scanned in or typed into an accounting integrated software that prints the business document and automatically updates all the related records
Speed advantage	Slow in entering and retrieving data	Faster than manual accounting in retrieving data	Fastest and very efficient in entering and retrieving data
Access to records	Business documents and accounting records limited by locks on drawers, fireproof cabinets and safes	Business documents stored in locked drawers, fireproof cabinets and safes	Data is saved on computer's server (main system) and soft copy backed-up and stored on or offsite securely
Changes to data	Not limited to any employee entering the data but restrictions based on internal control system	At preparation of business documents it is possible for all employees to make changes but access to data may be restricted by locked office or password restriction	Every employee has a unique password to access the system and enter data. Supervisor password required to change data
Controls over and access to business / accounting records	Documents and certain books limited to authorised personnel only. Information double-checked by accountant by preparation of control accounts and bank reconciliation statements	Documents limited to authorised personnel only. Accountant double-checks information by preparation of control accounts and bank reconciliation statements	Accessed by senior employee at a distant terminal. Software provides lists of data entered and by which employee. The accountant and internal auditor use the bank reconciliation programme to do bank reconciliation and trace entries

Limitations to internal controls

Internal controls may be limited as follows:

1. Collusion among employees.
2. The cost of implementation might seem to be more than the benefits that can be derived from implementing it or the cost may be prohibitive.
3. The size of the organisation may not allow for effective implementation.

Test Your Knowledge

In each of the following scenarios,

a. Identify the internal control principle being violated. **[6 marks]**

b. Indicate what can be done to correct the scenario. **[6 marks]**

1. Paula's Preserves, manufacturer of preserved plums and cherries, sells goods to retailers on credit. The accountant, Joanne Thomas collects cash from customers, verifies the receipts and enters the information to update customer balances.

2. Catherine Computers bookkeeper orders merchandise and approves payment.

3. Alexander Electronics salespersons record customers' requests in the company's integrated computer system. Each salesperson uses the same password to enter that data.

4. Wesley's Woodworking Co has a cashier that has not been on vacation for the past 8 years.

5. Paid invoices of customers at Sylvester's Shoe Store are stored in the accountant's unlocked drawer.

6. Cheques at Pierre's Sports Store are not numbered.

MULTIPLE CHOICE QUESTIONS

1. A good internal control system:

    I safeguards assets

    II ensures records prepared are accurate and reliable

    III encourages efficient use of resources.

    (A) I and II

    (B) II and III

    (C) I and III

    (D) I, II and III

2. Which of the following internal control principles attempts to limit fraud and safeguard assets?

    (A) segregation of duties

    (B) establishment of responsibilities

    (C) adequate documentation procedures

    (D) independent internal verification.

3. Which of the following internal control tasks would be considered as a priority in an inventory environment for documents?

    (A) updated and verified regularly

    (B) stored in a locked room

    (C) pre-numbered and prepared in duplicate

    (D) prepared by one person.

4. Internal auditors report:

    I directly to the Board of Directors

    II to shareholders at the Annual General Meeting

    III to trade union workers/representative.

    (A) I

    (B) II

    (C) I and II

    (D) II and III

5. One of the many benefits of a computerised accounting system is that:

    I it is slow in entering and retrieving data

    II it is fast and efficient in entering and retrieving data

    III information is more accurate.

    (A) I

    (B) II

    (C) III

    (D) I and III

6. Drawbacks of internal controls are:

    I There may be collusion among employees.

    II Implementation costs may be higher than benefits.

    III The size of the organisation may impede effective implementation.

    (A) I

    (B) I and II

    (C) II and III

    (D) I, II and III

Chapter 4

Forms of business organisations

Features of business organisations

The recognition of different forms of businesses and ownership patterns is of critical importance to the reporting of financial information. The major forms of businesses are sole proprietorship, cooperatives, partnerships, non-governmental organisations and corporations. Table 4.1 below shows the various types of business organisations and features that distinguish one type from the other in the private sector.

Table 4.1 Characteristics of private sector business organisations

	Sole proprietorship	Cooperatives	Partnerships	Non-governmental organisations (Not for profit)	Corporations/Limited liability companies
Ownership	Owned by one person called the **proprietor**	Groups of persons, called **members,** form an organisation to represent themselves	Co-owned by two or more persons called **partners** (2–20)	Run by a group of private individuals or group of organisations	Owned by investors called stockholders/ shareholders. Indefinite number of shareholders
Legal status	No separate legal entity	Separate legal entity	No separate legal entity	Separate legal entity	Separate legal entity
Motive for operating	Making profit	Improving the financial status and welfare of members	To make profits	To help people	For some corporations, to make profit for shareholders
Transfer of ownership	Sale of business by owner	Shares cannot be transferred	Changes in partners – admission and retirement	Cannot be transferred	Shares are easily transferable **only** in public companies. Board approval required for private companies
Lifespan (continuity) of business	Not continuous. Business closes at the owner's wish or death	Continuous. The firm has separate legal entity	Not continuous. Existing agreement ends when partners retire, die or new partners are admitted	Continuous. The firm has separate legal entity	Continuous. Firm will not be affected by changes in ownership because the firm has separate legal entity
Management of business	Owner controls and manages the business by his or herself	Operations managed by members	Operations managed by general partners	Operations managed by a board of directors	Operations managed by a board of directors
How capital is acquired	Owner (through personal savings, loans or family)	Purchase of shares by members	Investments made by partners	May acquire through public support – donors/ government grants. Others through subscriptions received from members and surpluses	Issuance of shares or stock
Regulations and rules	Relevant local laws	Rules relating to the Co-operatives Act	Rules relating to the Partnership Act	Incorporated and governed by the Act of Parliament/Companies Act/Business Act. Depends on laws of the jurisdictions	For creation, will file specific documents with the Registrar of Companies and comply with the Companies Act
Taxation	Owner pays personal income tax	Some cooperatives may have tax exemption; others may have to pay corporation tax	Each partner pays personal income tax	Guided by legislation relating to income tax of that jurisdiction	Pays corporation tax on its net income

Table 4.1 continued

	Sole proprietorship	Cooperatives	Partnerships	Non-governmental organisations (Not for profit)	Corporations/Limited liability companies
Composition of equity (capital)	Capital + Profit (or subtract losses)	Ordinary shares + Reserves + Undistributed surplus	Each Partner's Capital + Current Accounts Balances	Accumulated Fund + Surpluses	Ordinary shares (par or no-par value) + Preference shares (par or no-par value) + Share premium + Reserves
Profit/losses sharing	Receives all profits/absorbs all losses	Receives dividends and patronage refund	Profits and losses shared among partners	Members do not receive dividends. The income is used to further enhance the organisation's objectives	Receives dividends

Table 4.2 Characteristics of government-run corporations

Management of ownership	Acquisition of capital	Continuity of corporation	Formation	Ownership	Composition of equity (capital)
Run by elected board of directors	Shares quoted on the stock exchange and sold to the public	Continues, does not close down on the death of shareholder(s)	Incorporated	Owned by shareholders	Shareholder equity and financial institutions

Table 4.3 Advantages and disadvantages of different types of business organisations

Type of business organisation	Advantages	Disadvantages
Sole proprietorship	• Owner has complete control of the business • Small startup capital needed • More personal services are given to customers • Changes and decisions are made quickly without consulting others	• Owner has unlimited liability • Owner has difficulty in adapting to market conditions • Owner has difficulty in raising capital • Owner may have difficulty in transfer of ownership
Partnership	• Easy to form • More capital is available • Each partner contributes his or her skills and experience in the running of the business	• All partners stand to lose if a partner makes a bad business deal • No continuity of business if a partner dies or leaves the business • Not easy to transfer ownership
Cooperatives	• Sharing of knowledge, skills and efforts • All profits are shared among the membership	• Membership may not have the expertise to build the organisation • Decision-making process is very slow in the organisation

Test Your Knowledge

1. Copy the table below and list one advantage and disadvantage of the following businesses.   **[6 marks (1 mark for each correct entry)]**

Types of business organisations	Advantages	Disadvantages
Sole proprietorship		
Non-governmental organisations		
Partnership companies		

2. In the table below, distinguish between a company and a cooperative.

[6 marks (1 mark for each correct entry)]

	Company	Cooperative
Membership		
Ownership		
Transfer of ownership		

3. The following is a list of businesses and some characteristics of **each** business. Using the definitions given for public and private companies, classify the business in the space provided.

[3 marks (1 mark for each correct entry)]

Name of business	Characteristics	Classification
First Class Food Chain	Shares are owned by the Teek family	
Herry Sisters Incorporated	Shares owned by five sisters and the company are listed on the stock exchange	
Shants Dental Care Unit	Shares are owned by Shants Austrene	

MULTIPLE CHOICE QUESTIONS

1. Corporations (limited liability companies) are owned by:

(A) proprietor

(B) members

(C) shareholders

(D) partners.

2. Personal income taxes are paid by:

I sole trader

II shareholders

III partners.

(A) I

(B) I and II

(C) I and III

(D) I, II and III

3. Public limited companies and organisations raise capital or equity from:

(A) shareholders' personal savings

(B) investment made by partners

(C) subscriptions received from members

(D) shares issued on the stock market.

4. The advantage(s) of owning a sole proprietorship business is/are:

I Decisions are made quickly.

II More capital is available.

III Profits made are shared.

(A) I

(B) II

(C) I and II

(D) I and III

5. The advantage(s) of persons forming a cooperative organisation is/are:

I transferring ownership is difficult

II members needs are met

III raising capital is difficult.

(A) I

(B) II

(C) III

(D) I, II and III

Chapter 5

Preparation and presentation of statement of comprehensive income (income statement) and statement of retained earnings

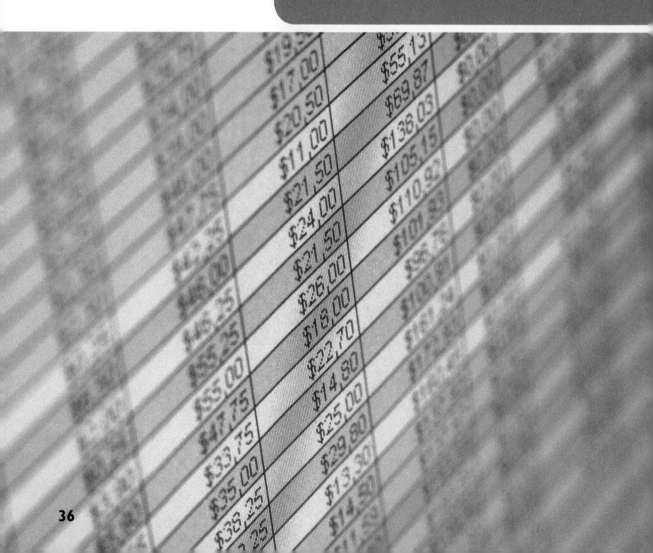

Revenue (IAS 18 and Section 23 of the IFRS for SMEs)

Definition: the gross inflow of economic benefits during the period arising **in the course of ordinary activities** of an entity.

Questions and answers

Question: What does not constitute revenue?
Answer: Sale of shares or the sale of non-current assets will not be considered revenue.
Question: How should revenue be measured?
Answer: Measure revenue at the fair value of the consideration received or receivable.

Conditions to be satisfied for recognising revenue

The conditions to be satisfied for recognising revenue are as follows:

1. Significant risks and rewards of ownership of the goods transferred to the buyer.
2. Neither continual managerial involvement nor effective control over the goods sold by the seller.
3. Revenue can be measured reliably.
4. Economic benefits associated with the transaction will flow to the entity.
5. The costs incurred or to be incurred in respect of the transaction can be measured reliably.

Main categories of revenue

The four main categories of revenue are:

1. Sale of goods
2. Rendering of services
3. Franchise fees
4. Interest, royalties and dividends earned.

Revenue for the sale of goods format:

Sales	XXXX
Less: Sales returns and allowances	(XXXX)
Less: Sales discounts	(XXXX)
Revenue (Turnover/net sales)	XXXX

Test Your Knowledge

1. Given the following information, what is the value of total revenue in each case?
   a. Sales $10 000, sales discounts $4000 and sales returns $530. **[3 marks]**
   b. Sales discounts $640, sales $9890 and sales returns and allowances $1200. **[3 marks]**
2. List two of the four main categories of revenue. **[2 marks]**
3. Define revenue. **[3 marks]**
4. List any three conditions for recognising revenue. **[3 marks]**

Inventories: IAS 2 (Section 13 of the IFRS for SMEs)

Inventories are assets:

1. held for sale in the ordinary course of business
2. in the process of production for such sale, or
3. in the form of materials or supplies to be consumed in the production process or in the rendering of services.

The cost of inventories shall include all costs of purchase, costs of conversion and other costs incurred in bringing the inventories to their present location and condition.

Inventory valuation methods

Inventory valuation methods are as follows:

1. Specific identification
2. FIFO
3. LIFO
4. Weighted average.

Don't forget

LIFO is not an acceptable format for IAS 2 (IFRS for SMEs Section 13).

Example

Stephens Ltd provided you with the following information.

Date	Details	Unit quantity	Unit cost $
January	Beginning Inventory	270	10.00
April	Purchases	300	11.00
July	Purchases	250	12.00
September	Purchases	320	13.00
November	Purchases	290	15.00

Number of units available for sale – Number of units sold = Number of units in ending inventory

Sales for the year were 1000 units at $22.00 each.

Required

Find the total value of the closing inventory at the end of the year under LIFO, FIFO and weighted average methods of inventory valuation.

Solution

1. FIFO

140 units	×	$13.00	$1 820.00
290 units	×	$15.00	$4 350.00
Total closing inventory			$6 170.00

2. LIFO

270 units	×	$10.00	$2 700.00
160 units	×	$11.00	$1 760.00
Total closing inventory			$4 460.00

3. Weighted average

Total value of inventory
$$\frac{\text{available for sale}}{\text{Total number of units}} = \frac{\$17\,510}{1430\ \text{units}} = \$12.25\ \text{per unit}$$
available for sale

Total closing inventory: 430 units × $12.25 = $5268 (rounded to the nearest whole number)

Test your Knowledge

1. Identify three items that can use the specific identification method of inventory valuation. **[3 marks]**

2. Identify two of the three characteristics of inventories by IAS 2 (IFRS for SMEs: Section 13). **[2 marks]**

3. Find the value of ending inventory under FIFO, LIFO and weighted average methods using the information in the table given below. **[8 marks]**

Date	Details	Unit quantity	Unit cost $
January	Beginning Inventory	250	10.00
April	Purchases	320	10.00
July	Purchases	270	12.00
September	Purchases	300	14.00
November	Purchases	290	15.00

Sales for the year were 1000 units at $20.00 each.

The lower of **cost** and **net realisable value (NRV)**

An entity shall measure inventories at the lower of **cost** and **NRV;** that is, the estimated selling price **less** costs to complete and sell. The cost to complete and sell includes all further costs to completion and the costs that would be incurred in marketing, selling and distribution of the inventory.

Example

Cellnetics Ltd retails cellphones. The current inventory of cellphones has a cost of $20 000. Due to the recent introduction of more up-to-date cellphones in the market, the company can sell its current inventory for $22 000 only after investment in a marketing campaign of $7 000.

Required

At what price should Cellnetics Ltd record its inventory?

Solution

Cost $20 000   Net realisable value: 22 000 – 7 000 = $15 000

Cellnetics Ltd should record its inventory at $15 000 (NRV).

Test Your Knowledge

JJ Company Limited sells appliances and electronics and has the following inventory data.

Determine the value at which the company will record its inventory of each item, at cost or NRV, showing the value of inventory under each.

Item no.	Details	Cost $	Selling price $	Cost to complete and sell $	
1	Refrigerators	679 000	792 000	104 000	[3 marks]
2	Televisions	432 000	454 000	25 000	[3 marks]
3	Stove ranges	526 000	616 000	100 000	[3 marks]
4	Automatic washing machines	292 000	387 000	88 000	[3 marks]
5	Dryers	301 000	298 000	4 000	[3 marks]

Don't forget	
When inventories are sold	Record as expense in the period in which related revenue is recognised
Goods on consignment	Seller is the owner
Goods FOB – shipping point	Buyer is the owner while in transit
Goods FOB – destination	Seller is the owner while in transit

Cost of purchases

The costs of purchase of inventories comprise:

- the purchase price
- import duties and other taxes
- transport, handling and other directly attributable costs
- trade discounts, rebates and other similar items are **deducted** in determining the costs of purchase.

Cost of sales (cost of goods sold) schedule format

Opening inventory		XXX
Purchases	XXX	
Less: Purchases returns and allowances	(XXX)	
Less: Purchase discounts	(XXX)	
Net purchases	XXX	
Add: Carriage inwards, transportation on purchases, excise duties and freight-in	XXX	
Cost of goods purchased		XXX
Cost of goods available for sale		XXX
Less: Ending inventory		(XXX)
Cost of sales		XXX

Test Your Knowledge

1. What items are included in finding the cost of goods purchased? [4 marks]
2. To whom does inventory in transit FOB-shipping point belong: the buyer or seller? [1 mark]
3. Copy and complete the following formulae: [5 marks]

   a. Cost of sales = _____ – Ending inventory

   b. Net purchases = _____ – Purchase discounts – _____

   c. Opening inventory = Cost of goods purchased – _____

   d. Cost of goods purchased = Net purchases – _____

4. From the following information find the cost of sales in the schedule for Broom Company. [8 marks]

Opening inventory	4230	Ending inventory	5725
Excise duties	230	Purchases	17235
Purchase discounts	1050	Purchases returns and allowances	4200

Statement of retained earnings: IAS 1 (Section 6 of the IFRS for SMEs)

Retained earnings are the accumulation of the balance of undistributed profits over the company's existence. All profits belong to the owners of the company (shareholders). The use of these profits is determined by the board of directors as revenue reserves, profits set aside for the future continuance and growth of the company, and/or for distribution to shareholders as dividends.

Example

The Marlon Metal Works Corporation started operations on 01 January 2010. The company only has ordinary shares. The following information was supplied at the current year ended 31 December 2013.

Profit for the year	$45 000	Retained Earnings 01 January 2013	$89 000
Prior year adjustment: understatement of 2012 depreciation expense before tax	$10 000	Cumulative decrease in income from changes in inventory valuation method before tax	$9 000
Interim dividend (dividend paid)	$4 000	Dividend declared	$15 000
Effective tax rate	32%		

Required

Prepare the statement of retained earnings.

Solution

Marlon Metal Works Limited
Statement of Retained Earnings
For the year ended 31 December 2013

Profit for the year		45 000
Retained earnings 01 January 2013		89 000
		134 000
Prior year adjustment understatement of 2012 depreciation expense ($10 000 × (100% − 32%))	6 800	
Change in inventory valuation method resulting in cumulative decrease in income (9 000 × (100% − 32%))	6 120	(12 920)
		121 080
Dividend declared		
Interim dividend	4 000	
Proposed dividend	11 000	(15 000)
Retained earnings 31 December 2013		106 080

Statement of comprehensive income: IAS 1 (Section 5 of the IFRS for SMEs)

Example

The following is information from Ade Company.

Administrative expenses	
Office salaries	4 600
Depreciation of office furniture and equipment	3 620
Cost of goods sold	57 630
Rent revenue	23 130
Selling expenses	
Transportation out	2 110
Depreciation on sales equipment	5 920
Sales commissions	6 570
Sales revenue	109 800
Income tax expense	9 920
Interest expense	2 540
Dividend paid	13 500
Retained earnings 01 January 2013	61 000
Loss on sale on motor vehicles	12 000
Bank charges	1 070

a. Prepare the statement of comprehensive income for the year ended 2013 using the multi-step method.

b. Prepare the statement of comprehensive income using the single-step format.

Solution

a. Multi-step format

ADE Company

Statement of Comprehensive Income for the year ended 31 December 2013

Sales revenue			109 800
Cost of goods sold			(57 630)
Gross profit			52 170
Other revenues			
Rent revenue		23 130	23 130
			75 300
Selling expenses			
Transportation out	2 110		
Depreciation on sales equipment	5 920		
Sales commissions	6 570	14 600	
Administrative expenses			
Office salaries	4 600		
Depreciation of office furniture and equipment	3 620	8 220	
Other expenses			
Loss on sale of motor vehicles	12 000	12 000	
Finance costs			
Interest Expense	2 540		
Bank Charges	1 070	3 610	(38 430)
Profit before tax			36 870
Income tax expense			(9 920)
Profit for the year			26 950
Retained earnings 01 January 2013			61 000
			87 950
Dividend declared			
Dividend paid		13 500	(13 500)
Retained Earnings 31 December 2013			$74 450

Solution

b. Single-step format

ADE Company

**Statement of Comprehensive Income for the year ended
31 December 2013**

Sales revenue			109 800
Cost of goods sold			(57 630)
Gross profit			52 170
Other revenues			23 130
			75 300
Selling expenses		14 600	
Administrative expenses		8 220	
Other expenses		12 000	
Finance costs		3 610	(38 430)
Profit before tax			36 870
Income tax expense			(9 920)
Profit for the year			26 950
Retained earnings 01 January 2013			61 000
			87 950
Dividend declared			(13 500)
Retained earnings 31 December 2013			$74 450

Test Your Knowledge

1. What is the section of the IFRS for SMEs or IAS that deals with the reporting of the Statement of Comprehensive Income? **[1 mark]**

2. What line items must be shown in a statement of comprehensive income? **[5 marks]**

3. At the end of its financial year, 31 December 2013, Ali Chemical Company made a profit of $92 000. Its retained earnings at 31 December 2010 were $56 200. The company has 45 000 ordinary shares at par $1 and 2000 5 per cent preference shares at par $3. The company paid an interim dividend of $0.05 per share to ordinary shareholders. The directors decided to transfer $8000 to a general reserve, $11 000 to its foreign exchange reserve and declared a dividend of $0.30 per share to ordinary shareholders. Prepare the statement of retained earnings for the company. **[7 marks]**

4. The accountant for Brandon Bicycle Products, Inc. has compiled the following information from the company's records as a basis for a statement of comprehensive income for the year ended 31 December 2012.

Net sales	970 000		
Dividends declared	14 400	Rent revenue	30 000
Interest on notes payable	17 000	Merchandise purchases	421 000
Transportation-in—merchandise	37 000	Merchandise inventory, 1 January 2002	82 000
Merchandise inventory, 31 December 2002	81 000		
Purchase returns and allowances	11 000	Wages and salaries—sales	95 000
Materials and supplies—sales	11 400	Income taxes	45 000
Wages and salaries—administrative	135 900	Other administrative expenses	46 700
Advertising expense	20 000	Express mail	6 000
Depreciation on plant assets (60 per cent selling, 40 per cent administrative)			70 000

a. Prepare a multiple-step income statement. **[18 marks]**

b. Prepare a single-step income statement. **[10 marks]**

MULTIPLE CHOICE QUESTIONS

1. IAS 2 (Section 13 of IFRS for SMEs) identifies four inventory valuation methods. Which of the following methods is not an acceptable format according to the standards?

   (A) First in first out (FIFO)

   (B) Last in last out (LIFO)

   (C) Specific identification

   (D) Weighted average.

2. Which of the following statements report/record the change in equity?

   (A) Statement of comprehensive income

   (B) Statement of owner's equity

   (C) Statement of financial position

   (D) Cash flow statement.

3. The four categories of revenue are:

   I   Sales of goods and rendering of services

   II Purchase and sale of goods

   III Franchise fees and dividends earned

   (A) I

   (B) II

   (C) I and II

   (D) I and III

4. Cost of inventories include ALL:

   I   purchase costs

   II conversion costs

   III administrative costs.

   (A) I

   (B) II

   (C) I and II

   (D) II and III

5. Which section of the IFRS for SMEs deals with the use of undistributed profits?

   (A) Section 5

   (B) Section 6

   (C) Section 13

   (D) Section 23

6. Which of the following sections of the IFRS for SMEs refers to the Statement of comprehensive income?

   (A) Section 5

   (B) Section 6

   (C) Section 13

   (D) Section 23

7. Which of the following financial reports indicate the financial performance of a firm?

   (A) Statement of comprehensive income

   (B) Statement of financial position

   (C) Cash flow statement

   (D) Statement of changes in owner's equity.

Chapter 6

Preparation of financial statements

Introduction

At the end of a business's financial year, every business owner wants to know the result of his or her financial position and performance. This information is prepared in financial statements known as statement of comprehensive income, statement of owner's equity, statement of financial position and statement of cash flow. Before preparing the financial statements, it is usual to prepare a listing of a trial balance. Formats for the trial balance and some of the financial statements (in accordance with the standards) are shown in other chapters of the guide.

Statement of comprehensive income (income statement/ trading and profit and loss account)

This statement is a financial report listing the revenues, expenses of its daily operations, other expenses and income (for some firms) and net income or net loss of a business for a specified period of time. It indicates the financial performance of the firm. The statement of comprehensive income provides the ending figure used in preparing the statement of owner's equity. Income statements are generally presented using the multiple-step statement format or the single-step format. The format of the multiple-step statement is presented in other sections of this guide. A format of the single-step income statement is presented below:

XYZ
Statement of Comprehensive Income
As at 31 December 2014

	$	$
Revenues and gains		
Sales (net of discounts and returns)		xxx xxx
Rent revenue		xx xxx
Interest revenue		xx xxx
Total revenues		xxx xxx
Less: Expenses and losses		
Cost of goods sold	xxx xxx	
Distribution expenses	xx xxx	
General and administrative expenses	xx xxx	
Income tax expense	xx xxx	
Total expenses and losses		xxx xxx
Net income		xx xxx

Statement of owner's equity

The statement of owner's equity reports the cause of change in owner's equity for a specific period of time. The owner's equity provides the ending figure used to prepare the balance sheet. The statement is presented as follows:

XYZ
Statement of Owner's Equity
As at 31 December 2014

	$
Balance 01 January 2014	xxx xxx
Add net income (deduct net loss)	xxx xxx
Balance at 31 December 2014	xxx xxx

Statement of financial position (balance sheet)

The statement of financial position reports the assets, liabilities and owner's equity at a specified date. The owner's equity ending balance is used to prepare this statement. The statement of financial position cash balance reconciles with the ending figure in the statement of cash flow.

Statement of cash flow

The statement of cash flow provides information on the cash inflows (receipts) and cash outflows (payments) for a specific period of time. The statement reports a business's:

- effects of cash operations
- investing activities
- financing activities
- net increase or decrease in cash during the period
- cash amount at the end of the period.

The format for the statement of cash flow is presented in Chapter 8 of this guide.

Test Your Knowledge

Match the financial statements with the phrases listed in the following table.

[4 marks (1 mark for each correct statement)]

Financial statements	Phrases
(i) Statement of cash flow	Reports assets, liabilities and owner's equity
(ii) Statement of owner's equity	Reports financing activities
(iii) Statement of comprehensive income	Provides ending figure for statement of financial position
(iv) Statement of financial position	Determines net income or net loss

Preparation of financial statements from incomplete records

Key issues to remember when preparing financial statements from incomplete records are:

1. Calculate net profit using **ONLY** balances of assets and liabilities at the start and at the end of an accounting period:
   a. Capital at close less capital at start less capital introduced during the year add drawings for the year. (See example below.)

   Jack, owner of Beanstore Enterprises began his business with $20 000 cash. During the year he made an additional investment of $15 000 in cash and withdrew $4 500 for personal use. His closing capital was valued at $32 000. Jack's profit earned during the period is:

   Closing capital + drawings – investment – opening capital = net profit
   $32 000   + $4 500   – $15 000   – $20 000   = $1 500

2. Use ratios to prepare the statement of comprehensive income (SOCI) and statement of financial position (SOFP)
   a. Use ratios such as receivables collection period, payables payment period, stock turnover, current and acid test ratios, fixed asset turnover and others.
   b. Ensure that you are able to convert gross margin to mark up or vice versa (see formula and example below).

   > Mark up = gross profit ÷ cost of sales (goods sold)
   > Margin = gross profit ÷ sales
   > If mark up is 30 per cent then
   > Gross profit = sales – cost of sales
   > 30 = 130 – 100
   > Margin is 30/130

3. Prepare the receivables control account in order to calculate:
   a. credit sales
   b. amounts collected from receivables
   c. closing balance
   d. opening balance

4. Prepare the payables control account in order to calculate:
   a. credit purchases
   b. amounts paid for payables
   c. closing balance
   d. opening balance

5. Prepare statement of comprehensive income

6. Prepare statement of financial position

Example

Samantha is the owner of a clothing store. Owing to a fire on her business premises, some of the records and vouchers for the year ended 31 December 2014 were destroyed. The following information was available from the records that were salvaged:

	01 January	31 December
Cash	3 844	5 927
Inventory	4 792	4 068
Receivables	5 630	4 315
Payables	3 266	4 787
Machine	46 000	See note 4
Receipts from receivables		71 084
Payments for payables		42 518
Operating expenses (excluding depreciation)		5 718

Additional information:

1. Cash purchases for the year $7 779
2. Cash sales for the year $5 291
3. Operating expenses outstanding $2 150
4. During December new machine purchased at a cost of $8 400. Fixed assets are to be depreciated by 10 per cent of the balance at the beginning of the year
5. Assume that gross profit was earned throughout at the uniform rate of 30 per cent on sales
6. Drawings for the year amounted to $9 877

Required

Prepare a statement of comprehensive income for the year ended 31 December 2014, statement of changes in owner's equity and statement of financial position on that date.

Solution

1. *Calculation of sales*

Balance on 31 December 2014	$ 4 315
Add receipts from receivables	71 084
	75 399
Less balance on 01 January 2014	5 630
Credit sales for the year	69 769
Calculation of total sales	
Credit sales	69 769
Add cash sales	5 291
Total sales for the year	75 060

2. *Calculation of purchases*

Balance on 31 December 2014	$4 787	
Add payments for payables	42 518	
	47 305	
Less balance on 01 January 2014	3 266	
Credit purchases for the year	44 039	
Calculation of total purchases		
Credit purchases	44 039	
Add cash purchases	7 779	
Cash purchases for the year	51 818	
Calculation of operating expenses		
Operating expenses	5 718	
Add outstanding expenses	2 150	
Operating expenses for the year	7 868	

3. *Statement of comprehensive income*

Samantha Statement of Comprehensive Income
For the year ended 31 December 2014

Sales		$75 060
Opening stock	4 792	
Purchases	51 818	
Available for sale	56 610	
Closing inventory	(4 068)	
Cost of goods sold		(52 542)
Gross margin		22 518
Operating expenses	7 868	
Depreciation expenses	4 600	
Total expenses		(12 468)
Net margin		10 050

4. *Statement of owner's equity*

Calculation of capital as at 01 January 2014

Assets – liabilities = capital

$60 266 – $3 266 = $57 000

Samantha Statement of Owner's Equity

Capital 01 January 2014	57 000
Add net margin	10 050
	67 050
Less drawings	(9 877)
Owner's equity at 31 December 2014	57 173

5. *Statement of financial position*

Samantha Statement of Financial Position
As at 31 December 2014

Plant, property and equipment		
Machine (net depreciation)		$49 800
Current assets		
Inventory	4 068	
Receivables	4 315	
Cash	5 927	
Total current assets		14 310
Total assets		64 110
Owner's equity and liabilities		
Owner's equity		57 173
Current liabilities		
Outstanding expenses	2 150	
Payables	4 787	
		6 937
Total owner's equity and liabilities		64 110

Test Your Knowledge

1. What is the formula used to convert gross margin to mark up? **[1 mark]**
2. What are the elements used to calculate credit purchases? **[4 marks]**
3. What are the elements used to calculate the owner's capital at end of an accounting year? **[4 marks]**
4. Alice Wonderland does not keep proper accounting records and she presents you with the following information pertaining to her last accounting period.

	2013	2014
	$	$
Machinery	40 000	40 000
Inventory	9 800	
Bank	12 000	12 160
Payables	7 750	14 780
Receivables	8 400	7 500
Utilities owing	300	200

Her bank records for the period show the following receipts and payments:

		$
Receipts:	Sales	7 380
Payments:	Creditors	12 595
	Utilities	1 800
	Rent	3 000
	Equipment	5 000

Additional information:

Alice Wonderland's gross profit is 30 per cent of sales

Required:

Prepare the statement of comprehensive account for the year ended 2014 and a statement of financial position as at that date. **[25 marks]**

Bank reconciliation

A bank reconciliation statement reveals the correct balance on a bank account. The statement ensures that the correct balance is shown in the statement of financial position. Usually, for effective internal controls in a business, the reconciliation is prepared by somebody other than the cashier, to minimise fraud or stealing of funds. Internal controls were discussed in more detail in Chapter 3 of this revision guide.

Bank reconciliation identifies the reasons why the bank account's (in the cash book) ending balance does not agree with the bank statement ending balance. The reasons are:

1. Errors made by the firm and items not recorded in the bank account.
   Process: use these items to update the bank account. Start with bringing down the balance carried (opposite side of the account).
   Examples include:
   a. bank charges (Cr)
   b. standing orders (Cr)
   c. direct debit (Cr)
   d. direct credit (Dr)
   e. NSF cheques (Cr)
2. Errors made by the bank and items not recorded in the bank statement.
   Process: use these to prepare the bank reconciliation statement
   Examples include:
   a. bank lodgments or unrecorded deposits
   b. unpresented cheques

Steps to follow when preparing a bank reconciliation statement

1. Compare the entries in the cash book with bank statements. Tick items that appear in both the cash book and the bank statement.
2. Enter in the cash book any items that remain unticked in the bank statements. Calculate the new cash book balance.
3. Prepare the reconciliation statement. Begin with the final balance in the new cash book and adjust it for any items that remain unticked in the cash book. The result should equal the balance on the bank statement.

Format of the bank reconciliation statement

Updated bank (cash book) account balance	x
Add unpresented cheques	x
Less bank lodgments/unrecorded deposits	(x)
Bank statement balance	x

Alternative format

Bank statement balance	x
Add bank lodgments/unrecorded deposits	x
Less unpresented cheques	(x)
Updated bank (cash book) account balance	x

> **Don't forget**
>
> 1. A debit in the bank account is equal to a credit in the bank statement.
> 2. A credit in the bank account is equal to a debit in the bank statement.

Example

The cash book of a ZEDCO shows a favourable bank balance of $3 856 at 30 June 2014. After comparing the entries in the cash book with the entries on the related bank statement you find that:

1. Cheques amounting to $218 entered in the cash book have not yet been presented for payment to the bank.

2. An amount of $50 entered on the debit side of the cash book has not been banked.

3. An amount of $95 has been credited by the bank to the account in error.

4. The bank has debited and then credited the bank statement with an amount of $48, being A. Dad cheque which it forwarded on 01 July 2014 marked 'insufficient funds – return to drawer'.

5. Interest of $10 has been charged by the bank, but not yet entered in the cash book.

6. A cheque from a customer incorrectly entered in the cash book as $88 had been correctly entered by the bank as $188.

Required

a. Record the additional entries to be made in the cash book (remember to bring down the corrected balance).

b. Prepare a bank reconciliation statement.

Solution

a. Additional entries to be made in the cash book:

Statement form

ZEDCO Adjustments to the cash book	
Bank balance shown in the cash book	3 856
Deduct amounts paid out which are on the bank statement but not in the cash book	(10)
	3 846
Adjust for other errors identified in the cash book	
Credit, cash debit A. Dad	(48)
Debit cash $100, credit customer	100
Revised cash book balance	3 898

Alternative cash book (T account) form

Balance brought forward	3 856	Amounts paid out which are on the bank statement but not in the cash book	10
		Errors identified in the cash book – credit, cash debit A. Dad	48
Debit cash $100, credit customer	100	Balance carried down	3 898
	3 956		3 956

b. Bank reconciliation statement:

Bank reconciliation statement as at 30 June 2014

Balance as per cash book	3 898
Add unpresented cheques	218
	4 116
Deduct payments into bank and not shown on bank statement	(50)
Balance at bank	4 066

Test Your Knowledge

1. Explain the reasons for preparing a bank reconciliation statement.   **[3 marks]**
2. Give brief explanations of the following: **[3 marks]**
    a. unpresented cheques
    b. bank lodgments
    c. standing orders.
3. The information below was taken from Readytogo Associates for the month of April 2014.

Readytogo Associates

Cash book (bank columns only)

	$		$
Balance brought down	15 890	Payments	109 290
Receipts	120 450	Balance carried down	27 050
	136 340		136 340
Balance brought down	27 050		

The following differences were spotted in the bank statement:

a. The bank deducted $3470 for loan payments.

b. Two direct payments of $3890 and $1980 for payables were made.

c. $7360 for receivables were deposited in the account.

d. Banks charges of $420 were entered on the bank statement.

Required: Prepare the updated cash book for Readytogo Associates for the month of April 2014.   **[7 marks]**

4. On 31 May 2014, the bank statement of Tryon Enterprises showed a balance of $5670. After updating the cash book the updated balance was $4130. The following differences remained to be reconciled:

    1. Cheques drawn, not yet presented to the bank for payment $2140.

    2. Cash deposited but not appearing on the bank statement $600.

    Required: Prepare the following for the month of May 2014:   **[6 marks]**

    a. Adjusted cash book balance.

    b. The bank reconciliation statement.

Preparation of financial statements for non-profit organisations

Like profit-making organisations, non-profit and non-governmental organisations need to record financial transactions and prepare financial reports. This section of the guide will seek to address the preparation of financial records and statements for non-profit organisations. The records kept and reports made are the receipts and payments account, statement of comprehensive account and statement of financial position.

Receipts and payments account

This account provides a summary listing of cash and bank receipts and payments during the period, indicating the opening and closing balances. The account can be shown in either statement form or T account form.

Statement of comprehensive account

The statement of comprehensive account may include, at times, transactions when there is a fund-raising activity. These transactions will be netted to determine whether the activity made a gross profit or loss. Other than the latter, this account shows all the institution's revenue receipts and revenue expenditure that are used to calculate the organisation's SURPLUS (profits) or DEFICIT (losses) for a specific period. The account is similar to the statement of a sole proprietorship business.

Statement of financial position

The preparation of the statement of financial position is done in the same way as that of the sole proprietor. However, the word 'capital' is replaced by the term 'accumulated fund'. Therefore the calculation of opening capital will be handled the same way; that is, total assets less total liabilities.

Don't forget

1. To use the correct terms and record them correctly for this topic.
2. Ensure to treat your adjustments correctly especially subscriptions, depreciation, loss or sale of property, plant and equipment and losses or gain from investing activities.

MULTIPLE CHOICE QUESTIONS

1. Which of the following statements report the assets, liabilities and owner's equity at a specified date?

   (A) Statement of financial position

   (B) Statement of comprehensive income

   (C) Cash flow statement

   (D) Statement of owner's equity.

2. Which of the following groups would be entered in the equity section of the balance sheet?

   (A) common stock, retained earnings and paid-in capital

   (B) accounts payable, notes payable and loans payable

   (C) cash, accounts receivable and inventory

   (D) retained earnings, common stock and long-term investment.

3. Elements used to calculate closing balance of accounts receivable are:

      I   credit sales

      II credit purchases

      III amounts paid by receivables.

   (A) I

   (B) II

   (C) I and II

   (D) I and III

4. Items used to prepare bank reconciliation statements are:

      I   NSF cheques

      II bank lodgments

      III unpresented cheques.

   (A) I

   (B) II

   (C) I and II

   (D) II and III

The following information refers to Questions 5 and 6.

Fitzroy commenced his business on 01 January with $200 000 with a loan of $5 000. His assets and liabilities at 31 December were as follows:

	$
Building	600 000
Motor van	50 000
Inventory	4 000
Loan from bank	20 000
Accounts payable	18 000

5. Fitzroy's capital on 01 January is:

   (A) $68 000

   (B) $200 000

   (C) $205 000

   (D) $250 000

6. Fitzroy's capital at 31 December is:

   (A) $54 000

   (B) $92 000

   (C) $616 000

   (D) $654 000

7. In non-profit organisations, capital is replaced by the term:

   (A) deficit

   (B) surplus

   (C) share capital

   (D) accumulated fund.

Chapter 7

Accounting for partnerships

Chapter 4 of this revision guide looked at the major forms of business organisations. It covered the organisation's unique features such as formation, ownership, laws and regulations, equity and many other characteristics. This chapter reviews accounting for one of those major business organisations; that is, a partnership. Accounting content areas addressed are:

- creation (formation) of a partnership
- sharing of profits and losses
- admission of partners (that is, deals involving individual partners)
- revaluation of assets
- admission of partners (that is, deals involving the partnership)
- retirement of partner
- sale (conversion) of partnership to a limited liability company and sale of partnership **(only)**.

Creation (formation) of a partnership company

Individuals may form a partnership for reasons such as:

- sharing workload, knowledge and experiences
- sharing of debts
- increasing equity (that is, the capital base)
- increasing products/services offered (which will increase the customer base)
- increasing profits (in order to be a stronger competitor in the market).

Accounting for the formation of a partnership company

Entries relating to the start (creation) of a partnership company are similar to those of a sole trading business. Steps for recording the creation of a partnership are as follows:

1. Add the common assets and liabilities of each partner forming the company.
2. Use fair value of assets.
3. Calculate and create the capital account for each partner (use the accounting equation: assets less liabilities).

The example below illustrates the above steps and accounting journal entries relating to the creation of a partnership company.

Example

Ainsley has been operating a roll-on-roll-off car business in Hardbargain for many years. To increase services offered he has decided to merge with Patrick, the local car alarm specialists. Ainsley's business has the following assets: cash $200 000; inventory $40 000; accounts receivable $30 000; and equipment $60 000. Patrick's assets and liabilities are as follows: cash $150 000; inventory $20 000; accounts receivable $10 000; premises $600 000; equipment $60 000; and notes payable $700 000.

Solution

Key point: Total assets − Total liabilities = Capital/owners' equity

Ainsley's capital = $330 000 − $0 = $330 000

Patrick's capital = $840 000 − $700,000 = $140 000

General Journal

Particulars	Dr $	Cr $
Cash	350 000	
Inventory	60 000	
Accounts receivable	40 000	
Equipment	120 000	
Premises	600 000	
Notes payable		700 000
Ainsley's capital		330 000
Patrick's capital		140 000
	1 170 000	1 170 000
Opening balances for the start of partnership		

Test Your Knowledge

1. List two reasons why individuals might form partnership companies.

    [2 marks]

2. Frank and Franka entered into partnership on 1 January 2011. They agreed to contribute an equal amount of capital and share profits and losses equally. The partners agreed to contribute the following assets.

	Book value	Fair value
Frank		
Machinery	$200 000	
Land and buildings	300 000	$400 000
Accounts receivable	40 000	
Franka		
Cash	60 000	
Equipment	70 000	$75 000
Inventory	20 000	
Notes payable	50 000	

Prepare the journal entry to record the formation of Frank and Franka Partnership.

[10 marks]

Sharing of profits and losses

Partnership agreement

The partnership agreement is a key element in the formation of a partnership company. The agreement will usually be made in writing or verbally. Some of the common provisions contained in the agreement are:

- each partner's contribution of capital to the firm
- ratio for sharing of partnership profits and losses among the partners
- the rights and responsibilities of each partner
- admission of new partners
- rate of interest on capital
- rate of interest to be charged on partner's drawings
- salaries to be paid to partners.

In a partnership, the distribution of net income or loss between partners is influenced by factors such as recognition of experience (including special skills), recognition of each partner's capital and the time committed (devoted) by partners in the business.

If there is no written agreement, the company will use the Partnership Act (1890). The Partnership Act includes the following provisions:

- Partners are not entitled to interest on capital.
- Partners are not entitled to salaries.
- Partners are not to be charged interest on their drawings.
- Partners will share profits and losses equally.

Appropriation (sharing) of partnership profits and losses

Example

To illustrate the appropriation of net income, assume that Chevanese and Vimala partnership agreement provides for:

a. salary allowances of $10 400 to Chevanese and $6 000 to Vimala

b. interest allowance of 10 per cent on capital balances at the beginning of the year, and

c. the remaining income/loss to be shared equally.

The capital balances on 1 January 2014 were Chevanese $40 000, and Vimala $25 000. The partnership net income is $60 000 on 31 December 2014.

Required

Prepare a partial statement of comprehensive income showing the appropriation (sharing) of profits and the journal entry to record the division of net income to partners.

Solution

Net income				60 000
	Chevanese	**Vimala**	**Total**	
Salary allowance	$10 400	$6 000	$16 400	
Interest allowance on partners' capital				
Chevanese ($40 000 × 10%)	4 000			
Vimala ($25 000 × 10%)		2 500		
Total interest			6 500	
Total salaries and interest	14 400	8 500	22 900	(22 900)
Remaining income ($60 000 – $22 900)				37 100
Chevanese ($37 100 × 50%)	18 550			
Vimala ($37 100 × 50%)		18 550		
Total remainder			37 100	(37 100)
Total division of net income	$32 950	$27 050	$60 000	

Recording the division of net income

The journal entry to record the division of net income is:

Date	Particulars	Dr	Cr
31 Dec	Income summary	60 000	
	Chevanese, Capital		32 950
	Vimala, Capital		27 050
	To close Income Summary		

Test Your Knowledge

1. Carl and Carla are discussing how income and losses should be divided in a partnership they plan to create. What factors should be considered in determining the division of net income or net loss? **[5 marks]**

2. Bookers, Jones and James Partnership reports a net income of $60 000. The partners' income ratios are 50 per cent, 30 per cent, and 20 per cent respectively. Prepare the following:

   a. Bookers, Jones and James Partnership Partial Statement of Comprehensive Income, showing each partner's appropriated division of net income. **[8 marks]**

   b. The journal to record the partners' division of net income. **[5 marks]**

3. Three years ago three partners formed a partnership called 'Beautiful Things'. A dispute arose among the partners. One partner invested more assets in the company than the other two partners and, as such, believes that the net income and net losses should be shared with capital ratios. What guides the division of net income and net loss and what does it state? **[6 marks]**

Admission of partners

New partners are admitted in a partnership company for several reasons including: for additional funds/resources, expansion or reduction of operations, and to share risk. A new partner may join the business in one of the following ways:

1. through the purchase of an interest from an existing partner, or
2. by the investment of assets in the partnership.

The steps/journal entry for each of the above will be given below.

Purchase of an interest from existing partner

A new partner can purchase an interest in a partnership company either from a partner leaving the business or through being admitted to the partnership by purchasing part of an existing partner's interest. The steps and journal entry for the latter is illustrated below.

Steps/journal entry

1. Ignore the cash exchanged.
2. Make the following journal entry:
   a. Debit capital account of the existing partner according to the interest purchased from the partner
   b. Credit capital account of incoming partner with the interest purchased.

Example			

Sherrain, one of the partners of WeLegal, has a capital of $40 000. On 1 July, she decides to sell her share in the partnership to Adrianna for $50 000 cash. Caleb, Wendy and Clunis, the other partners at WeLegal, have agreed to admit Adrianna into the partnership.

Required

Prepare the journal entry to record Adrianna's purchase of interest in the company.

Solution

Date	Details	Dr $	Cr $
1 July	Capital (Sherrain)	40 000	
	Capital (Adrianna)		40 000

You will notice that the $50 000 Adrianna received as cash has not been recorded in the partnership's books. This is a private agreement between Sherrain and Adrianna. As far as the business is concerned it is only necessary to transfer Adrianna's capital of $40 000.

Test Your Knowledge

Joan Als decides to pay $60 000 privately to Frank James for a one-third interest in an existing partnership company. What effect does this transaction have on partnership net assets? **[1 mark]**

Investment of assets in the partnership

Investment of assets in a partnership can be dealt with in several ways. The examples below deal with the goodwill method and the bonus method.

Goodwill method

Goodwill is created because of a good location, excellent reputation, excellent contact with suppliers or customers and the superior distribution channel, or the partnership's ability to create value. Two entries are necessary when goodwill is created:

1. To record the investment of the new partner and another
2. To record the goodwill of the partnership.

Steps/journal entry

1. Make journal entry to admit new partner:
   a. Debit asset introduced by new partner
   b. Credit liabilities introduced by new partner
   c. Credit capital of new partner.
2. Calculate partnership goodwill:
   (Capital introduced by incoming partner ÷ stake of partnership acquired) **less** (Capital and current accounts of existing partners + the capital of incoming partner)
3. Make journal entry for goodwill created:
   a. Debit goodwill with the value of goodwill calculated
   b. Credit capital accounts of existing partners (with the value of goodwill to be shared using the old profit and loss sharing ratio)

Example

Grace and Campbell are in partnership with $40 000 capital each, sharing profit and loss equally. On 31 July they agree to admit Soup to one-quarter interest in the partnership as a partner upon investment of $30 000.

Required

You are required to:

a. Make the journal entry to Soup's investment.

b. Calculate goodwill.

c. Record the partnership goodwill.

Solutions

Calculation of goodwill:		$
Value of business ($30 000 × 4)		$120 000
Capital of old partners ($40 000 × 2)	80 000	
Capital of new partner	30 000	110 000
Goodwill		10 000

Journal Entries:

Date	Details	Dr $	Cr $
31 July	Cash	30 000	
	Capital, Soup		30 000
	Goodwill	10 000	
	Capital, Grace		5 000
	Capital, Campbell		5 000

Bonus method

The bonus method requires that a new partner pays a bonus to the existing partners. The bonus acts as compensation to the old partners for the hard work they have put into the company over the years. The bonus is shared among the partners in the old profit sharing ratio. Steps and journal entry for the bonus method are listed below.

Steps/journal entry

1. Make journal entry to admit new partner:
   a. Debit asset introduced by new partner
   b. Credit liabilities introduced by new partner
   c. Credit new partner capital (**Key point: Assets less liabilities = capital**)
2. Calculate bonus:
   a. Add the capital and current accounts of existing partners to the capital introduced by the new partner.
   b. Multiply the answer of (a) above by the interest of the partnership to be acquired by the new partner.
   c. Deduct the answer in (b) above from the contribution of the new partner.
3. Make journal entry
   a. If the answer to (2.c) above is positive, then the surplus will be shared among the existing partners as a bonus. The journal entry is:
      i. Debit: new partner capital accounts
      ii. Credit: Capital accounts of existing partners (bonus will be shared using the old profit and loss sharing ratio)
   b. If the answer to (2.c) is negative, then the new partner must receive a bonus from the existing partners. The journal entry is:
      i. Debit: Capital account of existing partners (bonus will be deducted using the old profit and loss sharing ratio)
      ii. Credit: new partner capital account

Example

Jim and Jones are partners of a very profitable business, sharing profits and losses in the ratio 1:3, respectively. In January their capital accounts were: Jim $60 000 and Jones $90 000. In July they agree to admit Gysai upon investment of $200 000 for one-fifth interest in the business.

Required

You are required to:

1. Calculate the total capital upon Gysai's entry.
2. Calculate Gysai's one-fifth interest.
3. Calculate the bonus to be divided between Jim and Jones.
4. Calculate the new capital accounts for each partner.
5. Make the journal entry to record the admission of Gysai into the partnership and the payment of a bonus to the existing partners.

Solutions

1. Total capital upon Gysai's entry:

	$
Capital Jim	60 000
Capital Jones	90 000
Investment by Gysai	200 000
	350 000

2. One-fifth interest:
   $350 000 ÷ 5 = $70 000

3. Bonus to be divided:
   Bonus = $200 000 − $70 000 = $130 000
   Jim   ¼ × $130 000 = $32 500
   Jones   ¾ × $130 000 = $97 500

4. Calculate the capital of each partner:

Jim   60 000 + $32 500) = $92 500

Jones   ($90 000 + $97 500) = $187 500

Gysai   = $70 000

5. Journal entry to record the admission of Gysai:

Date	Details	Dr	Cr
July	Cash	200 000	
	Capital Jim		32 500
	Capital Jones		97 500
	Capital Gysai		70 000

Test Your Knowledge

Lemon and Lime are partners in Lemlime Partners. The balance sheet balances of the partnership are as follows:

Fixed assets	$300 000	Liabilities	$50 000
Current assets	$100 000	Capital, Lemon	$200 000
		Capital, Lime	$150 000

All profits and losses are to be shared equally.

Orange purchased a 15 per cent interest in capital for $90 000 cash.

Prepare the journal entry to record the admission of Orange (a) under the bonus method and (b) under the goodwill method. **[10 marks]**

Don't forget

Read your questions very carefully to see whether to use the goodwill method or the bonus method.

Dissolution of partnership

Apart from the admission of partnership, partnership companies may close (dissolve) for such reasons as bankruptcy of a partner, retirement of a partner, sale or conversion of partnership company and death of a partner. Illustrated in the section below are steps and entries for the retirement of a partner and sale or conversion of a partnership company.

Retirement of partner

When a partner dies or retires from a continuing partnership, the partner or estate of the deceased partner must be paid what is due to them. In the steps and journal entries below, you will notice that in the case of the retiring partner payment may be less than or in excess of the capital balance. Read your questions carefully for the correct treatment of the latter.

Steps/ journal entry

1. Check to see if assets have changed in value (been revalued).
2. Make journal entries to revalue assets:
   a. **Increase:**
      i. Debit assets with the **increase** in the value of the assets.
      ii. Credit revaluation/capital adjustment account with the **increase** in the value of the assets.
   b. **Decrease:**
      i. Debit revaluation/capital adjustment account with the **decrease** in assets.
      ii. Credit assets with the **decrease** in the value of the assets.
3. Share the balance of the revaluation/capital adjustment account among existing partners using old profit and loss sharing ratio.
   Make journal entries for sharing the balance of the revaluation/capital adjustment account:
   a. **Credit balance of revaluation/adjustment account:**
      i. Debit: revaluation/capital adjustment account
      ii. Credit: individual account(s) of existing partners
   b. **Debit balance of revaluation/adjustment account:**
      i. Debit individual account(s) of existing partners
      ii. Credit revaluation/capital adjustment account
4. If retiring partner is entitled to profit, share profit and update the current accounts.
5. Make journal entry to transfer the current account of the retiring partner to his or her capital account.
   a. Debit current account with a positive/credit balance.
   b. Credit capital account of retiring partner. (Entries will be reversed if the balance of the current account is a negative/debit balance.)
6. Make journal entry to show cash or loan used to close off retiring partner capital account:
   a. Debit capital
   b. Credit cash or loan.

Example

a. Personal transaction

Prem, Makesi and Kirk are partners in PMK and Associates. Their capital balances are $100 000, $80 000 and $60 000 respectively. They share profits and losses 2:5:3 respectively. All assets are valued at fair market value. Kirk decides to retire from the partnership.

Required

Prepare the journal entry to record where Kirk sells his interest to Makesi for $50 000.

Solution

Date	Details	Dr	Cr
	Kirk capital	$60 000	
	Makesi capital		$60 000

Note: You will have seen a transaction like this before. The transaction has no impact on the records of PMK. It is a personal transaction between Makesi and Kirk, so it results in a transfer of capital from Kirk to Makesi.

Example

b. Goodwill

Brittany, Dana, Manisha and Priyaka are in partnership sharing profits and losses equally. Brittany decides to retire on 31 December 2014; the balance sheet at that date is as follows:

Balance sheet of BDMK as at 31 December 2014

	$		$
Assets	250 000	Capital – Brittany	40 000
		Capital – Dana	56 000
		Capital – Manisha	60 000
		Capital – Priyaka	80 000
		Current – Brittany	5 000
		Current – Dana	4 000
		Current – Manisha	3 000
		Current – Priyaka	2 000
	250 000		250 000

Goodwill is to be valued at three times the average of the preceding 3 years' profits, which are as follows:

	$
2012	5 000
2013	15 000
2014	25 000

Brittany agrees that the amount due to her should be recorded as a loan.

Required:

1. Make journal entries to record the retirement of Brittany. (Hint: record the goodwill created.)
2. Prepare a revised balance sheet.

Solution

1. Calculate goodwill

   Average annual profits for the past 3 years
   $$= (5\ 000 + 15\ 000 + 25\ 000) \div 3 = \$15\ 000$$
   Goodwill $= (3 \times \$15\ 000)$ $= \$45\ 000$

Journal entries to record the retirement of Brittany:

Details	Dr	Cr
Goodwill	45 000	
Capital – Brittany		11 250
Capital – Dana		11 250
Capital – Manisha		11 250
Capital – Priyaka		11 250
Record of goodwill adjustment		
Current – Brittany	5 000	
Capital – Brittany		5 000
Transfer of current accounts balance to capital account		
Capital – Brittany	56 250	
Loan – Brittany		56 250
Convert Brittany's capital account to a loan account		

2. Dana, Manisha and Priyaka Balance Sheet as at 1 January 2015:

	$		$
Assets	250 000	Capital – Dana	67 250
Goodwill	45 000	Capital – Manisha	71 250
		Capital – Priyaka	91 250
		Current – Dana	4 000
		Current – Manisha	3 000
		Current – Priyaka	2 000
		Loan from Brittany	56 250
	295 000		295 000

Key points to note

1. Brittany's current account has been credited to her capital account since she is leaving the partnership.
2. The capital accounts of Dana, Manisha and Priyaka have been increased by $11 250. This reflects their share of goodwill in the profit-sharing ratio.

Example

c. Bonus

   1. A retiring partner may receive a bonus when:

      a. The fair market value of the partnership assets is more than their book value.

      b. There is unrecorded goodwill. Or

      c. The remaining partners remove the retiring partner from the firm.

   2. The bonus is deducted from the remaining partners' capital balances on the basis of their income ratios at the time of the withdrawal. The procedure for determining the bonus to the retiring partner and the allocation to the remaining partners is as follows:

      a. Determine the amount of the bonus (that is, subtract the retiring partner's capital account balance from the cash payment made by the partnership company).

      b. Allocate the bonus to the remaining partners on the basis of their income ratios.

Test Your Knowledge

1. List two of the possible reasons why a business partnership may be dissolved. **[2 marks]**

2. Annie, Cheryl and Joyce have capital balances of $120 000, $60 000 and $50 000 respectively. They share profits and losses 4:3:3, respectively. All assets are valued at fair market value. Joyce decides to retire from the partnership. Prepare the journal entry to record where Joyce sells her interest to Cheryl for $40 000. **[2 marks]**

Sale (conversion) of partnership to a limited liability company (corporation)

A partnership business may be sold to a limited liability company, or the partners may convert the business to a corporation in order to obtain the benefits as a limited liability company (corporation). When a corporation retains the partnership books, the assets and liabilities are adjusted to fair market values and a valuation adjustment (realisation) account is created to accumulate the gains and losses. The steps/journal entries in the books of the buyer and seller for the sale of the partnership company are given below.

Books of the buyer (that is, the limited liability company)
Steps

1. Identify all the assets and liabilities required.
2. Use the fair value for all assets and liabilities required.
3. Calculate the value of goodwill (purchase consideration less the fair value of net assets [assets less liabilities] acquired).
4. Calculate the share premium (fair value of net assets acquired less par value of shares issued).

Books of the seller (that is, the partnership)
Steps/journal entry

1. Prepare a realisation (valuation adjustment/capital adjustment) account to calculate the gain or loss on sale or conversion of partnership:
   a. Debit all assets (at book value) sold or transferred.
   b. Debit loss on assets taken over by partners.
   c. Debit any dissolution expenses paid.
   d. Credit all liabilities (at book value) sold or transferred.
   e. Credit gain on liabilities settled by the partnership.
   f. Credit the amount of the purchase consideration (amount paid for the partnership). The purchase consideration may be a combination of cash, loan or shares, the accounts of which must be debited.
   g. The balance is shared among partners using the profit sharing ratios.
2. Make entry to record the shared loss or gain on realisation to partners' capital account
   a. Debit: the shared loss on realisation to partners' capital account, or
   b. Credit: the shared gain on realisation to partners' capital account
3. Make entry to record the value of assets taken over:
   Debit: capital account with the value of any assets taken over
4. Make journal entry to transfer current accounts of the partners' capital accounts
   a. Debit: current account with a positive/credit balance.
   b. Credit: capital account of partners. (Entries will be reversed if the balance of the current account is a negative/debit balance.)

Sale of partnership (ONLY)

1. Prepare a realisation (valuation adjustment/capital adjustment) account to calculate the gain or loss on sale or conversion of partnership:
   a. Debit all assets (at book value) sold or transferred
   b. Debit loss on assets taken over by partners
   c. Debit any dissolution expenses paid
   d. Credit all liabilities (at book value) sold or transferred
   e. Credit gain on liabilities settled by partnership
   f. Credit the amount of the purchase consideration
   g. The balance is shared among partners using the profit sharing ratios

Note: All the above are the same elements of the sale or conversion of a partnership company.

2. Make entry to record the shared loss or gain on realisation to partners' capital account
   a. Debit the shared loss on realisation to partners' capital account, or
   b. Credit the shared gain on realisation to partners' capital account.

Note: If any partner ends up with a debit balance, he or she must introduce cash to close off his or her account. However, if this partner is insolvent, the remaining solvent partners must share the debit balance in the ratio of their fixed capitals.

3. Close off remaining partners' capital accounts with cash.

Don't forget

When a corporation retains a partnership's books, the assets and liabilities are adjusted at fair market value and a valuation adjustment account/capital adjustment account (realisation account) is created to appropriate the gains and losses.

MULTIPLE CHOICE QUESTIONS

1. The information below is for the formation of a partnership company by two sole traders.

Partner A	Assets
	$
Cash	100 000
Inventory	50 000
Accounts receivable	20 000

Partner B	Assets and Liabilities
	$
Cash	200 000
Inventory	30 000
Premises	300 000
Notes payable	50 000

The capital for each partner is:

(A) A $150 000 B $480 000

(B) A $150 000 B $530 000

(C) A $170 000 B $480 000

(D) A $170 000 B $530 000

2. The distribution of net income or loss between partners is influenced by the recognition of:

    I   experience

    II time devoted by partners

    III each partner's capital.

(A) I

(B) II

(C) I and II

(D) I, II and III

3. Trevene, one of the partners of Ede and Trevene Partnership company, has capital of $50 000. She decides to sell her share of the partnership to Akousa for $60 000 cash. The journal entry to record Akousa's purchase of interest is:

(A) Dr Trevene $50 000 Cr Akousa $50 000

(B) Dr Trevene $60 000 Cr Akousa $60 000

(C) Dr Trevene $110 000 Cr Akousa $110 000

(D) Dr Akousa $110 000 Cr Trevene $110 000

4. G and C are in partnership with $50 000 capital, sharing profits and losses equally. They agree to admit S to one-quarter interest in the partnership as a partner upon investment of $30 000 using the goodwill method. The goodwill is:

(A) $20 000

(B) $30 000

(C) $40 000

(D) $120 000

5. Partnership businesses may close down/dissolve for:

    I   retirement of a partner

    II sale or conversion

    III death of a partner.

(A) I

(B) II

(C) I and II

(D) I, II and III

6. A retiring partner may receive a bonus when:

    I   There is unrecorded goodwill.

    II Fair market value is greater than book value.

    III The retiring partner is a senior partner.

(A) I

(B) II

(C) I and II

(D) I and III

7. When a corporation retains a partnership's books:

    I   Assets and liabilities are adjusted at fair market value.

    II A valuation adjustment account is created.

    III The gains and losses are appropriated.

(A) I

(B) II

(C) III

(D) I, II and III

Chapter 8

Preparation of cash flow statement (indirect method only)

IAS 7 *Statement of Cash Flows*

IAS 7 *Statement of Cash Flows* requires an entity to present a statement of cash flows as an integral part of its primary financial statements. Cash flows are classified and presented with the following subheads:
operating activities (either using the 'direct' or 'indirect' method), investing activities, or financing activities.

Objective of IAS 7 (IFRS for SMEs 7.1)

The objective of IAS 7 and the IFRS for SMEs Section 7 is to require the presentation of information about the historical changes in cash and cash equivalents of an entity by means of a statement of cash flows, which classifies cash flows during the period according to operating, investing, and financing activities. The statement of cash flows provides this information.

Under the IFRS for SMEs Section 7.2, cash equivalents are short-term, highly liquid investments held to meet short-term cash commitments rather than for investment or other purposes. An investment normally qualifies as a cash equivalent only when it has a short maturity, less than one year from the date of acquisition. Bank overdrafts are normally considered financing activities similar to borrowings. However, if they are repayable on demand and form an integral part of an entity's cash management, bank overdrafts are a component of cash and cash equivalents. Some examples of cash and cash equivalents are:

- cash in hand
- cash at bank
- short-term investment
- marketable securities
- short-term fixed deposits
- bank overdraft.

All entities that prepare financial statements in conformity with IFRSs are required to present a statement of cash flows. [IAS 7.1and IFRS for SMEs Section 7.3]

The statement of cash flows analyses changes in cash and cash equivalents during a period. Guidance notes to the financial statements will indicate if an investment meets the definition of a cash equivalent. An investment that has a maturity of three months or less from the date of acquisition is considered a short-term investment. Equity investments are normally excluded, unless they are in substance a cash equivalent (e.g. preferred shares acquired within three months of their specified redemption date). [IAS 7.7–8]

Presentation of the statement of cash flows

Key principles specified by IAS 7 for the preparation of a statement of cash flows are as follows:

Operating activities

Operating activities are the main revenue-producing activities of the entity that are not investing or financing activities, so operating cash flows include cash received from customers and cash paid to suppliers and employees[IAS 7.14].

This will include the organisation's cash inflows and outflows from normal operations (found in the income statement) and changes in working capital (found in the balance sheet).

Investing activities

Investing activities are the acquisition and disposal of long-term assets and other investments that are not considered to be cash equivalents. [IAS 7.6]

Financing activities

Financing activities are activities that alter the equity capital and borrowing structure of the entity [IAS 7.6]; interest and dividends received and paid may be classified as operating, investing, or financing cash flows, provided that they are classified consistently from period to period [IAS 7.31]; cash flows arising from taxes on income are normally classified as operating, unless they can be specifically identified with financing or investing activities [IAS 7.35].

The indirect method adjusts accrual-basis profit for the year, or loss, for the effects of non-cash transactions. The operating activities cash flows section of the statement of cash flows under the indirect method would appear something like this:

Profit before interest and income taxes		xx xxx
Add: depreciation – non-cash flow		xx xxx
Add: impairment of assets–non-cash flow		xx xxx
Less: gain on sale of non-current asset		(xx xxx)
Add: loss on sale of non-current asset		xx xxx
(Increase)/ Decrease in current assets		(xx xxx)/xx xxx
Increase/ (Decrease) in current liabilities		xx xxx/(xx xxx)
Interest expense	xx xxx	
Less: Interest accrued but not yet paid	xx xxx	
Interest paid – Cash outflow		(xx xxx)
Income taxes paid – Cash outflow		(xx xxx)
Net cash from operating activities – Can be either positive or negative		$xx xxx

> **Don't forget**
>
> • The statement of cash flow can start with net income.
> • In the changes in working capital area, adjust for the change in income tax payable and interest expense payable.

Non-cash transactions (IAS 7.43 and IFRS for SMEs Section 7:18 and 7:19)

An entity *shall exclude* from the statement of cash flows investing and financing transactions that do not require the use of cash or cash equivalents. *An entity shall disclose such transactions elsewhere in the financial statements in a way that provides all the relevant information about those investing and financing activities.* The exclusion of non-cash transactions from the statement of cash flows is consistent with the objective of a statement of cash flows because these items do not involve cash flows in the current period. Examples of non-cash transactions are:

• the acquisition of assets either by assuming directly related liabilities or by means of a finance lease
• the acquisition of an entity by means of an equity issue
• the conversion of debt to equity.

Other disclosures IAS 7.21

An entity shall disclose, together with a commentary by management, the amount of significant cash and cash equivalent balances held by the entity that are not available for use by the entity. Cash and cash equivalents held by an entity may not be available for use by the entity because of, among other reasons:

• foreign exchange controls, or
• legal restrictions (statutory requirements).

Limitations of statement of cash flows

The limitations of the statement of cash flows are as follows:

• Cash flow information is historical in nature and therefore not a prediction of the future.
• Cash flows can be manipulated.

- Much of the detailed information is disclosed in the notes and therefore the notes must be reviewed carefully.
- It may not always be so easy to distinguish between cash and cash equivalent.

Test Your Knowledge

1. What is the objective of IAS 7 statement of cash flows?   **[4 marks]**

2. List four items that make up cash and cash equivalents.   **[4 marks]**

3. List three limitations of statements of cash flows.   **[3 marks]**

4. Give two examples of non-cash investing and financing activities that although not shown in the cash flow statement are to be reflected in the notes to the accounts.   **[2 marks]**

5. Why are non-cash investing and financing activities reflected in the notes to the accounts?   **[4 marks]**

6. Give a reason why a significant amount in cash and cash equivalents held by an entity may not be available for the entity's use.   **[1 mark]**

7. Define financing activities under IAS 7.   **[1 mark]**

8. Define investing activities under IAS 7.   **[1 mark]**

9. Under which heading in the statement of cash flows does changes in working capital fall?   **[1 mark]**

10. Is a gain on the sale of property a cash inflow, outflow or a non-cash flow?   **[1 mark]**

Format for the statement of cash flows (indirect method)

ABC Company Ltd
Statement of Cash Flows for the year ended 20X5

Cash flows: Operating activities		
Net income before interest and tax		xxx
Adjustments:		
Add: Depreciation		xxx
Add: Loss on sale of non-current asset		xxx
Less: Gain on sale of non-current asset		(xxx)
Add: Impairment of non-current assets		xxx
		xxx
Changes in working capital		
Add: Decrease in current assets		xxx
Less: Increase in current assets		(xxx)
Add: Increase in payable accounts (except interest payable and tax payable)		xxx
Less: Decrease in payable accounts (except interest payable and tax payable)		(xxx)
Interest expense	xxx	
Less: Interest accrued	(xxx)	
Less: Interest paid		(xxx)
Less: Taxes paid		(xxx)
Net cash flows from operating activities (this figure can be positive or negative)		xxx
Cash flows: Investing activities		
Proceeds from sale of non-current assets	xxx	
Purchase of non-current asset	(xxx)	
Net cash flows from investing activities (this figure can be positive or negative)		xxx
Cash flows: Financing activities		
Proceeds from general or rights issue of common stock (ordinary shares)	xxx	
Proceeds from issue of preference shares	xxx	
Redemption of shares (Treasury Stock)	(xxx)	
Issue of Treasury Stock	xxx	
Proceeds from sale of debentures /bonds	xxx	
Redemption of debentures /bonds	(xxx)	
Proceeds from note payable	xxx	
Repayment of note payable	(xxx)	
Dividends paid	(xxx)	
Net cash flow from investing activities (this figure can be either positive or negative)		xxx
Net increase/ (decrease) in cash (this figure can either be positive or negative)		xxx
Opening cash and cash equivalents balance (as seen in the previous year balance sheet)		xxx
Closing cash and cash equivalents balance (as seen in the current year's Balance Sheet)		xxx

Example

Stony Hills Corporation
Balance Sheet as at 31 December 2015

	2015 $	2014 $
Assets		
Current assets		
Cash	33 000	4 500
Accounts receivable	33 000	34 500
Merchandise inventory	52 500	51 000
Non-current assets		
Plant assets	229 800	145 800
Accumulated depreciation – Plant assets	(40 800)	(37 800)
Total assets	**307 500**	**198 000**
Liabilities and stockholders' equity		
Liabilities		
Current liabilities		
Account payable	52 500	39 000
Accrued expenses	10 500	13 500
Income tax payable	15 000	15 000
Non-current liabilities		
Bonds payable	126 000	79 500
Total Liabilities	204 000	147 000
Stockholder's equity		
Common stock	78 000	30 000
Retained earnings	40 500	28 500
Treasury stock	(15 000)	(7 500)
Total stockholders' equity	103 500	51 000
Total liabilities and stockholders' equity	**307 500**	**198 000**

Stony Hills Corporation
Income Statement for the year ended 31 December 2015

	$	$
Sales revenue		993 000
Less: Cost of goods sold		(840 000)
Gross profit		153 000
Operating expenses		
Salaries and wages expense	69 000	
Depreciation expense	15 000	
Rent expense	3 000	
Total operating expenses		(87 000)
Operating income		66 000
Other revenue and expenses:		
Loss on disposal of plant assets	(3 000)	
Total other revenues and expenses		(3 000)
Net income before income taxes		63 000
Income tax expense		(24 000)
Net income		**39 000**

Additional information

Purchase of equipment	210 000
Dividends paid	27 000
Proceeds from issuance of common stock	28 500
Issuance of bonds	66 000
Receipt from sale of equipment	
(Cost $126 000; Accumulated depreciation $12 000)	111 000
Cash paid for purchase of treasury stock	7 500

Required

Prepare Stony Hill's Corporation statement of cash flows for the year ended 31 December 2015 according to IAS 7 using the indirect method.

Solution

Stony Hills Corporation
Statement of Cash Flows for the year ended 31 December 2015

	$	$
Cash flows from operating activities		
Net income		39 000
Add: Depreciation expense		15 000
Add: Loss on disposal of plant assets		3 000
		57 000
Working capital changes		
Decrease in account receivable	1 500	
Increase in merchandise Inventory	(1 500)	
Increase in accounts payable	13 500	
Decrease in accrued expenses	(3 000)	10 500
Net cash flow from operating activities		67 500
Cash flows from investing activities		
Payment from purchase of equipment	(210 000)	
Sale of plant assets	111 000	
Net cash flow from investing activities		(99 000)
Cash flow from financing activities		
Dividends paid	(27 000)	
Proceeds from issuance of common stock	48 000	
Proceeds from issuance of bonds	46 500	
Cash paid for purchase of treasury stock	(7 500)	
Net cash flow from financing activities		60 000
Net increase/(decrease) in cash		28 500
Opening cash balance		4 500
Closing cash balance		33 000

Test Your Knowledge

1. Copy and complete the table below; the first row has been completed as an example. **[11 marks]**

	Type of activity	Inflow, outflow or non-cash flow
Depreciation expense for the period	Operating	Non-cash flow
Increase in accounts receivables		
Proceeds from issue of bonds		
Issue of common stock in exchange for a partnership business		
Cash purchase of a motor vehicle for use in the business		
Decrease in merchandise inventory		
Loss on sale of long-term investment		
Bonus issue of shares		
Gain on sale of land		
Payment of dividends		
Decrease in accrued liabilities		

2. The following is data extracted from the financial statements of DOM Industries Ltd:

Income Statement	
	$
Net income	45 000
Depreciation expense	8 360
Balance Sheet	
Increase in accounts receivable	7 500
Decrease in accounts payable	4 750

Compute net cash from operating activities for DOM Industries Ltd. **[5 marks]**

3. BBSSA Ltd has supplied the following data for 31 December 2015.

	$		$
Depreciation expense	14 000	Net income	65 000
Cash payment of dividends	20 000	Increase in current assets other than cash	12 000
Proceeds from issuance of common stock	7 300	Decrease in current liabilities	19 000
Cash receipt from sale of office equipment	41 000	Cash purchase of land	25 000

Compute the following for BBSSA Ltd:

a. Net cash flow from operating activities   **[4 marks]**

b. Net cash flow from investing activities   **[2 marks]**

c. Net cash flow from financing activities.   **[2 marks]**

4. Prepare Casablanca Corporation Statement of Cash Flows for the year ended 31 December 2017. **[25 marks]**

Casablanca Corporation
Balance Sheet as at 31 December 2017

	2017 $	2016 $
Assets		
Current assets		
Cash	55 000	7 500
Accounts receivable	55 000	57 500
Merchandise inventory	87 500	85 000
Non-current assets		
Plant	383 000	243 000
Accumulated depreciation - Plant	(68 000)	(63 000)
Total assets	512 500	330 000
Liabilities and stockholders' equity		
Liabilities		
Current liabilities		
Account payable	87 500	65 000
Accrued expenses	17 500	22 500
Income tax payable	25 000	25 000
Non-current liabilities		
Bonds payable	210 000	132 500
Total liabilities	340 000	245 000
Stockholder's equity		
Common stock	130 000	50 000
Retained earnings	67 500	47 500
Treasury stock	(25 000)	(12 500)
Total stockholders' equity	172 500	85 000
Total liabilities and stockholders' equity	512 500	330 000

Casablanca Corporation
Income Statement for the year ended 31 December 2017

Sales revenue		1 655 000
Less: Cost of goods sold		(1 400 000)
Gross profit		255 000
Operating expenses:		
Salaries and wages expense	115 000	
Depreciation expense	25 000	
Rent expense	5 000	
Total operating expenses		(145 000)
Operating income		110 000
Other revenue and expenses:		
Loss on disposal of plant assets	(5 000)	
Total other revenues and expenses		(5 000)
Net income before income taxes		105 000
Income tax expense		(40 000)
Net income		65 000

Additional information:

Purchase of equipment	350 000
Dividends paid	45 000
Proceeds from issuance of common stock	80 000
Issuance of bonds	77 500
Receipt from sale of equipment	
(Cost $210 000; Accumulated depreciation $20 000)	185 000
Cash paid for purchase of treasury stock	12 500

MULTIPLE CHOICE QUESTIONS

1. Cash and cash equivalents include:

    I   cash in hand and short-term investment

    II bank overdraft and marketable securities

    III equity investment and accounts payable

    (A) I

    (B) II

    (C) I and II

    (D) I and III

2. In which of the following categories/sections would altering of equity capital and borrowing payables of an entity be shown?

    (A) financing

    (B) investing

    (C) operating

    (D) non-cash

3. Which of the following adjustments are added to profit before interest and tax?

    (A) depreciation and impairment of assets

    (B) gain on sale of non-current assets

    (C) depreciation and gain on sale of non-current assets

    (D) impairment of assets and gain on sale.

4. Issue of Treasury Stock may be classified as:

    (A) operating activity

    (B) planning activity

    (C) financing activity

    (D) investing activity.

5. Non-cash transactions include:

    I   acquisition of assets by means of a finance lease

    II acquisition of an entity by means of an equity issue

    III conversion of a debt to equity.

    (A) I

    (B) II

    (C) I and II

    (D) I, II and III

Chapter 9

Financial statement analysis: ratios

Financial statement analysis (or financial analysis) is the process of reviewing and analysing a company's financial statements to make better economic decisions. These statements include the balance sheet, statement of comprehensive income (income statement, a statement of retained earnings) and statement of cash flows. Financial statement analysis is done for a number of reasons that are useful for users; they are usually analysed using the four groups of ratios. The following ratios are recommended for the use of the CAPE Accounting Syllabus.

Liquidity ratios

Liquidity ratios are set out in Table 9.1.

Table 9.1 Liquidity ratios

Name of ratio	Formula	Purpose
Current ratio	$\dfrac{\text{Current assets}}{\text{Current liabilities}} = x:1$	Measures the firm's ability to cover its short-term obligations. Current international standard 1.5:1
Acid test (Quick Ratio)	$\dfrac{\text{Cash + Bank + Short-term investments + Accounts Receivable + Short-term notes receivable}}{\text{Current liabilities}} = y:1$	Measures the ability of the firm to pay its short-term obligations should creditors demand payment immediately

Benefits of strong liquidity ratios to the company

The benefits of strong liquidity ratios to the company are as follows:

1. More liquid assets available for use by the firm for:
   a. purchase of non-current assets for future revenue and cash generation
   b. turning it into stronger interest-bearing short-term investments for further revenue and cash generation
   c. paying dividends
   d. redeeming shares (treasury stock)
   e. paying off debts.
2. Increased shareholders' confidence due to:
   a. potential cash dividends
   b. funds to replace assets and further investment for greater future returns.
3. Increased confidence by potential investors:
   a. a sign of excess liquidity provides potential cash dividends
4. Increased confidence by creditors as there is the possible payment of short-term debt on-time or earlier, which may result in:
   a. willingness to extend lines of credit
   b. willingness to offer new lines of credit.

Demerits of weak liquidity ratios

The demerits of weak liquidity ratios are:

1. Lack of cash to:
   a. pay short or even long-term obligations as they become due
   b. meet running expenses/overheads of the firm
   c. pay cash dividends
   d. meet expansion plans of the organisation.
2. Poor liquidity may result in:
   a. loss of creditor confidence resulting in reduced or no lines of credit and balance due being demanded
   b. loss of shareholder/potential investor confidence as cash may not be available for payment of dividends
   c. insolvency and resulting bankruptcy.

Profitability ratios

Profitability ratios are set out in Table 9.2.

Table 9.2 Profitability ratios

Name of ratio	Formula	Purpose
Gross margin percentage	$\dfrac{\text{Gross profit} \times 100}{\text{Net sales}} = a\,\%$	The percentage profit that the firm makes before period costs (administrative, selling and finance costs) are deducted
Net income percentage or net margin percentage	$\dfrac{\text{Net income} \times 100}{\text{Net sales}} = b\,\%$	The percentage profit the business makes for the year after all costs are deducted
Return on assets (ROA)	$\dfrac{\text{Net income} + [\text{Interest expense} \times (1 - \text{tax rate})]}{\text{Total assets}} = c\,\%$	Measures the firm's return from its investment in assets, indicating the measure of efficiency of the assets
Return on capital employed (ROCE)	$\dfrac{\text{Net income} \times 100}{\text{Capital employed*}} = d\,\%$ *Non-current liabilities + Shareholders' Equity	Shows the efficiency of the use of capital employed in the accounting period. This is the return to current investors in the firm
Earnings per share	$\dfrac{\text{Net income}}{\text{Average number of ordinary shares in issue*}} = \$d \text{ per share}$ *(opening number of shares in issue + closing number of shares in issue) ÷ 2	Shows the potential earnings (maximum possible dividend) that the shareholders (stockholders) can receive from the net income.
Price earnings ratio	$\dfrac{\text{Market price per share*}}{\text{EPS}} = e$ *Available from the stock exchange	The ratio show the relationship between potential dividend and market price per share
Dividend payout ratio	$\dfrac{\text{Total common stock dividend} \times 100}{(\text{Net income} - \text{preferred dividend})} = f\,\%$	Measures the percentage of net income that has been paid out to shareholders
Dividend per share	$\dfrac{\text{Total common stock dividend*}}{\text{Number of common stock in issue}} = \$g \text{ per share}$ *This is dividend declared by the board of directors	Shows the amount of dividend each share gets

Results of strong profitability ratios

Strong profitability ratios result in:

a. increased investor (shareholders and potential investors) confidence in the management of the resources of the organisation

b. company ranking increased

c. increase in the price of the share in the market

d. increased creditor confidence in the longevity of the company, which may result in willingness to provide debt funding.

Solvency ratios

Solvency measures the firm's financial health in relation to its debt, therefore measuring its ability to remain in business over the long term. Solvency ratios are set out in Table 9.3.

Table 9.3 Solvency ratios

Name of ratio	Formula	Purpose
Debt to total assets	$\dfrac{\text{Total liabilities} \times 100}{\text{Total assets}} = h\ \%$	Reflects the level of control creditors have on the business's assets. This can be easily compared to the level of control by the owners.
Debt to equity or gearing	$\dfrac{\text{Total liabilities}}{\text{Total stockholders' equity}} = i\ \text{times}$	Indicates how many times that creditors have control in relation to stockholders.
Time interest earned or interest cover	$\dfrac{\text{Net income before interest and tax*}}{\text{Interest expense}} = j\ \text{times}$ *Net income + Interest expense + Income Tax expense	Shows the firm's ability to meet the current year's interest payments out of current year's earnings.

Activity ratios

Activity ratios are set out in Table 9.4.

Table 9.4 Activity ratios

Name of Ratio	Formula	Purpose
Inventory turnover	$\dfrac{\text{Cost of sales}}{\text{Average inventory*}} = k\ \text{times}$ *$\dfrac{\text{(Opening inventory + Closing Inventory)}}{2}$	Shows the average holding of inventory over the accounting period therefore measuring the efficiency of inventory management.
Average payables or payment period	$\dfrac{\text{Average accounts payables} \times 365\ \text{days}}{\text{Cost of sales}} = l\ \text{days}$	Measures the length of time that the business takes to pay its creditors.
Average receivables or collection period	$\dfrac{\text{Average accounts receivables} \times 365\ \text{days}}{\text{Credit sales}} = m\ \text{days}$	Measures the average length of time a business must wait before being paid by debtors.

Don't forget

The use of the closing accounts payables and closing accounts receivables is also used.

Vertical analysis versus horizontal analysis

Vertical analysis is the analysis of financial statements in one accounting period, whereas horizontal analysis compares financial statements over two or more periods, or two or more organisations. Vertical analysis has some inherent weaknesses:

1. There is a lack of comparison to indicate whether the company has improved, or its status has weakened in relation to a previous period.
2. There is a lack of comparison to industry benchmarks and in relation to other companies to identify the position in the industry.

Example

Income Statement
For the year ended 31 December 2015

	Denn Co. $ (in millions)	Harps Co. $ (in millions)
Revenue	20 885	19 953
Operating expenses:		
Cost of revenue	5 638	4 833
Research and development	2 371	2 185
Sales and marketing	3 762	3 825
General and administrative	1 120	945
Total operating expenses	12 891	11 788
Operating income	7 994	8 165
Other income	245	332
Income before income taxes	8 239	8 497
Provision for income taxes	1 615	1 863
Net income	6 624	6 634

Balance Sheet as at 31 December 2015

	Denn Co. $ (in millions)	Harps Co. $ (in millions)
Assets		
Current assets:		
Cash, cash equivalents, and short-term investments	51 736	52 772
Accounts receivable (net)	13 643	14 987
Inventories	1 351	1 372
Deferred income taxes	2 169	2 467
Prepaid expenses	3 614	3 320
Total current assets	72 513	74 918
Property and equipment, net of accumulated depreciation	8 010	8 162
Equity and other investments	7 550	10 865
Goodwill	19 670	12 581
Intangible assets net	2 581	744
Other long-term assets	1 919	1 434
Total assets	112 243	108 704

Liabilities and stockholders' equity			
Current liabilities:			
Accounts payable	3 884		4 197
Accrued compensation	2 677		3 575
Income taxes	921		580
Short-term unearned revenue	13 985		15 722
Securities lending payable	849		1 208
Other	3 057		3 492
Total current liabilities	25 373		28 774
Non-current liabilities:			
Long-term debt	11 932		11 921
Long-term unearned revenue	1 349		1 398
Deferred income taxes	1 082		1 456
Other long-term liabilities	8 386		8 072
Total non-current liabilities	22 749		22 847
Total liabilities	48 122		51 621
Commitments and contingencies			
Stockholders' equity:			
Common stock and paid-in capital	(average shares in issue – 8 382 m) 63 902		(average shares in issue – 8 376 m) 63 415
Retained earnings (deficit)	219		(6 332)
Total stockholders' equity	64 121		57 083
Total liabilities and stockholders' equity	$ 112 243		$ 108 704

Ratio calculations

(Calculate the ratios that can be done based on the data available in the financial statement of the companies)

Liquidity ratios

Name of ratio	Denn Co. (in millions)	Harps Co. (in millions)
Current ratio	$\dfrac{72\,513}{25\,373} = 2.86{:}1$	$\dfrac{74\,918}{28\,774} = 2.60{:}1$
Acid test	$\dfrac{(51\,736 + 13\,643)}{25\,373} = 2.58{:}1$	$\dfrac{(52\,772 + 14\,987)}{28\,774} = 2.36{:}1$

Vertical analysis

Denn Co.
Denn. Co. has favourable liquidity positions as both the current ratio and acid test ratio reflect figures above 2. The current ratio is above the recognised international standard by $1.36: 1 and by 1.63:1 in relation to the acid test. Denn Co. should invest the excess cash in short or long-term investments to generate revenue. Shareholders, potential investors and creditors will be happy with these results, as they may carry benefits to all.

Harps Co.
Harps Co. has a current ratio that indicates it can cover and pay its short-term obligations comfortably. Both the current ratio and acid test are above international standards by 1.1 and 1.41 respectively.

Horizontal analysis

Denn Co. to Harps Co.
In both ratios Denn Co. has a stronger liquidity position than Harps Co. In relation to the current ratio, Denn Co. is greater by $0.26 and $0.22 in relation to the acid test. Creditors may favour Denn. Co. as it has the better liquidity position in extending lines of credit. Potential investors may consider investing in Denn Co., as it has the greater potential for paying cash dividends.

Profitability ratios

Name of ratio	Denn Co. (in millions)	Harps Co. (in millions)
Gross margin percentage	$\dfrac{(20\ 885 - 5\ 638) \times 100}{20\ 885} = 73\ \%$	$\dfrac{(19\ 953 - 4\ 833) \times 100}{19\ 953} = 76\ \%$
Net margin percentage	$\dfrac{6\ 624 \times 100}{20\ 885} = 32\ \%$	$\dfrac{6\ 634 \times 100}{19\ 953} = 33\ \%$
Return on assets (ROA)	$\dfrac{6\ 624 \times 100}{112\ 243} = 5.9\ \%$	$\dfrac{6\ 634 \times 100}{108\ 704} = 6.1\ \%$
Return on capital employed (ROCE)	$\dfrac{6\ 624 \times 100}{(22\ 749 + 64\ 121)} = 7.6\ \%$	$\dfrac{6\ 634 \times 100}{(22\ 847 + 57\ 083)} = 8.3\ \%$
Earnings per share (EPS)	$\dfrac{6\ 624}{8\ 382} = \$0.79$ per share	$\dfrac{6\ 634}{8\ 376} = \$0.79$ per share

Vertical analysis

Denn Co. performance showed a gross margin of 73 per cent of which a significant amount of that profit is eaten up by the firm's period cost (41 per cent). At the end of 2015, however, there seems to be a significantly large net margin percentage of 32 per cent. The assets of the firm showed a 5.9 per cent efficiency level and there was a return of 7.6 per cent on capital invested. Shareholders' potential earnings at the end of the period was $0.79 per share.

Harps Co. performance 2015 showed that the period cost incurred by the firm was 43 per cent, which resulted in a net margin percentage of 33 per cent. Its use of assets for 2015 was 6.1 per cent efficient and shareholders and long-term creditors seemed to generate a return of 8.3 per cent. The potential earning capability of shareholders was $0.79 per share.

Horizontal analysis

Denn Co. to Harps Co.
Harps Co. gross margin was greater than Denn Co. by 3 per cent and by 1 per cent with respect to its net margin percentage. Both organisations had an asset efficiency of approximately 6 per cent as reflected in their return on assets. However, Harps Co. capital employed seemed to be more efficient than that of Denn Co. by 0.7 per cent. Both entities have an earnings per share of $0.79. This shows that both entities had consistently the same level of performance. Investors in both organisations may not have any reason to change their level of investment for the other company. Potential investors looking at both entities' performance will be at odds to invest although Harps Co. insignificantly outperformed Denn Co.

Solvency ratios

	Denn Co.	Harps Co.
Debt to total assets	$\dfrac{48\ 122 \times 100}{112\ 243} = 42\ \%$	$\dfrac{51\ 621 \times 100}{108\ 704} = 47\ \%$
Debt to equity	$\dfrac{48\ 122}{64\ 121} = 0.75$	$\dfrac{51\ 621}{51\ 083} = 0.9$

Vertical analysis

Denn Co. had significantly high debt in the organisation; this is reflected in a debt to total assets ratio of 42 per cent and a high gearing of 0.75. This indicates that creditors have a 42 per cent claim on the company's resources and for every dollar invested by shareholders (the owners of the company) it is matched with $0.75 of creditor interest. This may result in decisions being made by managers more in favour of the creditors to reduce significant debt. This may result in there being no cash dividend paid to shareholders.

Harps Co. solvency ratios reflected significantly high debt to assets of 47 per cent and a gearing of 0.9. This shows that the company creditors had significant interest in it, almost 50 per cent. This is also reflected in the fact that its debt to equity was approximately 1:1. Creditors with that much interest may quickly affect cash flow as the company is committed to the contractual arrangement of meeting its obligations as they become due. One strategy a company can employ to reduce debt is to convert it into equity.

Test Your Knowledge

1. Vertical analysis:

Roaches Records Limited

Income Statement for the year ended 31 December 2015

Net sales	600 000
Cost of goods sold	(288 000)
Gross profit	312 000
Operating expenses	(217 200)
Operating income	94 800
Other revenues and expenses	
Gains on sale of machinery	13 200
Income before taxes	108 000
Income tax expense	(43 200)
Profit for the year	64 800

Compute the following ratios and comment on Roaches Records Limited.   [12 marks]

Gross margin
Operating expense as a percentage of sales
Cost of goods sold as a percentage of sales
Net margin percentage

2. Horizontal analysis: The following information is from the books of Linden Marketing Limited.

	Current year	Preceding year
Balance Sheet		
Cash	6 600	8 800
Short-term investments	4 840	11 770
Net accounts receivables	23 760	32 120
Merchandise inventory	33 880	30 360
Total current assets	69 080	83 050
Total current liabilities	58 520	40 920
Income Statement		
Net sales revenue	184 000	216 000
Cost of goods sold	126 000	168 000
Credit sales	98 000	108 000

Compare the following ratios for both years and comment on the company's liquidity position.

i. Current ratio

ii. Acid test

iii. Inventory turnover

iv. Average collection period [16 marks]

3. Perform a horizontal analysis and vertical analysis of Berbice Sugar Manufacturers Limited. State whether 2018 was a good or bad year and give your reasons to support your position. [12 marks]

Berbice Sugar Manufacturers Limited

Income Statement

For the year ended 31 December

	2018	2017
Revenues		
Net sales	600 000	500 000
Other revenues	0	2 000
Total revenue	600 000	502 000
Expenses		
Cost of goods sold	482 400	340 000
Engineer, selling and administrative expenses	54 000	96 000
Interest tax expense	12 000	10 000
Income tax expense	18 000	6 000
Other expenses	5 400	0
Total expenses	571 800	452 000
Net income	28 200	50 000

4. **Juices Inc.**

Four-year selected financial data

For the year ended 30 September 2017–2014

Income Statement results	2017	2016	2015	2014
	All figures in thousands			
Net sales	31 884	31 736	26 351	19 450
Cost of goods sold	25 644	27 112	17 996	11 582
Interest expense	910	575	544	461
Income from operations	5 401	7 648	3 118	1 576
Income tax expense	885.5	1 133.25	293.5	129.5
Net income	3 542	5 289	1 174	518
Financial position information				
Merchandise inventory	6 717	4 019	2 641	1 650
Total assets	9 179	7 210	5 891	6 339
Stockholders' equity (Par value: $20.00)	2 754	2 570	2 440	2 150

Using the above data for 2017–2014, compute the following ratios and evaluate Juices Inc.'s:

i. Net margin ratio

ii. Earnings per share

iii. Inventory turnover

iv. Times interest earned ratio

v. Rate of return on common stockholder's equity

vi. Gross profit percentage [36 marks]

5. The following is the income statement and balance sheet of Lystra Lawn Care Services Limited.

Lystra Lawn Care Services Limited

Income Statement for the year ended 31 December 2015

	2015	2014
Net sales	350 250	321 000
Cost of goods sold	(177 750)	(163 500)
Gross profit	172 500	157 500
Operating expenses	(102 000)	(100 500)
Income from operations	70 500	57 000
Interest expense	(6 750)	(7 500)
Income before income tax	63 750	49 500
Income tax expense	(19 125)	(14 850)
Net income	44 625	34 650

Lystra Lawn Care Services Limited

Balance Sheet as at 31 December 2015

	2015	2014	2013*
Assets			
Current assets			
Cash	72 750	71 250	
Accounts receivables, net	84 000	88 500	76 500
Merchandise inventory	108 750	122 250	152 250
Prepaid expenses	9 000	3 750	
Total current assets	274 500	285 750	
Property, plant and equipment, net	158 250	134 250	
Total assets	432 750	420 000	448 500
Liabilities			
Total current liabilities	168 750	184 500	
Long-term liabilities	85 500	72 750	
Total liabilities	254 250	257 250	
Stockholders' Equity			
Preferred stock, 3 %	81 000	81 000	
Common stockholders' equity	97 500	81 750	60 000
Total stockholders' equity	178 500	162 750	
Total liabilities and stockholders' equity	432 750	420 000	

* Selected 2013 figures

1. The par value of common stock is $10.00.
2. The market price of the common stock is $14.50 at 31 December 2015 and $11.00 at 31 December 2014.

3. All sales are on credit.

Compute the following ratios for 2015 and 2014.

i. Current ratio

ii. Acid test

iii. Times interest earned ratio

iv. Inventory turnover

v. Gross profit ratio

vi. Debt to equity ratio

vii. Debt to total assets ratio

viii. Earnings per share

ix. Price earning ratio.   **[18 marks]**

MULTIPLE CHOICE QUESTIONS

1. A company with strong liquidity ratios at the end of a year increases:

    I   solvency and resulting in bankruptcy

    II potential shareholders' confidence

    III shareholders' confidence.

(A) I

(B) II

(C) I and II

(D) II and III

2. Which of the following profitability ratios measures a firm's return from investment?

(A) returns on assets (ROA)

(B) returns on capital employed (ROCE)

(C) earnings per share (EPS)

(D) price earnings ratio (PER).

3. Average receivables or collection period measures the:

(A) efficiency of inventory management

(B) percentage of net income that has been paid out to shareholders

(C) average length of time a business must wait before being paid

(D) length of time that a business will take in paying its debts.

4. Which of the following shows the maximum possible dividend that shareholders can receive from net income?

(A) earnings per share (EPS)

(B) price earnings ratio (PER)

(C) dividend payout

(D) dividend per share.

5. Makesi's financial position at the end of the year is as follows:

	$
Cash	15 000
Accounts receivable	25 000
Inventory	30 000
Accounts payable	40 000
Long-term notes payable	200 000

What is Makesi's current ratio?

(A) 0.292:1

(B) 1:1

(C) 1.75:1

(D) 6.75:1

Chapter 10

Notes, disclosures, and post balance sheet events, receivership and liquidation

Inflation and accounting

Current cost accounting

In current cost accounting, assets are valued at their current replacement cost rather than at the price originally paid for them, the approach taken by historical cost accounting. Current cost accounts are drawn up by adjusting the historical cost for inflation and the usual adjustments such as those for depreciation. Current cost accounting is usually used in economies with hyperinflation.

Fair value measurement

1. IFRS 13 *Fair Value Measurement* applies to IFRSs that require or permit fair value measurements or disclosures and provides a single IFRS framework for measuring fair value and requires disclosures about fair value measurement. The standard defines fair value on the basis of an 'exit price' notion and uses a 'fair value hierarchy', which results in a market-based, rather than entity specific, measurement.
2. Exit price: the price that would be received on selling an asset or paid to transfer a liability.
3. Fair value hierarchy has three levels:
   a. Level 1: which is the most reliable is based on observable inputs such as market prices for identical assets and liabilities.
   b. Level 2: this is less reliable than Level 1 and is based on market prices for similar assets and liabilities.
   c. Level 3: which is the least reliable uses unobservable inputs such as company data and assumptions.
4. Fair value as defined by the IFRS for SMEs (Section 2:34b) is the amount for which an asset could be exchanged, or a liability settled, between knowledgeable, willing parties in an arm's length transaction. These include:
   a. investments in non-convertible and non-puttable preference shares, and
   b. non-puttable ordinary shares that are publicly traded or whose fair value can otherwise be measured reliably, which are measured at fair value.
5. Changes in fair value are recognised in profit or loss.

IFRS for SMEs (Section 2.50)

1. For the following types of non-financial assets, this IFRS permits or requires measurement at fair value:
   a. investments in associates and joint ventures that an entity measures at fair value
   b. investment property that an entity measures at fair value
   c. agricultural assets (biological assets and agricultural produce at the point of harvest) that an entity measures at fair value less estimated costs to sell
2. The use of the fair value hierarchy is also complied with under this IFRS.

Test Your Knowledge

1. When may current cost accounting be used?   **[2 marks]**
2. Define fair value measurement in accordance with IFRS 13.   **[2 marks]**
3. List two non-financial assets that are measured at fair value in the financial statements.   **[2 marks]**
4. Where are changes in fair value recorded?   **[1 mark]**
5. Outline the fair value hierarchy used in recording items at fair value. **[4 marks]**

IAS 37: *Provisions, Contingent Liabilities and Contingent Assets*

IAS 37 outlines the accounting for provisions, together with contingent assets and contingent liabilities. Provisions are measured at the best estimate (including risks and uncertainties) of the expenditure required to settle the present obligation, and reflects the present value of expenditures required to settle the obligation where the time value of money is material.

Objective of IAS 37

To ensure that appropriate recognition criteria and measurement bases are applied to these and that sufficient information is disclosed in the notes to the financial statements to enable users to understand their nature, timing and amount.

Key principle of IAS 37

A provision should be recognised only when there is a liability, i.e. a present obligation resulting from past events. *Planned future expenditure, even where authorised by the board of directors or equivalent governing body, is excluded from recognition.*

Provisions

1. A liability of uncertain timing or amount. An entity must recognise a provision if, and only if a present obligation (legal or constructive) has arisen as a result of a past event (the obligating event), payment is:
   - probable ('more likely than not'), and
   - the amount can be estimated reliably.

2. An *obligating event* is an event that creates a legal or constructive obligation and, therefore, results in an entity having no realistic alternative but to settle the obligation. [IAS 37.10] A constructive obligation arises if past practice creates a valid expectation on the part of a third party, for example, a retail store that has a long-standing policy of allowing customers to return merchandise within, say, a 30-day period. [IAS 37.10] The amount recognised as a provision should be the best estimate of the expenditure required to settle the present obligation at the balance sheet date.

3. Provisions for one-off events (restructuring, environmental clean-up, settlement of a lawsuit) are measured at the most likely amount. [IAS 37.40] Provisions for large populations of events (warranties, customer refunds) are measured at a probability-weighted expected value. [IAS 37.39]

4. Both measurements are at discounted present value using a pre-tax discount rate that reflects the current market assessments of the time value of money and the risks specific to the liability. [IAS 37.45 and 37.47] In reaching its best estimate, the entity should take into account the risks and uncertainties that surround the underlying events. [IAS 37.42]

5. If some or all of the expenditure required to settle a provision is expected to be reimbursed by another party, the reimbursement should be recognised as a separate asset, and not as a reduction of the required provision, when, and only when, it is virtually certain that reimbursement will be received if the entity settles the obligation. The amount recognised should not exceed the amount of the provision. [IAS 37.53]

6. In rare cases, for example in a lawsuit, it may not be clear whether an entity has a present obligation. In those cases, a past event is deemed to give rise to a present obligation if, taking account of all available evidence, it is more likely than not that a present obligation exists at the balance sheet date.

A provision should be recognised for that present obligation if the other recognition criteria described above are met. If it is more likely than not that no present obligation exists, the entity should disclose a contingent liability, unless the possibility of an outflow of resources is remote. [IAS37.15]

7. In measuring a provision consider future events as follows:
   a. Forecast reasonable changes in applying existing technology. [IAS 37.49]
   b. Ignore possible gains on sale of assets. [IAS 37.51]
   c. Consider changes in legislation only if virtually certain to be enacted. [IAS 37.50]
   d. Remeasurement of provisions. [IAS 37.59]

Use of provisions

Provisions should only be used for the purpose for which they were originally recognised. They should be reviewed at each balance sheet date and adjusted to reflect the current best estimate. If it is no longer probable that an outflow of resources will be required to settle the obligation, the provision should be reversed. [IAS 37.61]

Disclosures for provisions

1. Reconciliation for each class of provision: [IAS 37.84]
   a. opening balance additions used (amounts charged against the provision)
   b. unused amounts reversed
   c. unwinding of the discount, or changes in discount rate closing balance.
2. A prior year reconciliation is not required. [IAS 37.84]
3. For each class of provision, a brief description of nature, timing, uncertainties, assumptions and reimbursement, if any. [IAS 37.85]

Table 10.1 Circumstances for recognising a provision

Circumstance	Recognise a provision
Restructuring by sale of an operation	Only when the entity is committed to a sale, i.e. there is a binding sale agreement [IAS 37.78]
Restructuring by closure or reorganisation	Only when a detailed form plan is in place and the entity has started to implement the plan, or announced its main features to those affected. A Board decision is insufficient [IAS 37.72]
Warranty	When an obligating event occurs (sale of product with a warranty and probable warranty claims will be made)
Land contamination	As contamination occurs for any legal obligations of clean-up, or for constructive obligations if the company's published policy is to clean-up even if there is no legal requirement to do so (past event is the contamination and public expectation created by the company's policy)
Customer refunds	If the entity's established policy is to give refunds (past event is the sale of the product together with the customer's expectation, at time of purchase, that a refund would be available)
Offshore oil rig must be removed and sea bed restored	For removal costs arising from the construction of the oil rig as it is constructed, add to the cost of the asset. Obligations arising from the production of oil are recognised as the production occurs
Abandoned leasehold, four years to run, no re-letting possible	For the unavoidable lease payments
Onerous (loss-making) contract	Recognise a provision

Table 10.2 Circumstances when a provision is not recognised

Circumstance	Do not recognise a provision
Staff training for recent changes in tax law	No provision is recognised (there is no obligation to provide the training, recognise a liability if and when the re-training occurs)
Major overhaul or repairs	No provision is recognised (no obligation)
Future operating losses	No provision is recognised (no liability)

Contingent liability

This is a possible obligation depending on whether some uncertain future event occurs, or a present obligation but payment is not probable or the amount cannot be measured reliably. A possible obligation (a contingent liability) is disclosed by way of notes to the financial statements but not accrued. However, disclosure is not required if payment is remote. [IAS 37.86]

Contingent asset

This is a possible asset that arises from past events, and whose existence will be confirmed only by the occurrence or non-occurrence of one or more uncertain future events not wholly within the control of the entity. Contingent assets should not be recognised – but should be disclosed where an inflow of economic benefits is probable. When the realisation of income is virtually certain, then the related asset is not a contingent asset and its recognition is appropriate. [IAS 37.31–35]

Test Your Knowledge

1. Define provision under IAS 37. **[3 marks]**

2. When is a provision recognised? **[2 marks]**

3. Give three examples of provisions. **[3 marks]**

4. What is an obligating event? **[2 marks]**

5. Define a constructive obligation and give one example. **[3 marks]**

6. Define contingent assets. **[1 mark]**

7. What criterion allows for contingent assets being recorded in the notes to the financial statements? **[2 marks]**

8. Define contingent liabilities. **[2 marks]**

9. What criterion allows for contingent liabilities being recorded in the notes to the financial statements? **[2 marks]**

10. Management in a board meeting on 20 December 2015 anticipates that it will be engaged in expenditure of $4 million dollars for a major overhaul project to take place in March 2016. They have approved the expenditure and ask the accountant to include it in the financial statement for 2015. Should it be included in the financial statement and why? **[3 marks]**

11. Zidane Industries have been sued by the nearby community of Edinburg 500 for polluting the water. Its lawyers have advised that it is possible that the community can win the case but cannot reliably estimate the cost. How should this be recorded in the financial statements at the end of the accounting period? **[3 marks]**

12. Electrico Manufactures, producers of generator turbines, supplies PowerE with a turbine on 27 December 2015 for $6 million dollars. The turbine has a 4-year warranty and on 15 January 2016 PowerE reported to Electrico Manufactures that the turbine was malfunctioning. The financial statements were signed on 4 February 2016.

    Should the cost be included in the financial statements of Electrico Manufactures on 31 December 2015? State reasons for your answer. **[4 marks]**

Events after the reporting period: IAS 10 and IFRS for SMEs Section 32

Events after the end of the reporting period are those events, favourable and unfavourable, that occur between the end of the reporting period and the date when the financial statements are authorised for issue. There are two types of events:

1. Those that provide evidence of conditions that existed at the end of the reporting period (adjusting events after the end of the reporting period), and
2. Those that are indicative of conditions that arose after the end of the reporting period (non-adjusting events after the end of the reporting period).

Standard accounting practice for post balance sheet events

1. Financial statements should be prepared on the basis of conditions existing at the statement of financial position date.
2. A material post-statement of financial position event requires changes in the amounts to be included in the financial statements, where it is either an adjusting event, or it indicates the application of a going concern concept to the whole or material part of the company is not appropriate.
3. A material post-statement of financial position event should be disclosed where:
   a. It is a non-adjusting event of such materiality that its nondisclosure would affect the ability of the users of financial statements to reach a proper understanding of the financial position, or
   b. It is the reversal or maturity after the year end of a transaction entered into before the year end, the substance of which was primarily to alter the appearance of the company's statement of financial position.
4. The disclosure should state, in note form, the nature of the event and the estimate of the financial effect, or a statement that it is not practicable to make such an estimate.
5. The estimate of the financial effect should be disclosed before taking into account taxation, and the taxation implications should be explained, where necessary, for a proper understanding of the financial position.
6. The date on which the financial statement are approved by the board of directors should be disclosed in the financial statements.

Test Your Knowledge

1. What IAS governs events after the reporting period? **[1 mark]**
2. What should the disclosure, in a note, of a post balance sheet event include? **[3 marks]**
3. According to IAS 10 and IFRS for SMEs Section 32, financial statements should be prepared on what basis? **[1 mark]**
4. Under what circumstances do material post-statements of financial position events require changes in the amount included in the financial statements? **[5 marks]**
5. What is an adjusting event? **[2 marks]**
6. What is a non-adjusting event? **[3 marks]**
7. Under what circumstances do material post-statements of financial position events need to be disclosed? **[4 marks]**

Table 10.3 Published financial statements: disclosures

Section in IFRS for SMEs	Source	Description	Financial reporting requirement
Section 3	IAS 1	Financial statement presentation	3.2 Financial statements shall present fairly the financial position, financial performance and cash flows of an entity. Fair presentation requires the faithful representation of the effects of transactions, other events and conditions in accordance with the definitions and recognition criteria for assets, liabilities, income and expenses. 3.17 A complete set of financial statements of an entity shall include all of the following: (a) A statement of financial position as at the reporting date (b) Either: (i) A single statement of comprehensive income for the reporting period, or (ii) A separate income statement and a separate statement of comprehensive income (c) A statement of changes in equity for the reporting period (d) A statement of cash flows for the reporting period (e) Notes, comprising a summary of significant accounting policies and other explanatory information. 3.18 If the only changes to equity during the periods for which financial statements are presented arise from profit or loss, payment of dividends, corrections of prior period errors, and changes in accounting policy, **the entity may present a single statement of income and retained earnings** in place of the statement of comprehensive income and statement of changes in equity.
Section 4	IAS 1	Statement of financial position	4.11 An entity shall disclose, either in the statement of financial position or in the notes, the following sub-classifications of the line items presented: (a) Property, plant and equipment in classifications appropriate to the entity (b) Trade and other receivables showing separately amounts due from related parties, amounts due from other parties, and receivables arising from accrued income not yet billed (c) Inventories, showing separately amounts of inventories: (i) Held for sale in the ordinary course of business (ii) In the process of production for such sale (iii) In the form of materials or supplies to be consumed in the production process or in the rendering of services. (d) Trade and other payables, showing separately amounts payable to trade suppliers, payable to related parties, deferred income and accruals (e) Provisions for employee benefits and other provisions (f) Classes of equity, such as paid-in capital, share premium, retained earnings and items of income and expense that, as required by this IFRS, are recognised in other comprehensive income and presented separately in equity. 4.12 An entity with share capital shall disclose the following, either in the statement of financial position or in the notes: (a) for each class of share capital: (i) The number of shares authorised (ii) The number of shares issued and fully paid, and issued but not fully paid.
Section 5	IAS 1	Statement of Comprehensive income and income statement	5.2 An entity shall present its total comprehensive income for a period either: (a) in a single statement of comprehensive income, in which case the statement of comprehensive income presents all items of income and expense recognised in the period, or (b) in two statements – an income statement and a statement of comprehensive income – in which case the income statement presents all items of income and expense recognised in the period except those that are recognised in total comprehensive income outside of profit or loss as permitted or required by this IFRS. 5.11 An entity shall present an analysis of expenses using a classification based on **either the nature of expenses or the function of expenses** within the entity, whichever provides information that is reliable and more relevant.

Table 10.3 continued

Section in IFRS for SMEs	Source	Description	Financial reporting requirement
Section 6	IAS 1	Statement of changes in equity	6.1 This section sets out requirements for presenting the changes in an entity's equity for a period, either in a statement of changes in equity or, if specified conditions are met and an entity chooses, in a statement of income and retained earnings. Information to be presented in the statement of income and retained earnings: 6.5 An entity shall present, in the statement of income and retained earnings, the following items in addition to the information required by Section 5 Statement of Comprehensive Income and Income Statement: (a) Retained earnings at the beginning of the reporting period (b) Dividends declared and paid or payable during the period. (c) Restatements of retained earnings for corrections of prior period errors (d) Restatements of retained earnings for changes in accounting policy (e) Retained earnings at the end of the reporting period.
Section 8	IAS 1	Notes to the financial statements	Structure of the notes 8.2 The notes shall: (a) present information about the basis of preparation of the financial statements and the specific accounting policies used, in accordance with paragraphs 8.5–8.7; (b) disclose the information required by IASs and IFRSs or IFRS for SMEs that is not presented elsewhere in the financial statements; and (c) Provide information that is not presented elsewhere in the financial statements but is relevant to an understanding of any of them. 8.3 An entity shall, as far as practicable, present the notes in a systematic manner. An entity shall cross-reference each item in the financial statements to any related information in the notes. 8.4 An entity normally presents the notes in the following order: (a) a statement that the financial statements have been prepared in compliance with the IFRS for SMEs or IASs; (b) a summary of significant accounting policies applied (see paragraph 8.5 of the IFRS for SMEs); (c) supporting information for items presented in the financial statements, in the sequence in which each statement and each line item is presented; and (d) Any other disclosures.
Section 22	IAS 1	Liabilities and equity	22.3 22.4 Equity is the residual interest in the assets of an entity after deducting all its liabilities. A liability is a present obligation of the entity arising from past events, the settlement of which is expected to result in an outflow from the entity of resources embodying economic benefits. Equity includes investments by the owners of the entity, plus additions to those investments earned through profitable operations and retained for use in the entity's operations, minus reductions to owners' investments as a result of unprofitable operations and distributions to owners.

Test Your Knowledge

1. List a full set of financial statements. **[5 marks]**

2. What statement can an entity prepare instead of the statement of comprehensive income and statement of change in equity? **[2 marks]**

3. List six sub-classifications shown in the statement of financial position. **[6 marks]**

4. What are the classes of inventory to be listed in the statement of financial position under IAS 1 and IFRS for SMEs Section 4.11? **[3 marks]**

5. Under IAS 1 and IFRS for SMEs Section 5.11, what are the two in which expenses can be classified? **[2 marks]**

6. List the order of presenting notes in the financial statements. **[5 marks]**

7. Define equity according to IAS 1. **[2 marks]**

8. Define liabilities according to IAS 1. **[2 marks]**

Receivership and liquidation

Terminology

Bankrupt: a person or business against whom the court has issued a receiving order, as a result of a creditor filing that the debtor has committed an act of bankruptcy.

Illiquid: the inability of a firm to meet its short-term obligations.

Insolvent: this is a firm that:

- is bankrupt and unable to meet its obligations as they become due
- has ceased paying its current obligations in the ordinary course of business as they become due
- has property, plant and equipment with a total value, at fair valuation, which if disposed of would be insufficient to enable the payment of all its obligations due and accruing due. This results in a negative net worth, that is, assets are less than liabilities.

Liquidity: a firm's ability to meet its short-term obligations (current payments).

Receiver: a person appointed by the court when a firm is considered to commit an act of bankruptcy.

Secured creditor: a person or business that a debt is owed to by a firm that is tied to a specific asset or assets of that firm.

Security agreement: a contract for a creditor to get the assigned asset, or the proceeds from the sale of an assigned asset, as payment of a debt, if the debtor is unable to pay.

Solvency: the firm's ability to generate enough cash to cover long-term debts as they mature.

Reasons for bankruptcy

Reasons for bankruptcy include:

a. Changes in the economy such as inflation causing major increased prices in inputs, or recession causing a major fall in selling prices
b. Difficulty in sourcing finance or financiers to continue
c. Poor planning
d. Being indecisive
e. Loss of key employees
f. Overwhelmed by competition
g. Lack of ability to change to suit current demand or advances in technology
h. Unforeseen circumstances such as floods, storms and fires
i. Fraudulent activity.

The receivership process

1. An act of bankruptcy is allegedly committed by a debtor, as the debtor is not meeting its obligation as they mature (become due).
2. The creditor verifies the petition by an affidavit and files it with a court of law.
3. The court dismisses the petition, then the action ends.
4. If the court allows the petition, then a receiving order is made and a receiver appointed. The receiver is limited by the receiving order in his or her management of the business. Generally, under the control of the receiver by law usually are: the inventory, accounts receivable and other property of the debtors. One of the highest priorities of the receiver is the statutory obligations of the bankrupted firm.
5. A receiver informs all the debtors and creditors of the firm of his appointment.
6. The receiver takes custody of the assets.

7. The receiver opens a bank account to facilitate receipts and payment under his or her management.
8. The receiver continues the business and disposes of assets where necessary.
9. The receiver assesses the claims made by the creditor.
10. The receiver prepares a monthly statement of affairs (balance sheet at market values).
11. The receiver, in an effort to carry out the instruction of the court, carries on the business by:
    a. safeguarding assets
    b. monitoring company activities
    c. disposing of assets
    d. discharging the firm's indebtedness.
12. If the business is successful then it is returned to the owners by the receiver as per the terms of the court. If not, then the business is liquidated by disposing of the assets in a commercial manner.

Test Your Knowledge

1.	Define liquidity.	[1 mark]
2.	Identify two ways of recognising an insolvent firm.	[1 mark]
3.	List five reasons for bankruptcy.	[1 mark]
4.	Who appoints the receiver to a bankrupted business?	[1 mark]
5.	Outline the role of the receiver.	[1 mark]

MULTIPLE CHOICE QUESTIONS

1. Current cost accounting value assets at:
   (A) historical cost price
   (B) current replacement cost
   (C) market price
   (D) fair price.

2. IFRS for SMEs Section 13 permits non-financial assets to be measured at fair value. The types of non-financial assets are
      I   investment in joint ventures
      II investment in property
      III agricultural assets add estimated costs to sell.
   (A) I
   (B) II
   (C) I and II
   (D) II and III

3. Which of the following statements recognises the changes in fair value?
   (A) balance sheet
   (B) profit and loss account
   (C) cash flow statement
   (D) statement of changes in owner's equity

4. Which of the following International Accounting Standards (IAS) outlines the accounting for provisions, contingent assets and contingent liabilities?
   (A) IAS 1
   (B) IAS 2
   (C) IAS 10
   (D) IAS 37

5. Which of the following circumstances will cause accounting personnel to recognise a provision?
      I   warranty
      II major overhaul
      III future operating losses.
   (A) I
   (B) II
   (C) III
   (D) I and II

6. Which of the following International Accounting Standards (IAS) outlines accounting for events after the reporting period?
   (A) IAS 1
   (B) IAS 2
   (C) IAS 10
   (D) IAS 32

7. Which of the terms below may be used to describe a firm's inability to meet its short-term obligations?
   (A) liquidity
   (B) illiquidity
   (C) solvency
   (D) efficiency.

8. Which of the following subsections of the IFRS for SMEs Section 3 requires that financial statements present fairly the financial position, financial performance and cash flow of an entity?
   (A) subsection 2
   (B) subsection 4
   (C) subsection 5
   (D) subsection 6

Chapter 11

Introduction to cost and management accounting

Have you ever wondered how businesses determine their prices? Or, how do their discounts and promotional campaigns affect their prices? How will these changes in price attract new customers? Managers need information to answer these questions and make decisions. A good managerial system will therefore help them in making those decisions. This chapter reviews the definitions of management accounting, financial accounting and cost accounting. Emphasis will also be placed on making distinctions between management accounting and financial accounting.

Management accounting

Management accounting focuses on the accounting tools managers can use internally to run a business. These tools can help managers to control day-to-day operations by comparing the performance of actual results with budgeted results.

Financial accounting

Financial accounting focuses on preparing financial records and reports for the use of external persons such as stockholders, suppliers, banks and government agencies.

Cost accounting

Cost accounting provides information for the day-to-day control of operations. It indicates information such as inefficiencies and wastage of materials. Costing analyses losses from plant and machinery breakdowns. In addition, it records actual costs which are compared with estimated or standard costs.

In today's world the role of cost accounting and management accounting are known as management accounting. It is important to remember as well, that both management accounting and financial accounting do reflect some similarities; however, there are some differences. With reference to their similarities, they both use the accrual basis of accounting and highlight a business's economic transactions.

There are several major differences between financial and managerial accounting even though they both rely on the same financial information. Table 11.1 summarises these major differences between financial and managerial accounting.

Table 11.1 Differences between management accounting and financial accounting

	Management accounting	Financial accounting
Users of accounting information	Internal users such as managers at all levels and employees	External users such as investors, creditors, and government agencies
Purpose of accounting information	Helps managers and employees to plan and control business operations	Helps investors, creditors and others make investments, give credit and make other decisions
Freedom of choice with reference to accounting measures	No constraints, information prepared contain both monetary and non-monetary transactions	Constrained by Generally Accepted Accounting Principles (GAAP). Information prepared contains mostly monetary transactions. Public companies must be audited by an independent auditor
Timing focus for the preparation of financial reports	Usage of both historical and future information such as formal use of budgets as well as financial records. In addition, the information used must be relevant	Use of historical information ONLY. The information evaluates a firm's yearly performance. The information used in the preparation of the reports contain characteristics such as relevance, faithful representation, and must be reliable and objective
Time span of financial reports	Time span of financial reports is flexible and may vary from, for example, hourly, daily or maybe yearly	The time span of financial reports is less flexible; it can be quarterly or yearly
Types of reports	Detailed reports and may include details about products, departments or territories	Summarised reports on an entire business

Test Your Knowledge

Identify the following characteristics that are primarily related to financial accounting (FA) or management accounting (MA).

1. Helps creditors to make lending decisions.   **[1 mark]**
2. Helps in planning and controlling operations.   **[1 mark]**
3. Is not required to follow Generally Accepted Accounting
    Principles (GAAP).   **[1 mark]**
4. Has a focus on the future.   **[1 mark]**
5. Summary reports prepared quarterly or annually.   **[1 mark]**

MULTIPLE CHOICE QUESTIONS

1. Financial accounting provides to external users a historical perspective, whereas management accounting:

    (A) enables managers to make accurate decisions

    (B) emphasises a current perspective

    (C) emphasises the future in addition to historical reports

    (D) allows the use of GAAP.

2. The users of cost and management accounting are:

    I   stockholders and suppliers

    II   managers and supervisors

    III government agencies.

    (A) I

    (B) II

    (C) I and II

    (D) I and III

3. Management accounting information helps:

    I   managers to plan and control operations

    II   investors to make decisions

    III creditors to give credit.

    (A) I

    (B) II

    (C) I and II

    (D) I and III

4. Financial accounting is prepared at prescribed times, for example annually, whereas management accounting:

    (A) follows GAAP in its preparation

    (B) is examined by external auditors

    (C) is required only once a year

    (D) is required as management request.

5. Management accounting and financial accounting reports are both:

    (A) examined by external auditors

    (B) rely on the same financial information

    (C) follow GAAP for their preparation

    (D) required once a year.

Chapter 12

Manufacturing accounts preparation

Businesses in the Caribbean and the rest of the world differ by nature in their day-to-day operations. Some may offer services to their customers, some may convert raw materials into finished products and others may buy the finished products and resell to their customers. These businesses are known as service industries, manufacturing industries and merchandising industries. Because of their differences by nature and operations, the formats and preparations of financial reports are not the same.

This chapter reviews how service industries, merchandising industries and manufacturing differ by identifying features such as their costs and inventories. In addition, the formats of each financial report for different industries, showing the cost classifications are reviewed.

Furthermore, there is a review of schedules for computing raw materials used in production, total manufacturing cost, cost of goods manufactured and, cost of goods sold. Table 12.1 briefly outlines costs differences within each industry.

Table 12.1 Features of service industry, merchandising industry and manufacturing industry

Service	Merchandising	Manufacturing
Offer sales services, time, skills and knowledge	Purchase products from suppliers and resell them	Labour, equipment, and supplies convert raw materials into finished products
Examples of service industries – accounting firms, cleaning firms and so forth	Major expenses are cost of goods sold. Keeps inventory	Three kinds of inventory may exist in the industry: raw materials, work in process and finished goods
All costs are classified as period costs	Some product costs are purchases and freight in (carriage in)	Some product costs are raw materials, direct labour and manufacturing overheads

Test Your Knowledge

Match the accounting terminologies to the types of industries in the examples listed below:

Types of industries	Accounting terminologies	
1. Service	a. Salaries paid to accounts personnel	[1 mark]
2. Merchandising	b. Company that makes cast iron rods	[1 mark]
3. Manufacturing	c. Raw materials and labour used in making cars	[1 mark]
4. Period cost	d. Rendering janitorial services	[1 mark]
5. Product cost	e. Selling jeans in a department store	[1 mark]

Formats for financial statements within different industries

Although differences are seen, managers will be able to determine firms' profitability and performance and will be able to compare the differences of the three industries. Examples of income statements and balance sheets for the each of the industries are highlighted below

Income statements or statements of comprehensive income

a. **Service industry**

Service revenue	x
Expenses	(x)
Operating income	x

b. **Merchandising industry**

Sales revenue	x
Cost of goods sold:	
Beginning merchandise inventory	x
Purchases	x
Freight	x
Goods available for sale	x
Ending merchandise inventory	(x)
Cost of goods sold	(x)
Gross margin	x
Expenses	x
Operating income	x

c. **Manufacturing industry**

Sales revenue	x
Cost of goods sold:	
Beginning finished goods inventory	x
Cost of goods manufactured	x
Ending finished goods inventory	(x)
Cost of goods sold	(x)
Gross profit	x
Operating expenses:	
Selling expenses	x
Administrative expenses	x
Total expenses	(x)
Operating income	x

Balance sheet or statements of financial position

The balance sheet or statement of financial position of a merchandising company is similar to that of a manufacturing company. However, the differences are in the inventory accounts. The manufacturing company has three classes of inventories – raw materials, work in process and finished goods. In contrast, the merchandising company has only one class of inventory – finished goods.

Don't forget

1. Service companies offer sales services instead of products.
2. Merchandising companies purchase goods from suppliers for resale to customers.
3. Manufacturing companies produce goods as well as sell them.

Schedules

Cost of goods manufactured schedule

The cost of goods manufactured schedule contains three elements of products: direct materials, direct labour and manufacturing overhead. The total of these three elements is not the cost of goods manufactured. The reason for this is that some of these elements, incurred during the firm's accounting period, are goods (inventories) not yet completed, which are known as work in process. For the purposes of your course, two examples of computing the cost of goods manufactured schedule are shown here.

Example (1)	
Computation of raw materials used in production:	
Beginning raw materials inventory	x
Add purchases of raw materials	x
Less ending raw materials inventory	x
Raw materials used in production	x
Computation of total manufacturing cost:	
Raw materials used in production	x
Add direct labour	x
Total manufacturing overhead cost	x
Total manufacturing cost	x
Computation of cost of goods manufactured:	
Beginning work in process inventory	x
Add total manufacturing cost	x
Less ending work in process inventory	x
Cost of goods manufactured	x
Computation of cost of goods sold:	
Beginning finished goods inventory	x
Add cost of goods manufactured	x
Less ending finished goods inventory	x
Cost of goods sold	x

Example (2)	
Beginning work in process inventory	x
Direct materials:	
Raw materials, beginning	x
Add raw materials purchased	x
Total raw materials available for use	x
Less raw materials, ending	x
Raw materials used	x
Direct labour	x
Manufacturing overheads:	
Depreciation – factory	x
Indirect labour	x
Maintenance – factory	x
Total manufacturing overheads	x
Total manufacturing costs	x
Total work in process	x
Less ending work in process inventory	x
Cost of goods manufactured	x

Don't forget

1. Opening work in process can be either at the beginning of the cost of goods manufactured schedule or at the end.
2. Use the appropriate terminologies within the schedule.
3. Remember to show in your computations raw materials used in production, total manufacturing cost, cost of goods manufactured and, cost of goods sold.

Test Your Knowledge

1. What are the three types of inventory given on a manufacturing company's balance sheet?   **[3 marks]**

2. Explain how income statements for manufacturing and merchandising companies differ.   **[6 marks]**

3. Explain the links of the manufacturing statement to the financial statements.   **[4 marks]**

MULTIPLE CHOICE QUESTIONS

1. The following information was extracted from the records from Karlisha Step Inc.:

	$
Opening balance of finished goods	70 000
Cost of good manufactured	57 000
Cost of goods sold	107 000

The closing balance of balance of finished goods inventory is:

   (A) $20 000
   (B) $77 000
   (C) $127 000
   (D) $157 000

2. Service industries:

   I   convert raw material into finished products

   II   purchase products from suppliers and resell them

   III offer sales service, time, skills and knowledge.

   (A) I
   (B) II
   (C) III
   (D) I and III

3. Product costs in a manufacturing company are:

   I   raw materials

   II   direct labour

   III manufacturing overhead.

   (A) I
   (B) II
   (C) III
   (D) I, II and III

4. Which of the following is the correct format for a service industry?

   (A) service revenue less expenses

   (B) sales revenue less cost of goods sold less expenses

   (C) service revenue add expenses

   (D) sales revenue less cost of goods sold add expenses.

5. Which of the following is the correct format for computing raw materials in production?

   (A) beginning finished goods inventory less cost of goods manufactured add finished goods inventory

   (B) beginning raw materials inventory less purchases raw materials add ending raw materials inventory

   (C) beginning raw materials inventory add purchases of raw materials less ending raw materials inventory

   (D) beginning goods inventory and cost of goods manufactured less finished good inventory.

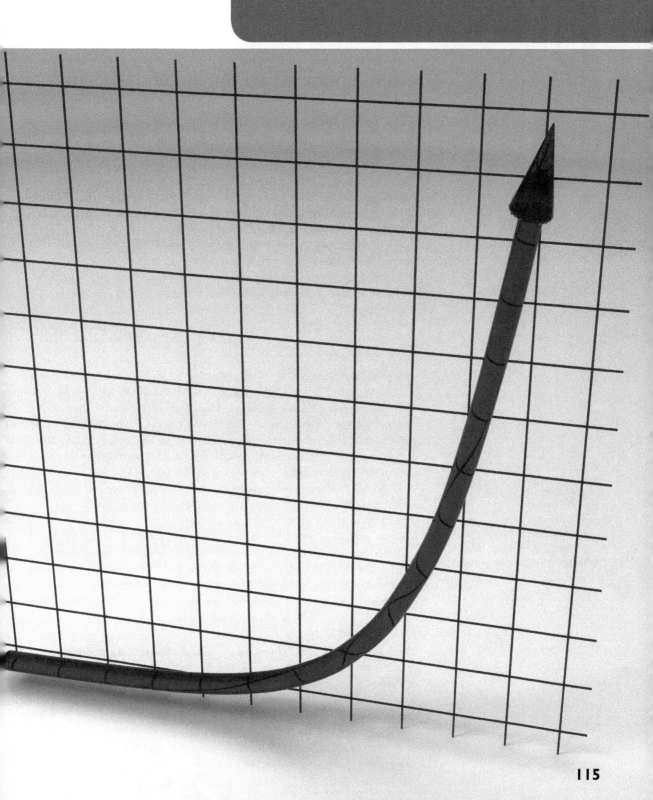

Chapter 13   Cost classification and cost curves

An organisation incurs many different types of costs. This chapter reviews cost classification and the sketching of curves. Goods produced or services offered all incur costs for material, labour and overheads. Cost as a definition is the monetary exchange of resources given up to acquire a product or service. In this guide, the cost definition may vary with the information such as time, changes in activity, classification in financial statements or impact on decision-making.

Cost classification is the process of arranging cost items into groups. Classification into groups will depend upon the purpose of cost. The purposes are: inventory valuation and income determination, decision-making, and planning and control.

Inventory valuation and income determination

Cost by function

It is important to separate costs for stock valuation and income determination purposes. For stock valuation, a distinction must be made between product costs and period costs, because product costs are assigned to inventory on the balance sheet and period costs are treated as expenses in the income statement.

Product costs, also known as inventoriable costs relate to making products or providing services that generate revenue for the firm. These costs include direct materials, direct labour and manufacturing overheads.

Period costs, also known as fixed costs (non-manufacturing costs, non-inventoriable costs) relate to a business's daily operating expenses, such as selling or administrative expenses. They are related to time, not to activity, and do not change in relation to the level of output or activity.

There are other classifications that are used to separate costs for profit-reporting and stock-valuation purposes. They are cost behaviour and traceable costs.

Cost behaviour

Cost behaviour is the way in which costs respond to changes in the volume of output or activity. Cost can be classified as fixed, variable or mixed costs. A fixed cost does not change within the relevant range of activity (that is, the total cost does not increase and decrease in the level of activity). However, a unit fixed cost will vary with changes in activity throughout the relevant range. Some examples of fixed cost are rental of a building, business rates, salary of a director, and straight line depreciation.

A variable cost changes in proportion to changes in the volume of activity. Some examples of variable costs are direct materials, direct labour and, sometimes, sales commission that varies with the volume of sales. However, the unit cost remains constant throughout the relevant range.

Mixed costs refer to a combination of fixed and variable costs. Examples include electricity and telephone bills. The fixed cost in one of these bills often includes a minimum amount and the variable costs are based on the amount of usage.

Traceable cost

Cost is traceable to a cost object, which can be a product, department, process or customer to which costs are assigned. Traceable costs assigned to one or more objects are known as direct and indirect costs. Direct costs are assigned to one specific cost object. For example, if a product is the cost object, the raw materials and labour used will be classified as the direct costs.

Indirect costs are assigned to more than one specific cost object. An example of an indirect traceable cost is a maintenance plan that benefits two or more departments. Examples of such costs are factory rent and factory light and heat.

Decision-making

Managers of businesses make decisions daily. They use costs to make certain decisions such as making or buying a product, dropping a product or adding a new product. Costs are classified as avoidable (relevant) or unavoidable (irrelevant) costs. Avoidable costs or relevant costs are costs that are critical to a particular decision in choosing one alternative over another. Unavoidable costs or irrelevant costs are costs that have no bearing on decisions to be made in the present or in the future. An example of such a cost is sunk cost.

There are other financial costs and non-financial factors to be considered in decision-making. The financial costs are out-of-pocket expenses, opportunity costs and future costs. Some non-financial factors may include social costs and environmental costs.

Planning and control

Planning and controlling requires firms' personnel to predict costs and then compare costs to actual costs incurred for the period. Therefore, costs are classified as planned costs and actual costs, fixed costs and variable costs, and controllable and non-controllable costs. Controllable costs are costs that are under the control of management. Some examples are controlling daily expenses such as supplies, maintenance and overtime, or large investments in land, buildings and equipment. Non-controllable costs are costs that are not under control of management such as depreciation and write-offs.

Table 13.1 Summary of cost classifications/terms for a manufacturing company

Cost unit	Unit of product or service that relates to costs, for example: • patient in a hospital (surgical procedure) • barrel (in beer industry) • room (in a hotel)
Direct materials	Materials that can be easily traced to a product
Direct labour (touch labour)	Labour costs that can be easily traced to a product
Prime cost	Sum total of direct material and direct labour
Manufacturing overhead (factory overhead/factory burden)	All manufacturing costs other than direct labour and direct materials
Conversion cost	Sum of total direct labour and manufacturing overhead

Test Your Knowledge

Identify each cost as a period cost or a product cost. If it is product cost, indicate if the cost is direct material, direct labour or manufacturing overhead. Then, determine if the product cost is a prime cost and/or a conversion cost.

1. Wages of car assembly plant workers   [4 marks]
2. Wages of an office secretary   [1 mark]
3. Property taxes on the factory   [3 marks]
4. Sugar and flour used to make cookies   [3 marks]
5. Salary of a factory maintenance supervisor   [3 marks]
6. Salary of a sales manager.   [1 mark]

Sketching of cost curves

This chapter has reviewed the classification of costs by behaviour. This section looks at sketching some of those costs. The graphs shown in the figures below illustrate variable costs, fixed costs, step costs and mixed costs.

Figure 13.1 Total variable cost

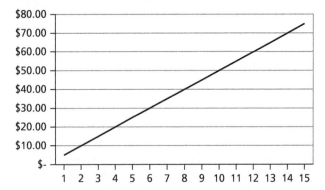

Figure 13.2 Total fixed cost

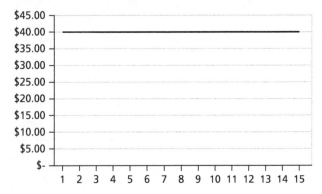

Figure 13.3 Total cost

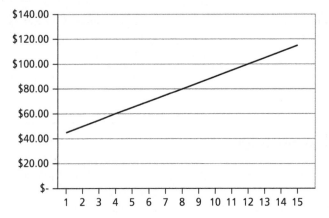

Figure 13.4 Total revenue

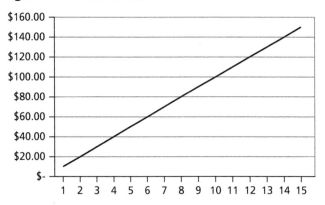

Figure 13.5 Average variable cost curve

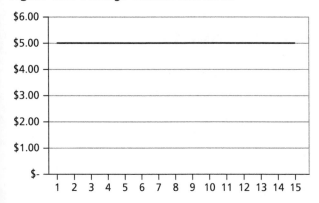

Figure 13.6 Average fixed cost curve

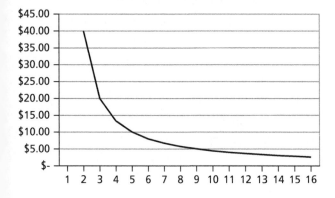

Figure 13.7 Total step cost curve

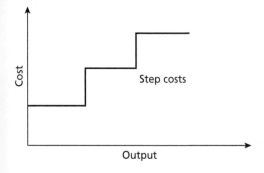

Figure 13.8 Total mixed cost curve

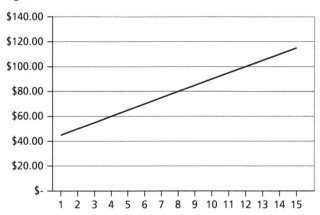

MULTIPLE CHOICE QUESTIONS

1. Conversion costs consists of:

(A) direct labour cost

(B) product costs

(C) manufacturing overhead cost

(D) direct labour and manufacturing overhead costs.

2. Cost that responds to changes in volume of output or activity is classified as:

(A) cost behaviour

(B) cost by function

(C) traceable cost

(D) controllable cost.

3. Fixed costs include:

I straight line depreciation

II rental of a building

III direct labour.

(A) I

(B) II

(C) III

(D) I and II

4. Which of the following costs has a combination of fixed and variable elements?

(A) mixed

(B) fixed

(C) variable

(D) traceable.

5. A cost object can be a:

I product

II process

III customer.

(A) I

(B) II

(C) III

(D) I, II and III

6. Controllable costs include:

I large investments in non-current assets

II daily operating expenses

III depreciation expenses and write-offs.

(A) I

(B) II

(C) I and II

(D) I and III

Chapter 14

Elements of cost: materials

Earlier chapters have introduced you to cost and management accounting and some of the terms, concepts, and elements of costs used in the preparation of final accounts. The purpose of costs accounts were considered and the forms of cost classification. This chapter looks at one of the components in the manufacturing process: raw materials.

Raw materials

Raw materials represent a significant percentage of a firm's outflow of cash. Therefore, it is important for businesses to record raw materials in their accounts. The procedure for recording raw materials is: storage of raw materials, purchase of raw materials, receipt of materials, issue of materials and the assignment of the cost of materials to cost objects. Figure 14.1 highlights the procedures, the departments responsible for each step and the documents involved in the process.

Figure 14.1 Steps to record raw materials

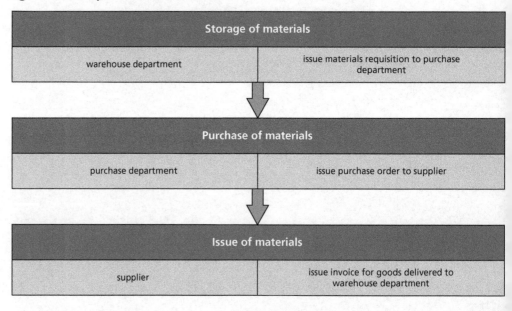

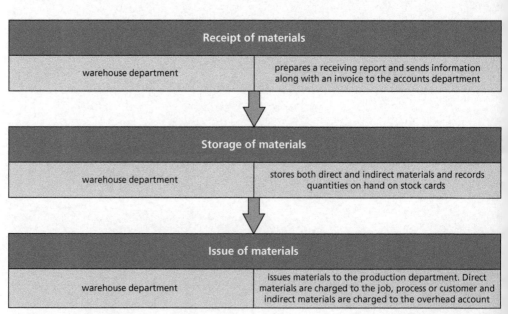

The charging of materials to a job, process or customer will be reviewed in later chapters of this guide.

Inventory planning and control are essential for profit planning in a business, as raw materials purchase is normally very high. Therefore, purchasing and accounting personnel must consider when to place an order and the most economical quantity to purchase. This section of the chapter examines the economic order quantity (EOQ), which is a technique that can be used to determine the most economic quantity to order and purchase. The EOQ model, as it is called, attempts to determine the order size that will minimise total inventory cost, based on six assumptions. These are:

1. The demand rate is uniform and known.
2. The item does not vary with order size.
3. All the order is delivered at the same time.
4. The lead time is known well enough in advance so that an order can be timed to arrive when inventory is exhausted.
5. The cost to place and receive an order is the same regardless of the amount ordered.
6. The cost of holding inventory is a linear function of the number of items held.

Common terms identified for inventory control and computing EOQ

Buffer stock (minimum stock or safety stock): the lowest quantity of inventory kept on hand by a company in the event of fluctuating usage or unusual delays in lead time. Safety stock of inventory is allowed to act as a buffer to protect the company against errors such as possible stock outs.

Lead or procurement time: the period of time between ordering and the time the goods arrive for usage or are produced by the company.

Maximum level: a stock level calculated as the maximum desirable which is used as an indicator to management to show when stocks have risen too high.

Reorder point: the level of inventory that triggers the placement of an order for additional units. It is determined by usage, lead time and safety stock.

Usage: refers to the quantity of inventory used or sold each day.

Economic order quantity (EOQ)

There are basic costs associated with the selection of the right level of inventories. These costs are purchasing cost of inventory, inventory ordering costs, inventory carrying costs, and the costs of not carrying sufficient inventory.

Purchasing cost of inventory

Purchasing cost of inventory is the quoted purchase price of inventory, less any sales discount, plus shipping (freight) charges.

Inventory ordering costs

Inventory ordering costs are the variable costs associated with preparing, receiving and paying for an order. Some examples of costs are:

- the administrative cost in preparing the order
- the communication cost involved in placing the order – telephone, email of delivery of purchase order costs
- the cost of ordering excess or too little inventory called Total Stocking Cost
- the cost of inspection of the received batches.

Inventory carrying costs

Inventory carrying cost is the total variable cost of carrying one unit of inventory in stock for one year. It includes storage costs, handling costs, property taxes, insurance and the opportunity cost of the capital invested in stocks.

- storage charges (rent, lighting, air conditioning and heating)
- stores – wages, equipment, maintenance and running costs

- material handling costs
- audit – stocktaking and stock recording costs
- insurance and security
- deterioration and obsolescence or pilferage
- evaporation and vermin damage.

Costs of not carrying sufficient inventory (stock-out costs)

Costs of not carrying sufficient inventory include:

- lost income through the loss of sales
- loss of future sales because customers may go elsewhere, or
- extra costs associated with expediting urgent orders.

Computing the EOQ: how much to order

There are two approaches to computing the EOQ: the formula approach and the tabular approach.

Formula approach

The formula used to calculate the EOQ is:

$$Q = \frac{\sqrt{2SO}}{C}$$

Where:
S = total demand in units
O = the costs of placing one order and
C = the cost of carrying one unit of inventory per annum

Tabular approach

This approach is used to determine the minimum total relevant cost, which is the EOQ. In the actual calculations, the total relevant cost is minimised (that is the order cost is equal to carrying cost).

The schedule for the tabular approach will appear as shown in Table 14.1.

Table 14.1 Schedule for the tabular approach

Order size (this column shows the order in lots)	Carrying cost (average inventory multiplied by carrying cost per unit)	Order cost (number of orders multiplied by the ordering cost)	Total relevant (carrying cost plus ordering cost)

Example

Kyehan's company has an annual demand of 5000 units. The company can order in lots of 100, 500, 1000 or 2 500. The carrying cost per unit is $2 and the cost to place an order is $200.

Required

a. Using the formula approach compute the EOQ.

b. Using the tabular approach compute the total relevant cost (Hint: EOQ).

Solutions

a. Formula approach

$$EOQ = Q = \frac{\sqrt{2 \times 5\,000 \times 200}}{2} = \sqrt{1\,000\,000} = 1\,000 \text{ units}$$

b. Tabular approach

Order size (this column shows the order in lots)	Carrying cost (average inventory multiplied by carrying cost per unit)	Order cost (number of orders multiplied by the ordering cost)	Total relevant (carrying cost plus ordering cost)
100	(100 ÷ 2) × 2 = $100	(5 000 ÷ 100) × 200 = $10 000	$10 100
500	(500 ÷ 2) × 2 = $500	(5 000 ÷ 500) × 200 = $2 000	$2 500
1 000	(1 000 ÷ 2) × 2 = $1000	(5 000 ÷ 1 000) × 200 = $1 000	$2 000
2 500	(2 500 ÷ 2) × 2 = $2 500	(5 000 ÷ 2 500) × 200 = $400	$2 900
5 000	(5 000 ÷ 2) × 2 = $5 000	(5 000 ÷ 5 000) × 200 = $200	$5 200

> **Don't forget**
>
> The EOQ is at 1000 units, that is where the order cost is equal to the carrying cost.

Test Your Knowledge

Tyrell Company uses 8000 units of a part each year. To gain better control over its inventories, the company is keen to determine the economic order quantity (EOQ) for this part.

The company has determined that it costs $40 to place an order for the part from the supplier and $4 to carry one part in inventory each year.

Required: Compute the EOQ for the part using:

a. The formula approach   [3 marks]
b. The tabular approach   [3 marks]

Computing reorder point: when to order
Constant usage during lead time

The formula below will be used when the rate of usage during lead time is known with certainty.

Reorder point = lead time × average daily or weekly usage

> **Example**
>
> Mason's company EOQ is 400 units, the lead time is 3 weeks, and the average weekly usage is 60 units.
>
> **Solution**
>
> Reorder point: 3 weeks × 60 units per week = 180 units

Variable usage during the lead time

The formula below will be used when companies experience problems in demand, delivery or processing of orders and place a buffer to guard against stock outs.

Reorder point = (Lead time × Average daily or weekly usage) + Safety stock

Example

Economic order quantity 400
Lead time 3 weeks
Average weekly usage 60 units
Maximum weekly usage 70 units
Safety stock 50 units

Solution

Safety stock = (maximum expected usage per week − average usage per week) × lead time

$(70 - 60) \times 3 = 30$

Reorder point = (3 weeks × 60 units per week) + 30 = 210 units

Test Your Knowledge

Vitaly sells 200 headphones sets. The purchase lead time is $1\frac{1}{3}$ per week and the economic order quantity is 500 units. The company maintains a safety stock of half the week's demand.

Required: Compute the safety stock and the reorder point.   **[5 marks]**

Disposal of hazardous materials

Hazardous waste is any waste material that poses a potential threat to society or the environment. Examples of waste material than can be discarded are cleaning fluids, pesticides, motor oil and many other materials. Waste material can be defined by one or more of the following:

*   ignitability
*   corrosivity
*   reactivity
*   toxicity.

The laws to regulate the disposal of waste may differ in the Caribbean; also the disposal of hazardous waste can cost industries (based on the type) a substantial sum of money. Apart from the disposal, preventative measures can be costly; for example, the storage of oil in tanks or containers above and underground.

Test Your Knowledge

Use the internet to research the step-by-step process for hazardous waste disposal in an industry of your choice in your own country. In your research identify costs that the firm will incur and the preventative measures to be employed.   **[10 marks]**

MULTIPLE CHOICE QUESTIONS

1. Which of the following departments is responsible for issuing a purchase order to a supplier?

    (A) Warehouse

    (B) Procurement

    (C) Accounting

    (D) Sales.

2. Materials stored are:

    (A) recorded on a stock card

    (B) charged to manufacturing overhead account

    (C) sent on an invoice to the accounts department

    (D) issued as a purchase order to supplier.

3. Buffer stock is also known as:

    I   maximum stock

    II   minimum stock

    III safety stock.

    (A) I

    (B) II

    (C) I and II

    (D) II and III

4. Inventory carrying costs include:

    I   quoted purchase price of inventory

    II   handling costs

    III lost income through the loss of sales.

    (A) I

    (B) II

    (C) III

    (D) I and II

5. Zylon Company requires 50 000 units of product Y for the year. The cost of placing an order is $50. Its carrying cost is $10 per unit. The economic order quantity (EOQ) rounded to the nearest whole unit is:

    (A) 43

    (B) 224

    (C) 707

    (D) 1581

Chapter 15

Elements of cost: labour

There are many methods of paying for work. They are based on time, production or some form of incentive scheme. Labour will be placed under two broad headings in this chapter and further categorised later on in the guide. The broad headings are remuneration and incentive (fringe benefits).

There are two common approaches: direct labour (touch labour) and indirect labour. Direct labour is defined as labour costs that can be easily traced to the making of specific products and indirect labour is labour costs that cannot be easily traced to the making of products. Some examples of workers who fall under the indirect labour category are:

- janitors
- supervisors
- material handlers
- security guards
- maintenance workers.

Apart from direct and indirect labour costs there are other labour costs. These include costs such as idle time, overtime premium and labour fringe benefits. Some of these costs may be treated as part of the manufacturing overhead cost, rather than as part of the direct labour cost.

Idle time

Idle time represents payments made to direct labour workers who are unable to complete their assignments due to machine breakdowns, materials shortages, power failures, and many other reasons. These costs are treated as part of the manufacturing overhead cost rather than as part of direct labour cost. The calculation of idle time is shown in the example below:

Example

Riaz, a machine operator, earns $20 per hour. He is paid for a normal 40-hour working week. During one day of the working week, there was a power failure and Riaz remained idle for 3 hours.

Required

Compute Riaz's labour cost for the week (including the allocations).

Solution

	$
Direct labour ($20 × 37 hours)	740
Manufacturing overhead (idle time; $20 × 3 hours)	60
Total cost for the week	800

Test Your Knowledge

Sergio a plant operator earns $30 per hour. He is paid for a normal 45-hour working week. On one day of the working week, there was a materials shortage and Sergio remained idle for 3 hours. Compute Sergio's labour cost for the week (including the allocations). **[5 marks]**

Overtime premium

These are payments made to skilled (direct) and unskilled (indirect) workers in a factory. Overtime premium is usually classified as a manufacturing overhead and not assigned to any particular order or batch of production. It is paid to all workers to complete an emergency production run that cannot be completed in a regular working week or to complete a special project. The example below illustrates how to compute overtime premium and allocate costs.

Objectives

At the end of this chapter you will be able to:

- categorise labour costs as direct or indirect
- identify the types of remuneration for employees
- discuss the advantages and disadvantages of the various payment methods
- calculate employee gross pay.

Don't forget

Always deduct the idle time from the regular working hours.

Example

Galieb earns $30 per hour in an assembly plant. He is paid time and a half for over-time in excess of a 40-hour working week. During the week, Galieb works 60 hours and has no idle time.

Required

Compute Galieb's labour cost for the week (including the allocations).

Solution

	$
Direct labour ($30 × 60)	1 800
Manufacturing overhead (overtime premium: $15 × 20)	300
Total cost for the week	2 100

Don't forget

1. Direct labour is calculated on the total hours worked.
2. Overtime premium is calculated on the excess of normal hours.
3. Remember that only the overtime premium is charged to the overtime premium and not the regular rate.

Test Your Knowledge

Stefan earns $40 per hour in a car assembly plant. He is paid time and a half for overtime in excess of a 40-hour working week. During the week, Stefan works 70 hours and has no idle time. Compute Stefan's labour cost for the week (including the allocations).   **[5 marks]**

Labour fringe benefits

Labour fringe benefits are paid by the employer; some of the costs include retirement (gratuity) payment plans, insurance programmes, hospitalisation plans, National Insurance (Social Security) workers' compensation and many other benefits. Some businesses treat these costs as indirect labour and others treat the benefit portion that relates to direct labour as additional direct labour. The latter approach is mostly used because the fringe benefits represent an added cost for services provided by the workers.

It is important to distinguish between remuneration and incentive. Remuneration is defined as the reward for labour and services, and incentive is the stimulation of effort and productivity by offering monetary inducement or enhanced opportunities.

Methods of remuneration and incentive systems

Some basic categories of labour remuneration are day work methods (time work), piece work (piece rates) and commissions.

Day work

Flat time (time rates or day rate)

The flat time or time rates (day rate) system operates by paying labour for the time worked; the payment is by the hour, day or week. Wages are calculated by multiplying the total hours worked by the rate per hour. The total number of hours worked is recorded on clock cards or time sheets. Overtime premiums due to workers are paid in this system.

Table 15.1 Advantages and disadvantages of day work methods of remuneration

Advantages	Disadvantages
Favoured where a worker is learning a job or trade	All workers (skilled and unskilled) are paid the same regardless of their quality of work
Workers are guaranteed a fixed wage each week for the agreed hours worked	There is no incentive offered to workers for making extra efforts
Quality of work is maintained throughout (and not sacrificed for increased earnings)	Workers may decide to work at a slower pace during normal working hours in order to work overtime for increased rates of pay

High day

This method pays a much higher day rate to workers than flat time. Most firms make this payment to attract good employees, whose output will continuously be productive and performance will be of a high standard.

Table 15.2 Advantages and disadvantages of the high day method of remuneration

Advantages	Disadvantages
Payments are much higher than other firms and will attract labour (and the firm is able to choose a better class of worker)	Problems occur when the target for production is not met
Simple to understand and administer	Standards must be continuously maintained and closely monitored
Firms benefit from high performance through lower unit costs	

Measured day

In this system, employees are paid above the time rate. The workers' output is measured over a period of time and they are paid on the basis of their performance and efficiency during that time. The advantages of firms using this system are listed below:

- It reduces paperwork.
- Although payment is based on the output for a period, the employee receives a regular rate per hour for a long period.

Piece rates

This method of payment is related to effort, and varies with production. Payment depends on results and inducements are offered to the worker to increase output. The monetary incentives offered for extra output are either individually to a worker, or collectively when employees share an earned bonus. This section looks at three common piece rate systems of payments: straight piece rate, piece rate with guaranteed pay and differential piece rate.

Straight piece rate

A straight piece rate is the payment of a fixed sum per fixed unit produced, per standard time.

Table 15.3 Advantages and disadvantages of a straight piece rate method of remuneration

Advantages	Disadvantages
It is simple to understand and calculate	No payment or allowance is normally made for unsuitable materials, variations in the efficiency of tools and machinery or production delays, which are matters outside the control of the worker
There is a direct incentive to increase output (because the system encourages greater efficiency)	Varying rates of output between different workers may result in labour troubles (trade unions may be contentious over fixing of piece rates)
Individual output can be easily and quickly determined	May not be suitable for all workers (only workers with specialised skills)
Unit costs are reduced	System may leave opening for spoilt production, lead to substandard work or unacceptable wastage of materials because of lack of monitoring and control
Wages are paid proportionate to production	
The work is completed more quickly and time wastage is not encouraged	

Example (1)

Kyle, a machine operator, is paid on piecework at the rate of $2.00 per 100 components produced. During a week, he produced 9 000 components, of which 50 were rejected by inspection. What were Kyle's wages for the week?

Solution

	Components
Output	9 000
Less rejects	50
Net good output	8 950

Wages for the week = 8 950 @ $2.00 per 100 = $179.00

Example (2)

Week No: 1

Employee name: Jadiel Martin

Clock hours: 50

Output:

200 units of A	Piecework time allowance	1.7 minutes/unit
300 units of B	Piecework time allowance	1.5 minutes/unit
400 units of C	Piecework time allowance	2.2 minutes/unit

Piece work rate: $0.15 cents per minute produced

Required

Compute the following

a. Total production piecework minutes

b. Jadiel Martin's gross wages

Solution

a. Total production: $(200 \times 1.7) + (300 \times 1.5) + (400 \times 2.2)$

$= 340 + 450 + 880 = 1\ 670$ piecework minutes

b. Gross wages $= 1670 \times \$0.15 = \$250.50$

Test Your Knowledge

Kevin is paid $10.00 per piecework hour produced. In a 40-hour week he produces the following output:

- 5 units of a product at a piecework time allowed per unit at 8.5 hours
- 3 units of another product at a piecework time allowed per unit at 3.0 hours

Required: Compute Kevin's pay for the week.   **[5 marks]**

Piece rate with guaranteed pay

This is offered to workers so that they do not suffer loss of earnings when production is low through no fault of their own. This is to safeguard earnings when there is a shortage of materials, unsuitable materials, power failures, machine breakdowns and delays caused by inefficient planning which makes it impossible for the employee to earn bonus pay.

Example

The following information is available for Jarron Wood:

Normal working day	8 hours
Guaranteed rate of pay (on time basis)	$6.50
Standard time allowed producing one unit	3 minutes
Piecework price	$0.15 per standard minute

Required

For daily production levels of 80, 120 and 210 units, calculate earnings for Jarron Wood on piecework, where earnings are guaranteed at 80 per cent of time-based pay.

Solution

Level of output (units)	80	120	210
Standard minutes produced (×3 minutes)	240	360	630
Piece work value (×0.15)	$41.60 (note)	$54	$94.50

Note: Earnings are guaranteed at 80% of time-based pay = 80% × 8 hours × $6.50 = $41.60. This is greater than the piece work earnings of $36.00, and will be the amount paid

Test Your Knowledge

Ty-Dy Corporation produced the information below pertaining to five workers and three products.

	Employee			
	A	B	C	D
Actual hours worked	35	45	55	65
Hourly rate of pay	$6.00	$2.00	$3.00	$3.60

Information for the three products and the employees that worked on those products are:

	Employee			
	A	B	C	D
Output unit L	42	120		120
Output unit M	72	76		270
Output unit N	92		50	

Standard time allowed for each unit: L – 5 minutes, M – 10 minutes and N – 20 minutes

Each minute earned is valued at $0.15 for piecework calculation.

Required: Calculate the following:

a. Guaranteed hourly rates only (basic pay) [12 marks]
b. Piecework, but earnings guaranteed at 80 per cent of basic pay where the employee fails to earn this amount. [15 marks]

Differential piece rate

This scheme offers incentives to employees as an encouragement to increase their output by paying higher rates for increased levels of production.

Table 15.4 Advantages and disadvantages of a differential piece rate as a method of remuneration

Advantages	Disadvantages
Provides a very strong incentive to fast workers	The beginner or slow learner is penalised
It is simple to understand and work	The quality of work may suffer as workers strive to reach a high output
Only the best workers are attracted to the firm	

Example

Leandro is paid by differential piecework and the following rates have been agreed:

Up to 500 units	$0.30 cents per unit
501–600 units	$0.35 cents per unit
601–700 units	$0.45 cents per unit
701 and above	$0.55 cents per unit

Leandro produced 645 good units.

Required

Compute Leandro's wages for the week

Solution

Leandro's wages:

	$
500 @ $0.30	150.00
100 @ $0.35	35.00
45 @ $0.45	20.25
Total wages	205.25

Test Your Knowledge

Virgil Harry is paid by differential piece rate work. The scheme is as follows:

Up to 60	units per day	$0.55 per unit
61–70	units per day	$0.60 per unit
71–80	units per day	$0.65 per unit
81–100	units per day	$0.75 per unit

Virgil's daily outputs for a 6-day week were: 60 units, 68 units, 83 units, 94 units, 47 units and 59 units.

Required: Calculate Virgil's gross pay for the week.   **[29 marks]**

Bonus

Bonuses are incentive systems which allow for the payment of a day rate plus a proportion of the time saved when a worker performs the task in less than the time allowed. Some examples are shift bonus, time-keeping bonus and continuous working bonus.

Example

Renaldo Dunks is employed by a manufacturing company. His basic pay rate is $15.00 per hour and he receives a bonus of half the hours saved on each job. In a 40-hour week, he completes two jobs as follows:

Job	Target time	Actual time
A	35 hours	25 hours
B	20 hours	15 hours
		40 hours

Required

Compute the following for Renaldo Dunks:

a.   Total bonus hours

b.   Total pay hours

c.   Total wages

Solution

Bonus hours:

Job A	$(35 - 25) \times \frac{1}{2}$	= 5 hours
Job B	$(20 - 15) \times \frac{1}{2}$	= 2.5 hours
Total bonus hours		7.5 hours

Total pay hours = 40 + 7.5 = 47.5 hours

Total wages = 47.5 × $15 = $712.50

Test Your Knowledge

A worker with a basic rate of $25 per hour receives a bonus of half the hours saved on each job. In a 60-hour week he completes three jobs as follows:

Job	Target time	Actual time
D	32	25
E	25	20
F	20	15
Total hours		60 hours

Work out his

a.	Total bonus hours	[4 marks]
b.	Total pay hours	[4 marks]
c.	Total wages	[3 marks]

Commission

Commission is paid to workers as a fixed percentage, or on a rate based on some particular unit of output, sales or revenue.

Impact of labour due to technology changes

Many manufacturing companies have more fixed costs and fewer variable costs including labour. This trend results in fewer persons being employed and therefore a decrease in direct labour costs (variable costs). On the other hand, because there are more fixed costs, there is an increase in automation and, as a result, depreciation and lease charges (fixed costs) increase.

MULTIPLE CHOICE QUESTIONS

1. Payment to workers when they are on lunch or when production is halted due to machine breakdowns is called:

   (A) overtime

   (B) labour fringe benefits

   (C) idle time

   (D) commission.

2. Which of the following is considered as a disadvantage for flat time (Time rates or day rates)?

   (A) Workers work at a slower pace during normal working hours.

   (B) Workers are guaranteed a fixed wage week for the agreed hours worked.

   (C) Workers produce quality work throughout.

   (D) New apprentices are employed to learn a trade.

3. The use of more technology in manufacturing companies will cause:

   I   the direct labour cost to decrease

   II noncurrent assets to increase

   III depreciation and maintenance costs to increase.

   (A) I

   (B) II

   (C) III

   (D) I, II and III

4. Horace normally works a 40-hour working week and is paid $80 per hour. He was unable to complete his task on a given day because of power failure. Horace was idle for 3 hours on that day. The direct labour cost to be allocated for the week is:

   (A) $0

   (B) $2960

   (C) $3200

   (D) $3440

5. Which type of remuneration method pays employees based on the number of items completed?

   (A) wage

   (B) salary

   (C) piece rate

   (D) commission.

Chapter 16

Elements of cost: overheads

Apportionment of service cost centre overheads to production centres (service department allocations)

Services departments such as stores, canteen and building maintenance are not directly involved in the manufacturing of goods; their overheads are re-apportioned to the production departments according to the use (or support) they make of the service departments. These service departments, incur costs and the costs from these departments must be allocated to the production departments. This section will review how to allocate service department costs to the production departments. The four methods of apportioning service cost centres overhead costs are: direct, step-down (sequential allocation), reciprocal and repeated distribution methods.

Direct method

The direct allocation method allocates each service cost (support) centre costs directly **ONLY** to the operating (production) departments (and not to any services areas provided among the support departments).

Example

Anesia Dass Limited budgets the following amounts for its Building Services and Business Lab Services departments. The costs for each department are as follows:

Building Services	$100 000
Business Lab Services	$250 000

Anesia Dass Limited has two service departments, the Building and Business Lab Services, and two production departments, Machining and Assembly. The Building and Business Lab Services provide services to the production departments as well as to each other in the following relationship:

Supplied by	Used by			
	Building Services	Business Lab Services	Machining	Assembly
Building Services	-	0.30	0.40	0.30
Business Lab Services	0.10	-	0.40	0.50

Required

Using the direct method, allocate the service departments' cost to the production departments.

Solution

Steps:

1. Reassembling of data to ignore any reciprocal services offered between the Buildings and Business Lab Services

Supplied by	Used by		
	Machining	Assembly	Total
Building Services	0.40	0.30	0.70
Business Lab Services	0.40	0.50	0.90

2. Allocate the Building Services costs of $100 000 using the ratio of 0.40: 0.30 or 4/7 to Machining and 3/7 to Assembly

Supplied by	Machining $	Assembly $
Buildings Services	$100\ 000 \times \frac{4}{7}$	$100\ 000 \times \frac{3}{7}$
	57 142.86	42 857.14

3. Allocate the Business Lab Services of $250 000 to Machining and Assembly using the ratio 0.40: 0.50 or 4/9 to Machining and 5/9 to assembly

Supplied by	Machining $	Assembly $
Business Lab Services	$250\,000 \times \frac{4}{9}$	$250\,000 \times \frac{5}{9}$
	111 111.11	138 888.89

Step-down method (sequential allocation method)

This method allows for partial recognition of services rendered by support departments to other services department. It requires support departments to be ranked with the highest percentage of its total services to other departments in the order of allocation.

Example

Anesia Dass Limited budgets the following amounts for its Building Services and Business Lab Services departments. The costs for each department are as follows:

Buildings $100 000

Business Lab Services $250 000

Anesia Dass Limited has two service departments, the Building and Business Lab Services, and two production departments, Machining and Assembly. The Buildings and Business Lab Services provide services to the production departments as well as to each other in the following relationship:

Supplied by	Used by			
	Building Services	Business Lab Services	Machining	Assembly
Buildings	-	0.30	0.40	0.30
Business Lab Services	0.10		0.40	0.50

Required

Using the step-down method, allocate the service departments' costs to the production departments.

Solution

Note:

This method requires you to look at the relationship between the services provided by Buildings to Business Lab Services. The Building Service provide 0.30 (30%) of its services to the Business Lab Services, while the Business Lab Services provides 0.10 (10%) of its services to the Buildings. Therefore in this method, you would allocate the Buildings department first, since it provides the highest level of support to the Business Lab Services department.

Steps

1. Allocate the buildings costs to all other departments:

Supplied by	Building Services $	Business Lab Services $	Machining $	Assembly $
Costs	100 000	250 000		
Allocation of buildings costs	(100 000)	30 000	40 000	30 000

2. Recalculate all department costs:

Supplied by	Building Services $	Business Lab Services $	Machining $	Assembly $
Costs	100 000	250 000		
Allocation of building costs	(100 000)	30 000	40 000	30 000
Recalculated costs	0	280 000	40 000	30 000

Note: The Business Lab Services now has a new total of $280 000.

3. Allocate the next service department costs (Business Lab Services) to the Machining and Assembly departments (using the ratio 0.40:0.50):

Supplied by	Building Services $	Business Lab Services $	Machining $	Assembly $
Costs	100 000	250 000		
Allocation of building costs	(100 000)	30 000	40 000	30 000
Recalculated costs	0	280 000	40 000	30 000
Allocation of Business Lab Services		(280 000)	124 444.44	155 555.56
Recalculated costs		0	164 444.44	185 555.56

Reciprocal method

In the reciprocal method, the service department remains open to receive costs from other departments. This is done by first using simultaneous equations for re-working new overhead costs for the service departments (only the service costs are used). Then the cost is allocated using the new overhead costs to all departments.

Example

Anesia Dass Limited budgets the following amounts for its Buildings and Business Lab Services departments. The costs for each department are as follows:

Building Services $100 000

Business Lab Services $250 000

Anesia Dass Limited has two service departments, the Building and Business Lab Services, and two production departments, Machining and Assembly. The Buildings and Business Lab Services provide services to the production departments as well as to each other in the following relationship:

Supplied by	Used by			
	Building Services	Business Lab Services	Machining	Assembly
Buildings	-	0.30	0.40	0.30
Business Lab Services	0.10		0.40	0.50

Required

Using the reciprocal method, allocate the service departments' costs to the production departments.

Solution

Let B = Building Services and L = Business Lab Services

B = 100 000 + 0.1L   Equation (1)

L = 250 000 + 0.3B   Equation (2)

Substitute Equation (1) in Equation (2)
Therefore:
L = 250 000 + 0.3(100 000 + 0.1L)
L = 250 000 + 30 000 + 0.03L
L – 0.03L = 280 000
0.97L = 280 000
L = 280 000/0.97
L = 288 660

Substituting L = 288 660 in Equation (1)
B = 100 000 + 0.1 × 288 660
B = 100 000 + 28 866
B = 128 866

Supplied by	Building Services $	Business Lab Services $	Machining $	Assembly $
Costs	100 000	250 000		
Allocation of Building Services costs	(128 866)	38 660	51 546	38 660
Recalculated costs	(28 866)	288 660	51 546	38 660
Allocation of Business Lab Services	28 866	(288 660)	115 464	144 330
Recalculated costs	0	0	167 010	182 990

Repeated distribution method

In the repeated distribution method, the service department remains open to receive costs from other departments. The order of allocation is the same as the step-down method (that is, it requires the support departments to be ranked with the highest percentage of its total service to other departments in the order of allocation) until the amount is minimal. Then that last amount is allocated directly to the production departments.

Example

Anesia Dass Limited budgets the following amounts for its Buildings and Business Lab Services departments. The costs for each department are as follows:

Building Services $100 000

Business Lab Services $250 000

Anesia Dass Limited has two service departments, the Building and Business Lab Services, and two production departments, Machining and Assembly. The Buildings and Business Lab Services provide services to the production departments as well as to each other in the following relationship:

Supplied by	Used by			
	Buildings	Business Lab Services	Machining	Assembly
Building Services	-	0.30	0.40	0.30
Business Lab Services	0.10		0.40	0.50

Required

Using the repeated distribution method, allocate the service departments' cost to the production departments

Solution

Supplied by	Buildings $	Business Lab Services $	Machining $	Assembly $
Costs	100 000	250 000		
Allocation of buildings	(100 000)	30 000	40 000	30 000
Adjusted balances (recalculated costs)	0	280 000	40 000	30 000
Allocation of Business Lab Services	28 000	(280 000)	112 000	140 000
Adjusted balances	28 000	0	152 000	170 000
Allocation of buildings	(28 000)	8 400	11 200	8 400
Adjusted balances	0	8 400	163 200	178 400
Allocation of Business Lab Services	840	(8 400)	3 360	4 200
Adjusted balances	840	0	166 560	182 600
Allocation of buildings	(840)	252	336	252
Adjusted balances	0	252	166 896	182 852
Allocation of Business Lab Services	25.20	(252)	100.80	126
Adjusted balances	25.20	0	166 996.80	182 978
Allocation of buildings	(25.20)	7.56	10.08	7.56
Adjusted balances	0	7.56	167 006.88	182 985.56
Allocation of Business Lab Services*	0	(7.56)	3.36	4.20
	0	0	167 010.24	182 989.76

* In the last allocation step, service cost is allocated directly to production departments because of the small amount.

Don't forget

1. Ensure that you apply the correct principle for the three methods.
2. Check all calculations carefully for each method; arithmetical mistakes cost marks.
3. Read the information carefully; the information presented is not always in a percentage form.

Test Your Knowledge

1. Belmont Company has two service departments and two production departments. The following information is provided in the table below:

	Service Departments		Production Departments	
	Finance	Administration	Moulding	Finishing
Total Overhead Cost	75 000	100 000	260 000	130 000
Overhead Allocation				
Finance		10%	50%	40%
Administration	20%		30%	50%

Allocate service department costs to production departments using:

a. Direct method   **[6 marks]**

b. Repetitive distribution method (limited to two steps).   **[10 marks]**

2. Providence Manufacturing Company has two service departments and two production departments. The following information is provided in the table below:

	Departments	Total overhead $	Overhead allocation Finance %	Overhead allocation Human resources %
Service departments	Finance	70 000		20
	Human resources	80 000	10	
Production departments	Mixing	90 000	45	40
	Baking	60 000	45	40

Allocate service department costs to production departments using:

a.   Step-down method   [7 marks]

b.   Reciprocal method   [15 marks]

3. BAHS Company has three service departments and two production departments. The company supplies the following information:

	Service departments Finance	Service departments Human resources	Service departments Marketing	Production departments Printing	Production departments Packaging
Total overhead costs $	40 000	70 000	60 000	135 000	87 000
Overhead allocation %					
Finance		20%	30%	25%	25%
Human resources	10%		20%	30%	40%
Marketing	15%	25%		40%	20%

Allocate overhead to the production departments from the service departments using:

a.   The direct method   [6 marks]

b.   The step-down method, starting with Finance.   [7 marks]

Under- over-absorption of overheads

Overhead absorption rates are calculated on planned levels of production and budgeted overhead expenditure. At times (even in job costing which you will review in later chapters) the actual volume of goods produced and the actual overhead expenditure will turn out to be different from the budgeted amounts. Those results will show that overhead expenditure will either be under-absorbed or over-absorbed.

Under-absorption (applied) of overheads

Under-absorption occurs when the actual expenditure is more than the budgeted and planned levels of production. This means that not enough overheads were charged to production.

Over-absorption (applied) of overheads

Over-absorption occurs when the actual expenditure is less than the budgeted and planned levels of production. This means that too many overheads were charged to production. Application of both methods will be reviewed in Chapter 19, Job costing.

MULTIPLE CHOICE QUESTIONS

1. Smart Company used labour hours to allocate manufacturing overhead to all jobs. The budgeted manufacturing overhead is $40 000 and budgeted machine hours and labour hours were 100 000 and 60 000 respectively. The predetermined overhead rate is:

   (A) $0.40 per labour hour

   (B) $0.67 per labour hour

   (C) $1.50 per labour hour

   (D) $2.50 per labour hour

2. Which of the following methods allocates service cost centres directly to operation (production) departments?

   (A) direct

   (B) step-down

   (C) reciprocal

   (D) repeated distribution.

3. Cost assignment is the process of:

   I   assigning cost to cost pools

   II   assigning cost from cost objects to cost pools

   III assigning costs from cost pools to cost objects.

   (A) I

   (B) I and II

   (C) I and III

   (D) II and III

   The following information relates to questions 4 and 5.

   The following table is provided by the Tom Tom Company

Type of department	Service departments		Production departments	
Name of department	Finance	Human resources	Mixing	Baking
Overhead Cost Assigned	$25 000	$40 000	$60 000	$80 000
Overhead cost allocation of Finance cost		20%	30%	50%
Overhead cost allocation of Human Resource cost	10%		40%	50%

4. Using the step-down method, what is the amount allocated to the mixing department from human resources if the human resource department is allocated first?

   (A) $15 000

   (B) $12 000

   (C) $16 000

   (D) $17 778

5. Using the direct method, what is the amount allocated to the mixing department?

   (A) $15 000

   (B) $12 000

   (C) $16 000

   (D) $17 778

6. Which allocation base is best suited for allocating rent cost among departments?

   (A) floor space

   (B) labour costs

   (C) labour hours

   (D) machine hours.

Chapter 17   Decision-making

Objectives

At the end of this chapter you will:

- know the various terms/ characteristics related to decision-making
- be able to calculate relevant costing data related to a short-term decision.

Managers have to make decisions for their business daily such as which customers to sell to, how much to charge customers, which products to make, and when it is better to buy a product or service rather than producing it in-house. This chapter reviews how managers use their knowledge of cost behaviour to make short-term decisions such as whether to accept or reject a special order, make or buy a product, and add or drop a product.

Decisions involve making choices among alternatives to meet objectives such as increasing profits or reducing losses. Therefore, managers use relevant cost information to conduct the following procedures:

- defining the objectives
- identifying alternative courses of action
- gathering, analysing relevant information and comparing with alternatives
- making a decision on the best course of action.

There are fundamental terms/characteristics that are critical in the decision-making process. Table 17.1 identifies and explains the role of each one.

Table 17.1 Terms/characteristics that are critical in the decision-making process

Terms/characteristics	Role in the decision-making process
Relevant cost (avoidable)	Gives data that is relevant in decision-making (hint: variable costs). The costs are future incremental cash flows and differ among alternatives.
Irrelevant cost (unavoidable)	The information given does not affect decisions to be made because it is not in the future or differs among alternatives.
Sunk cost	Sunk cost is past (historical) cost incurred. Therefore, it cannot be used in the decision-making process (considered as an irrelevant cost).
Relevant (qualitative) non-financial data	Qualitative data occurs in the future and differs among alternatives and is critical in the decision-making process. Plays a role in managers' decision; such examples may include: decision to buy or subcontract a product or service rather than produce it in-house; reduce control/over delivery time or product quality; offering discount prices to selected customers, and many other data.
Differential costs	These are used in the decision-making process. They are the differences in the cost of alternatives.
Incremental (differential) analysis	This method looks at the impact that alternative relevant costs would have on operating income.
Opportunity cost	This cost is critical in the decision-making process (because of the choice made). Opportunity cost is the benefit earned (from giving up something) by choosing one option instead of another.
Controllable cost	Controllable costs are items of expenditure that are directly influenced (by authority) within a period of time. These costs are critical in the decision-making process because they may changed by persons who are in direct control.
Uncontrollable cost	Items of expenditure that are not directly influenced or controlled. These costs, therefore, are not used in the decision-making process.
Fixed cost	These are assumed unless specified as non-relevant costs because they remained fixed within a relevant range.

Managers make decisions among alternative courses of action by using relevant information (which was gathered and analysed). This section reviews some of the short-term decisions made by managers, looking at factors to consider and the rule of thumb for each of them.

Special order

These are one-time (emergency or rushed) orders/jobs received to be done at a reduced or special price. Before accepting or rejecting a special order, managers should consider the following factors:

- Does the company have the excess capacity available to fill the orders?
- Will the sales price be high enough to cover the differential costs of filling the order? (Hint: the special price must be greater than the variable costs of filling the special order, and the contribution margin must be positive.)

- Will the special order affect the regular sales in the long run? (For example, if the regular customers find out, will they leave?)
- Will special order customers come again for the service offered?
- Will this job cause a price war in the market?

Example

Joy, who lives in Chase Village, makes netball uniforms for the regional netball competitions. Each uniform costs:

	$
Direct material	5
Direct labour	1
Fixed overhead	3
Total	9

Joy receives an order from the Canadian Netball Association to supply 700 uniforms of the same design at $7 each. Should she accept the special order?

Solution

Joy's Differential Income Statement

Sales (700 × $7)		$4 900
Less: Relevant costs		
Direct material (700 × $5)	$3 500	
Direct labour (700 × $1)	700	(4 200)
Differential profit		700

Decision: Based on the calculations, Joy should accept the order; she is able to make profit of $700.

Key points to note in the solution:

- The financial unit cost data was not used (because, at a glance, Joy would not have accepted the order as she will be making a loss of $2 ($9 – $7) for each uniform supplied.
- Fixed costs of $3 were not taken into consideration because it is an irrelevant cost.
- To determine total costs and revenue, the number of uniforms ordered was multiplied by each unit cost.

Guidelines for special order decisions

Guidelines for special order decisions are as follows:

1. Gather and analyse relevant costs (for example, variable costs). (Hint: focus on relevant revenues, costs and profits in the question.)
2. Ignore fixed costs (it is an irrelevant cost).
3. If there are mixed costs, isolate costs.
4. Prepare a differential income statement to determine differential profit or loss.
5. Make the decision to accept or reject using the rule of thumb. (Hint: for profit, look out for increase in revenue, increase in variable manufacturing overheads and increase in operating income.)

Rule of thumb

1. If revenue exceeds expenses – accept the special order.
2. If expenses exceed revenue – reject the special order.

Test Your Knowledge

Carlene makes a product that regularly sells for $12.50. The product variable manufacturing cost is $8.50 per unit and the fixed manufacturing cost is $2.00 per unit (this is based on fixed costs of $200 000 for the production of 100 000 units). The total product cost of the product is $10.50.

Carlene receives an offer from Dana for the purchase of 5 000 units at $9.00 each. Note: the selling and administrative costs and future sales will not be affected by the sale and Carlene does not expect to have any additional costs.

Required:

a. If Carlene has excess capacity, should she accept the offer from Dana? (Show your calculations.) **[8 marks]**

b. Does your answer change if Carlene is operating at capacity? Why or why not? **[8 marks]**

Make or buy

In the make-or-buy method managers decide whether to buy (outsource) or continue to produce. Factors to consider in this process before making the decision are:

- whether the firm has any spare capacity in making its own components instead of buying from others
- consider costs (variable costs only).

Example

Peter has been making 2 000 units of a component for the new wave mobile phones at the following cost:

	$
Raw materials	1 000
Direct labour	1 500
Variable overheads	500
Fixed overheads	4 000
Total cost	7 000
Total product cost	$3.50

Carl, a new manufacturer has offered to supply the components for the mobile phone at a special price of $1.50. Peter's cost accounting personnel informs him that if he purchases the components, it will enable the firm to avoid only 80 per cent of the variable overheads and 50 per cent of the fixed overheads.

Required

Should Peter make or buy the components for the mobile phones?

Solution

Peter's Comparative Cost Statement

Cost of 2 000 units of components for mobile phones	Make $	Buy $
Raw materials	1 000	-
Direct labour	1 500	-
Variable overheads (20% × $500)	500	100
Fixed overheads (50% × $4 000)	4 000	2 000
Manufacturer's price (2 000 × $1.50)	-	3 000
Total relevant cost	7 000	5 100

Key points to note in the solution
- Variable costs avoided were: all of the raw materials and the direct labour, 20 per cent of variable overheads and 50 per cent of fixed overheads.
- Comparison of make and buy total relevant costs: to determine cost saving or losses.

Guidelines for make-or-buy decisions

Guidelines for make-or-buy decisions are as follows:

1. Gather and analyse relevant costs (that is, direct material, direct labour and variable costs). (Hint focus on relevant data (variable costs and relevant fixed costs).)
2. Prepare comparative cost statements for the two alternatives to determine the costs saved.
3. Qualitative factors to consider are:
   a. whether there is spare capacity
   b. if the manufacturing of components is done at the expense of another product (this may be that the firm has no spare capacity)
   c. the quality of the supplier's work, and their after-sales service.
4. Compare the cost of manufacturing in-house with the price quoted by the supplier.
5. Determine the contribution lost (opportunity cost) as a result of not producing the original product.
6. Make the decision to make or buy using the rule of thumb. (Hint: compare the make or buy cost.)

Rule of thumb
1. If relevant cost is cheaper to make rather than outsource – make.
2. If relevant cost is cheaper to outsource rather than make – buy.

Test Your Knowledge

Caleb manufactures a variety of air-conditioning units. He currently manufactures all the parts on his own. An outside supplier has offered to produce and sell one of the parts at a cost of $20.00. Caleb's data for producing 15 000 parts internally is given below:

	$
Direct materials	6
Direct labour	8
Variable manufacturing overheads	1
Fixed manufacturing overheads	15 (the firm can avoid only 80%)
Total cost	30

Should Caleb accept the outside supplier's offer? Show all computations.   **[10 marks]**

Add or drop

Relevant information also plays an important role in decisions about adding or dropping products, services or departments (segments). The purpose of deciding whether to do the latter is to obtain the greatest contribution possible. The company will use contribution to pay the unavoidable costs because the unavoidable costs will remain the same regardless of any decision made. Therefore, for managers to decide which products to produce and to sell, the following factors must be considered when deciding to add or drop:

- Does the product, service or department provide a positive contribution margin?
- Will fixed costs continue to exist even if the company drops the product?
- Are there any direct fixed costs that can be avoided if the company drops the product?
- Will dropping the product affect sales of the company's other products?
- What would the company do with the fixed manufacturing capacity or storage space?

Example

Wendy Philly manufactures three different shades of eye shadow kits for targeted age groups. Data on sales and expenses for the past month are as follows:

	Total $	Eye shadow Ages 3–18 $	Ages 9–30 $	30 and over $
Sales	1 000 000	140 000	500 000	360 000
Less: variable expenses	410 000	60 000	200 000	150 000
Contribution margin	590 000	80 000	300 000	210 000
Less fixed expenses				
Advertising – traceable	216 000	41 000	110 000	65 000
Depreciation of special equipment	95 000	20 000	40 000	35 000
Assembly line supervisors' salaries	19 000	6 000	7 000	6 000
General factory overhead (allocated on the basis of sales)	200 000	28 000	100 000	72 000
Net operating income (loss)	60 000	(15 000)	43 000	32 000

Management is concerned about the continued losses shown by the 13–18 age group line and wants a recommendation as to whether or not the line should be dropped. The special equipment used to produce the eye shadow has no resale value. If the 13–18 age line is dropped, the services of two line supervisors assigned to the age group line would no longer be required and their contracts of employment with the company would be terminated.

Required

Should the production and sale of eye shadow for the 13–18 age group line be dropped? You may assume that the company has no other use for the capacity now being used to produce the eye shadows for the 13–18 age group. Show computations to support your answer.

Solution

	Keep 13–18 eye shadow $	Drop 13–18 eye shadow $	Difference: net income increase or (decrease) $
Sales	140 000	0	(140 000)
Less variable expenses	60 000	0	60 000
Contribution margin	80 000	0	(80 000)
Less fixed expenses			
Advertising – traceable	41 000	0	41 000
Depreciation of special equipment	20 000	20 000	0
Assembly line supervisors' salary	6 000	0	6 000
General factory overheads	28 000	28 000	0
Total fixed expenses	95 000	48 000	47 000
Net operating income (loss)	(15 000)	(48 000)	(33 000)

Alternative solution

Contribution margin lost if the 13–18 age group line is discontinued		(80 000)
Less fixed costs that can be avoided:		
Advertising – traceable	41 000	
Assembly line supervisors' salaries	6 000	47 000
Decrease in net operating income for the company as a whole		(33 000)

Decision:

Wendy Philly should not discontinue the production and sale of the 13–18 age group line because it would cause a decrease of $33 000 in net operating income for the entire company.

Keys points to note in the solution

- Depreciation of the special equipment represents a sunk cost and, therefore, it is not relevant in the decision-making process.
- The general factory overhead is an allocated cost and will therefore continue whether or not the 13–18 age group lines are dropped. These costs are also irrelevant.
- Use either solutions to determine net operating income or loss.

Guidelines to adding or dropping product, service or department

1. Gather and analyse relevant costs.
2. Prepare a comparative income statement (use the contribution approach) to determine net operating income (loss).
3. Make decision to add or drop product, service or department using the rule of thumb.

Rule of thumb

1. If lost revenues from dropping a line exceed the cost of savings from dropping – do not drop.
2. If total cost savings exceed the lost revenues from dropping a product – drop the product.

Test Your Knowledge

Shane has two product lines: furniture and accessories for the furniture. The manager is concerned about the recent loss situation of the accessories line and has threatened to close that product line, terminate its manager's contract of employment, and rent the space to a vendor who is willing to pay $1500 per month for the released space. The manager says that although the $5000 allocated cost of his salary and rent will remain it would be partly offset by the subleasing arrangement. The average monthly income data for the company is as follows:

	Furniture line $	Accessories for furniture line $	Total sales $
Sales	18 000	10 600	28 600
Cost of goods sold	9 800	6 360	15 360
Sales commission	1 800	1 060	2 860
Fixed costs	1 500	1 400	2 900 *
Allocated costs	2 500	2 500	5 000

*includes department manager's salary and benefits only.

Required: Should the manager carry out his threat?   [15 marks]

Qualitative (non-financial/relevant factors)

It is difficult at times for managers to quantify all the elements of a decision in monetary terms. In other instances, for managers to make a decision, both financial and non-financial factors are used in the process. These factors will be addressed in a later chapter in this revision guide.

MULTIPLE CHOICE QUESTIONS

1. Which of the following are considered as future incremental costs?

    (A) relevant

    (B) irrelevant

    (C) sunk

    (D) uncontrollable.

2. A sunk cost is a:

    I   relevant cost

    II   irrelevant cost

    III opportunity cost.

    (A) I

    (B) II

    (C) III

    (D) I and III

3. Differential (incremental) analysis is the process of identifying data that:

    (A) change under an alternative course of action

    (B) do not change under an alternative course of action

    (C) are mixed under alternative course of action

    (D) represents new fixed assets purchased.

4. In a make-or-buy decision, the key relevant costs to be considered are:

    I   variable manufacturing cost that will be saved

    II   purchase price

    III opportunity cost.

    (A) I

    (B) II

    (C) III

    (D) I, II and III

5. A company has decided to take up a one-time offer to supply its manufactured goods to another company. What kind of short-term decision is this called?

    (A) make-or-buy

    (B) invest in machinery

    (C) add and drop

    (D) special order.

Chapter 18

Traditional costing vs. Activity based costing

This chapter reviews indirect costs or overheads (factory burden). Overhead costs can be either manufacturing or non-manufacturing. Manufacturing overhead refers to costs indirectly associated with making a product. These costs can be fixed or variable. Some examples of fixed costs and variable costs are depreciation, rent, lubricants and power.

In addition, this chapter looks at the process of assigning indirect costs to cost objects (referred to as cost allocation) and methods for allocating support (service department) costs. While looking at the process, the following are reviewed: the structure of the overhead analysis sheet, the predetermined overhead rate, overhead absorbed, the concept of over and under applied and calculating the total unit cost.

Assignment of indirect costs

Indirect costs are accumulated to appropriate accounts for the provision of accurate and equitable allocation and appropriation of expenses to cost centres. A cost centre is any location in a business to which the costs can be attributed. Some examples of cost centres may include an item of equipment or even a person. These centres are divided into two main categories: production (operations) cost centres and service (support) cost centres.

The production cost centres are directly involved in producing goods; the service cost centres are not directly involved in the production of goods, but provide services for the production cost centres.

Terminology

The following terms are used in the process of charging and distributing overhead expenses to departments, cost centres, cost units, jobs and processes.

Allocation: is the process by which whole items are charged directly to cost centres or cost units. Examples include direct costs and indirect expenses which arise directly from the activity of a particular cost centre (food – canteen, or wood – production department)

Apportionment: is where separate totals of expenses are apportioned to production and similar cost centres (two or more) on the estimated basis of benefit received. The basis adopted for each expense takes into account the following:

- the nature of the expense
- the impact of the cost centre on the amount of the expense
- the relative benefit enjoyed by the cost centre.

Some common overheads and the basis of apportionment to cost centres are listed in Table 18.1.

Table 18.1 Some common overheads and basis of apportionment to cost centres

Overhead	Basis of apportionment to cost centres
Heating and lighting (when not separately metered to cost centres)	In proportion to the respective floor areas of the departments
Rent, insurance of buildings	In proportion to the respective floor areas of the departments
Power (if metered separately to cost centres)	Actual consumption (Note: this will be allocation rather than apportionment)
Depreciation of non-current assets	On cost or book value of assets in each department
Insurance of plant, machinery and other assets	On cost or replacement value of assets in each department
Costs of storekeeping	On number or value of stores requisitions raised by each cost centre
Costs of canteen, personnel department and administration	On number of personnel in each cost centre

Absorption: is the allotment of overhead to cost units by means of rates (usually predetermined) separately calculated for each cost centre. This rate is simply calculated by dividing the budgeted overhead costs by an activity base. The activity base can be in terms of hours, units or costs.

Overhead analysis sheet

Indirect costs are assigned to cost objects by allocation or apportionment. This is where all of the indirect costs are collected under various headings on some basis to all production and service departments. The collections, allocations and apportionments are made on an overhead analysis sheet. A review of the preparation of an overhead analysis sheet follows.

Example (1)

PC Incorporated is a manufacturing company which uses three production departments to make its product. It has the following factory costs which are expected to be incurred in the year to 31 December 2014:

	$
Indirect wages and salaries: Machining	300 000
Assembly	200 000
Finishing	70 000
Factory rent	500 000
Heating and lighting	400 000
Canteen	200 000

Other information available is:

	Machining	Assembly	Finishing
Number of employees	50	60	18
Floor space occupied	1 800	1 400	800
Number of labour hours	100 000	140 000	35 000
Number of machine hours	200 000	36 000	90 000

Required

Prepare the company's overhead analysis sheet for the year.

Solution

Overhead analysis sheet

Expense	Basis	Total	Machining	Assembly	Finishing
Indirect wages	Allocated	570 000	300 000	200 000	70 000
Rent	Floor area	500 000	225 000	175 000	100 000
Canteen	Number of employees	200 000	78 125	93 750	28 125
Heating and lighting	Floor area	400 000	180 000	140 000	80 000
Totals		1 670 000	783 125	608 750	278 125

Don't forget

1. Use the appropriate basis for apportionment.
2. Ensure that the totals at the end of each column equal the total column.

Predetermined overhead rates (POHR)

Now that you have reviewed the overhead analysis sheet (that is apportioning overheads to cost centres), it is time for you to review the next step, calculating the overhead absorption rates (OARs). These rates are used to calculate the amount of overhead to be attributed to each cost unit in each cost centre. This method of using one activity or base to determine the OAR is referred to as the *traditional method* of overhead allocation.

Overhead absorption rates are calculated for future periods because the cost of production must be known in advance to enable selling prices to be fixed. Calculations are based on two areas: planned volumes of output and budgeted overhead expenditure. You will notice in this review that the amount of overhead by a cost unit is usually calculated by reference to the time taken to produce it.

You were probably exposed to other OAR methods and were told that they were considered to be less satisfactory. Those methods will be reviewed later on in this chapter. The two methods about to be reviewed assume that a unit of production absorbs overhead proportionately to the time spent on processing it in the cost centres. This time is measured either in direct labour hours or machine hours.

Direct labour overhead absorption rate

There is an objective in this unit that requires you to discuss the impact of labour due to technological changes. It is therefore important for you remember the following:

- A process is labour intensive when it requires the use of labour rather than machines, and the labour cost is greater than the cost of using machinery.
- A cost centre is capital intensive when the operations carried out in the centre are mechanised and the machinery running cost is greater than the direct labour cost.

The above statements will help you to identify some of the changes/impact of labour.

Labour intensive industries measure their time in direct labour hours (DLH) and capital intensive firms' overhead will be absorbed using the machine hour OAR (MH).

The formula for OAR is $= \dfrac{\text{Estimated overhead during the period}}{\text{Estimated activity level during period (labour hours, machine hours or other methods)}}$

Example 2 (direct labour hour)

LemLime Ltd makes two products, Y and Z. The output for January 2014 is budgeted as follows:

Product Y   10 000 units
Product Z   8 000 units

Each unit of Y requires 1½ direct labour hour to make, and each unit of Z requires ¾ hour direct labour. LemLime Ltd overheads for the month of January is $131 250.

Required

a. Compute the total number of direct labour hours required to produce both products.

b. Calculate the OAR for LemLime Ltd.

c. Compute the total overhead absorbed.

Solution

a. Product Y (10 000 × 1½) + Product Z (8 000 × ¾) = 21 000

$\dfrac{\text{Total budgeted overhead expenditure}}{\text{Total budgeted number of direct labour hour}} = \dfrac{131\ 250}{21\ 000} = \$6.25\ \text{per DLH}$

b. Overhead absorbed by Y per unit = $6.25 × 1½ = 9.375
   Overhead absorbed by Z per unit = $6.25 × ¾ = 4.6875

c. The total overhead absorbed:
   Product Y: 10 000 × $9.375 = $93 750
   Product Z: 8 000 × $4.6875 = $37 500
   Total overhead absorbed $131 250

Example 3 (machine hour)

Realtime Ltd has six machines which are used in a 6-day working week. The number of machine hours used is 8000 hours. The overheads for one month is $160 000.

Required

Calculate the machine hour OAR.

Solution

$$\frac{\text{Overheads}}{\text{Machine hours}} = \frac{\$160\ 000}{8\ 000} = \$20.00 \text{ per MH}$$

Example 4 (Calculate total cost of each unit)

Product	R	S	
Number of units to be produced	5 000	6 000	
Cost of direct materials per unit	$18	$20	
Direct wages per unit	$15	$16	
Machine hours per unit			
Department I	3	2	
Department II	1	1	
Department III	2	3	
Direct labour hours per unit			
Department I	1	2	
Department II	2	3	
Department III	3	4	
Production departments	I	II	III
Budgeted overheads	$ 95 920	$ 86 250	$ 96 000
Budgeted machine hours	22 000	9 000	23 000
Budgeted labour hour	14 000	23 000	32 000

Required

Assume that Department I is machine intensive and Departments II and III are labour intensive, you are required to:

a. Calculate OAR for each department.

b. Calculate the overhead absorption for each unit of R and S.

c. Prepare a statement to show how the overheads of each department are absorbed by production.

d. Calculate the total cost of each unit of R and S.

Solution

a. Department I $\dfrac{\$95\ 920}{22\ 000} = \$4.36$ per MH

Department II $\dfrac{86\ 250}{23\ 000} = \$3.75$ per DLH

Department III $\dfrac{96\ 000}{32\ 000} = \$3.00$ per DLH

b. OAR per unit

OAR per unit	Department	I	Department	II	Department	III	Total
Product R	($4.36 × 3)	$13.08	($3.75 × 2)	$7.50	($3 × 3)	$9.00	$29.58
Product S	($4.36 × 2)	$8.72	($3.75 × 3)	$11.25	($3 × 4)	$12.00	$31.97

c. Total overhead absorbed (recovered)

Product	Department	I		II		III	Total
Product R	(5 000 × $13.08)	$65 400	(5 000 × $7.50)	$37 500	(5 000 × $9.00)	$45 000	$147 900
Product S	(6 000 × $8.72)	52 320	(6 000 × $11.25)	67 500	(6 000 × $12.00)	72 000	191 820
		117 720		105 000		117 000	339 720

d. Total cost per unit

	Product R $	Product S $
Direct material	18.00	20.00
Direct labour	15.00	16.00
Overhead	29.58	31.97
Total cost	62.58	67.97

Other bases for calculating OARs

The following bases are considered to be unsatisfactory for calculating OARs:

- direct material cost
- direct labour cost
- prime cost
- cost unit.

Test Your Knowledge

1. Describe **two** methods of re-apportioning service cost centres. **[2 marks]**
2. State **two** methods of overhead apportionment, other than labour or machine hours. **[2 marks]**
3. Dylon Ltd has two production departments, A and B, and two service departments, Packing and Canteen. Specific costs needing to be allocated to each cost centre are estimated to be as follows:

	$
Department A	10 000
Department B	8 000
Packing	5 998
Canteen	3 839

The total overhead costs for Dylon Ltd are estimated to be:

	$
Rent	40 000
Building repairs	6 000
Machinery insurance	3 600
Machinery depreciation	12 000
Machinery maintenance	5 000
Power	9 500

The following cost centre information is also available:

	A	B	Packing	Canteen
Floor space (square metres)	10 000	8 000	6 000	3 000
Power usage (%)	40	30	20	10
Machine value ($ 000)	100	80	60	–
Machinery hours (000)	60	40	–	–
Number of employees	30	20	4	2
Number of packages (000)	20	10	–	–

Required:

a. Prepare a schedule to allocate and apportion the costs over the **four** departments. [25 marks]

b. Re-allocate the service department costs to the **two** production departments. Assume that neither service department does work for the other service department. [10 marks]

c. Calculate suitable OARs for **each** production department, bearing in mind that Dylon Ltd is a highly mechanised company. [8 marks]

Activity based costing

Activity based costing (ABC) is the method of allocating overheads where each item of overhead cost is matched with its cost driver to arrive at individual overhead activity rates. The main difference between ABC and traditional costing systems is that ABC has individual overhead rates for each activity, whereas traditional costing has only one rate for applying overheads.

Example

Jahn Bean Manufactures estimated that its overhead costs for 2016 would be $600 000 and total direct labour of 50 000 hours. The firm uses the traditional method of allocating overheads using direct labour hours as its base in calculating its POHR. The firm provided the following information in relation to products K19 and N36.

Activity	Expected costs $	Activity driver	Total activity capacity
Machining	180 000	Machining hours	200 000
Setup equipment	150 000	Number of setups	300
Engineering	210 000	Engineering hours	20 000
Inspecting	60 000	Number of inspections	12 000
Total	600 000		

	K19	N36
Number of units produced	5000	3500
Direct materials per unit ($4.00 per lb)	5 lb	3 lb
Direct labour per unit	3 hours	1.5 hours

Jahn Bean Manufactures is considering the use of ABC. The firm supplies the following information in relation to its two products:

Per unit activity	K19	N36
Machining hours	2 hours	4 hours
Number of setups	5	6
Engineering hours	3	5
Number of inspections	2	3

Required

1. Calculate the overhead rate per labour hour using traditional costing.
2. Under traditional costing methods that Jahn Bean Manufactures uses, what is the total cost of the number of units produced for K19 and N36?
3. Calculate the activity rates for each of the four activities.
4. Using the answers in 3 above, calculate the cost of manufacturing the units under the ABC system.
5. Explain how the ABC can provide more accurate product costs than traditional costing systems.

Solution

5. ABC though more complex than traditional methods of allocating overheads:

- seeks to eliminate the allocation of irrelevant cost – cost that is not related to that department or product
- seeks to assign and allocate cost based on the activities of the various cost drivers rather than the activity of one common cost driver which can be disproportionate in its allocation
- is easier for benchmarking when determining standard cost and comparing it to actual outcomes
- is an easier and more precise interpretation of the organisation's overhead cost by internal management.

MULTIPLE CHOICE QUESTIONS

1. Indirect costs are assigned to:

    (A) cost pools

    (B) cost units

    (C) cost centres

    (D) cost objects.

2. The collections, allocations and apportionments are done on a/an:

    (A) overhead analysis sheet

    (B) work sheet

    (C) spreadsheet

    (D) pay sheet.

3. The basis of apportionment for heating and lighting to cost centres may be:

    I   in proportion to floor area of department

    II   the cost or book value of assets in each department

    III the number of personnel in each cost centre.

    (A) I

    (B) II

    (C) I and II

    (D) I and III

4. Which of the following allots overheads to cost units by means of rates calculated separately for each cost centres?

    (A) assignment

    (B) apportionment

    (C) allotment

    (D) absorption.

5. The difference between the traditional costing and activity based costing (ABC) is:

    (A) Traditional costing uses many bases whereas ABC uses only one base.

    (B) ABC uses the predetermined overhead rate.

    (C) Traditional costing uses one base whereas ABC uses many bases.

    (D) Traditional costing uses individual activity rates for applying each overhead.

Chapter 19   Job costing

Job costing is a cost accounting system. It is used when making products that are distinct from each other, or distinct groups or batches of identifiable, unique products. All costs are collected at each job.

- Direct materials and direct labour are assigned and manufacturing overhead is allocated using a pre-determined overhead rate (POHR) or overhead absorption rate using activity based costing.
- Jobs to which costs are assigned or allocated and are complete are considered work-in-process (WIP).
- All jobs that are completed at the end of the period are finished goods and incomplete jobs are ending WIP inventory.
- Finished goods that are sold are called cost of goods sold and unsold finished jobs of the end of the period are ending finished goods inventory.

The flow of costs for a job is outlined in Figure 19.1.

Figure 19.1 Flow of costs (job costing)

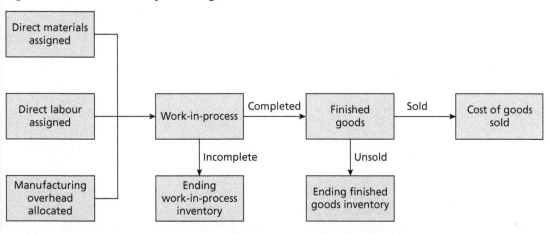

Example

Consider the Crespo Co. that upholsters and refurbishes furniture. In the month of March 2015 the company started seven jobs: numbers 363, 364, 365, 366, 367, 368 and 369. At the end of March 2015, jobs 363, 364, 367, 368 and 369 were completed and jobs 364 368 and 369 were sold.

Required

1. List the jobs that make up ending work-in-process inventory at the end of the period.
2. List the jobs that make up ending finished goods inventory at the end of the accounting period.
3. List the jobs that make up the cost of sales at the end of March 2015.

Solution

Figure 19.2. Crespo Co. Flow of costs (job costing)

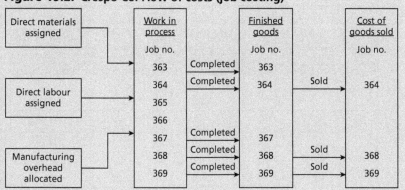

As seen in Figure 19.2 costs are assigned and allocated to the seven jobs. It also shows the movement of the five completed jobs from work-in-process to finished goods and the sale of the three finished goods.

1. Ending work-in-process inventory jobs are jobs 365 and 366.
2. Ending finished goods inventory are jobs 363 and 367.
3. Cost of sales consists of jobs 364, 368 and 369.

Calculating WIP and cost of jobs

Example

John Enterprises are manufacturers of special edition furniture. Each piece is made-to-order. On 1 July 2015 the company has a balance in work-in-process inventory of $4 200 for two jobs: job 476 – $2 200 and job 478 – $2 000. During the month of July, the following information was collected:

Jobno.	Materials $	Labour $
476	2 500	3 000
478	1 000	2 400
489	4 200	2 500
490	3 600	2 300
491	3 900	2 600

The company applies manufacturing overheads to jobs at a rate of 80 per cent of direct labour costs. Jobs 489 and 491 were incomplete at the end of the month.
Required

a. What is the total cost of manufacturing overheads to be incurred during the month of July 2010?
b. What is John Enterprises' total work-in-process at the end of July 2010?
c. What is John Enterprises' cost of goods manufactured at the end of July 2010?

Solution

a. Jobs 489 and 491 are incomplete at the end of the period.
Overhead costs calculation for completed jobs for July 2010

Job no.	Direct labour costs $	Manufacturing overheads (80% of direct labour) $
476	3,000	2,400
478	2,400	1,920
489	2,500	2,000
490	2,300	1,840
491	2,600	2,080
Total manufacturing overheads to be charged against finished goods for July 2005		10,240

b. Calculation of John Enterprises' work-in-process at the end of July 2005.

Incomplete Jobs	Direct materials $	Direct labour $	Manufacturing Overhead $	Total $
489	4200	2500	2000	8700
491	3900	2600	2080	8580
Total	8100	5100	4080	17280

c. Calculation of John Enterprises' cost of finished goods at the end of July 2005.

Direct materials	15 200
Direct labour	12 800
Prime cost	28 000
Manufacturing overhead	10 240
Cost incurred during July 2010	38 240
Add: Opening WIP	4 200
	42 440
Less: Closing WIP	(17 280)
Cost of goods manufactured	**$25 160**

Test Your Knowledge

1. How is the total cost of a job determined? **[1 mark]**
2. What are the two methods used to allocate overheads in jobs costing? **[2 marks]**
3. What are incomplete jobs called at the end of the period? **[1 mark]**
4. What are the unsold jobs of the end of the period called? **[1 mark]**
5. What is the name of jobs sold? **[1 mark]**
6. Jelani Adams Manufacturers makes and installs custom kitchen cupboards. The firm's job nos. 911 and 913 were incomplete at the end of May 2015. At the start of June 2015, the firm started job nos. 914, 915, 916, 917, 918, 919, 920 and 921. During June 2015 job nos. 911, 913, 916, 918, 919 and 920 were completed and moved into the nearby warehouse. Job nos. 911, 916, 918 and 920 were sold during June 2015.
   a. How many jobs were incomplete at the beginning of June 2015? **[2 marks]**
   b. How many jobs were started in June 2015? List them. **[2 marks]**
   c. List the ending work-in-process inventory at 30 June 2015. **[4 marks]**
   d. List the jobs that constitute finished goods inventory at 30 June 2015 **[4 marks]**
   e. If jobs are sold for $4500 each, what is the value of sales for June 2015? **[6 marks]**
7. May 2015 production generated the following activity in DVAK manufacturing work-in-process inventory:
   Work-in-process inventory

	$	$
01 May, Balance		16 000
Direct materials used	29 000	
Direct labour assigned to jobs	32 000	
Manufactured overhead allocated to jobs	12 000	

Completed production, not yet recorded, in September 2015 consists of jobs A21 and B56, with total costs of $41 000 and $37 000 respectively. Compute the cost of work-in-process at 31 May 2015. **[5 marks]**

8. Rajkumar's Car Repair Service job cost records yield the following information:

Job no.	Date			Total cost of job at 31 March $
	Started	Finished	Sold	
1	21 February	16 March	17 March	3 800
2	29 February	21 March	26 March	13 000
3	03 March	11 April	13 April	6 400
4	07 March	29 March	01 April	4 000
5	09 March	30 March	02 April	7 120
6	22 March	11 April	13 April	2 000

Compute Rajkumar's Car Repair Service cost of:
a. Work-in-process inventory at 31 March 2015.   [6 marks]
b. Finished goods inventory at 31 March 2015.   [6 marks]
c. Cost of goods sold at 31 March 2015.   [6 marks]

9. JJ Manufacturing Enterprises uses the job costing system. On 01 September 2015, the company has a balance in work-in-process inventory of $6400 and two jobs in process: job nos. 156 – $4000 and job no. 157 – $2400. The following information was supplied for the month of September 2015.

Job no.	Direct materials	Direct labour
158	2500	2400
159	2000	3000
160	4400	7600
161	800	1200

JJ Manufacturing Enterprises applies manufacturing overheads to jobs at a rate of 80 per cent of direct labour cost. Job nos. 159 and 160 were the only jobs incomplete at the end of September 2015.
Required: Calculate the following:
a. The cost of goods manufactured for September 2015.   [8 marks]
b. The ending work in process inventory at the end of September 2015.   [4 marks]
c. Jobs nos. 156, 157 and 161 were sold. What is the cost of goods sold?   [8 marks]

Under and over-applied overheads

Chapter 18 discussed the calculation of POHR as a comparison to the use of the activity based costing method for applying overheads to units. Under either method when the overhead applied is compared to the actual overheads incurred, overheads can either be over-applied or under-applied.
If overheads applied > actual overheads incurred = over-applied
If overheads applied < actual overheads incurred = under-applied

Test Your Knowledge

1. Selected cost data for Super Stickers Co. are as follows:

Expected manufacturing overhead cost for the year	$97 800
Expected direct labour cost for the year	$61 125
Actual manufacturing cost for the year	$104 600
Actual direct labour cost for the year	$63 900

a. Compute the POHR per direct labour dollar.   [3 marks]
b. Determine the over or under-applied manufacturing overhead for Super Stickers Company.   [5 marks]

2. Sammy Surveyors, an architectural firm uses job costing systems with a pre-determined overhead allocation rate, computed as a percentage of labour costs. At the beginning of 20X6, the managing director, Johnny Henry prepared the following budget for the year:

Direct labour hours (professionals)	17 000 hours
Direct labour costs (professionals)	$2 669 000
Office rent	$ 350 750
Support staff salaries	$1 194 000
Utilities	$ 324 000
Office supplies	$ 133 000

Bargain Hunters Inc. is inviting several consultants to bid for work. Johnny Henry estimates that this job will require about 220 direct labour hours.

a. Compute Sammy Surveyors:
   (i) hourly direct labour cost rate, and
   (ii) indirect cost allocation rate. **[6 marks]**
b. Compute the predicted cost of the Bargain Hunters Inc. job. **[4 marks]**
c. If Johnny Henry wants to earn a profit equal to 30 per cent of the job's cost how much should he bid for the Bargain Hunters job? **[3 marks]**
d. The actual cost of overhead for the job was as follows:

Office rent	$ 3 605
Support staff salaries	$18 587
Utilities	$ 3 784
Office supplies	$ 2 245

   Was the overhead over-applied or under-applied? **[5 marks]**

MULTIPLE CHOICE QUESTIONS

1. The source document used to record the hours worked on a job is called a:
   (A) Material requisition
   (B) Time sheet
   (C) Process work sheet
   (D) Memorandum.

2. In job costing, completed jobs are transferred to:
   (A) work-in-process inventory
   (B) finished goods inventory
   (C) cost of goods sold
   (D) raw materials inventory.

3. In job costing, jobs sold are transferred to:
   (A) work-in-process inventory
   (B) finished goods inventory
   (C) cost of goods sold.
   (D) raw materials inventory.

4. In job costing, incomplete jobs are transferred to:
   (A) work-in-process inventory
   (B) finished goods inventory
   (C) overheads
   (D) raw materials inventory.

5. Andon uses a job order costing system. Overheads are applied to jobs using direct labour hours. The rate per direct labour hour is $30. The data for job no. 200, an unfinished job, is listed below:

Job no.	200
Direct materials	$5 000
Direct labour cost	100 hours @ $15 per hour

   The value of ending work in process inventory is:
   (A) $4 500
   (B) $6 500
   (C) $8 000
   (D) $9 500

6. In a job costing system, the document used to account for the cost of an individual job is known as the:
   (A) Labour time ticket
   (B) Process work sheet
   (C) Material requisition form
   (D) Job cost sheet.

Chapter 20   Process costing

Process costing is a costing system used in manufacturing organisations, where units are continuously mass produced through various processes. In the mass production system, the product is a single homogeneous product and the output (finished goods) of one process becomes the input for the next process until the last process. Examples may include the production of oil, natural gas, sugar, flour, cement and bricks. The costing of a unit of product remains the same, consisting of direct materials, direct labour and applied manufacturing overhead. These organisations are usually highly capital intensive (more machinery in production than labour).

Terminology

Terms to note are set out below:

Term	Description
Normal loss	The normal expected wastage under usual operating conditions. This may be due to evaporation or expected rejects. This cost is not accounted for by the business. The cost of these units are absorbed by the other units in production.
Abnormal loss	These are losses that occur above that of the normal loss. This can be due to pilferage, employee negligence and faulty equipment. Reflected as a loss in the income statement.
Abnormal gain	This occurs when the actual loss is less than the normal loss. This may result from worker efficiencies, improved technology and more efficient controls in the use of direct material and direct labour and a more effective application of overheads. Reflected as a gain in the income statement.
Work-in-process (WIP)	The number of units that are incomplete in that process at the end of the period. Opening WIP refers to uncompleted units at the beginning of the process and ending WIP refers to uncompleted units at the end of the process.
Equivalent units	This refers to units fully 100% complete) or partly (less than 100% complete) completed, converted to an equivalent number of fully completed goods. For example, 1500 units of which 1000 units are 100% complete and 500 are 60% complete: 1000 units 100% complete = 1000 equivalent units 500 units 60% complete = 300 equivalent units Total equivalent units = 1300 equivalent units.
Scrap value	In some cases the units that are part of the normal or abnormal loss can be sold. This is referred to as the scrap value. This is shown as revenue to the company.

Process costing report

At each process or department a product report or worksheet is prepared to account for the units received and complete and their related cost. One of two approaches is used to prepare the report; FIFO (first-in, first-out) or weighted average.

Weighted average method

An example of the weighted average method is given below.

	Total	Direct materials	Direct labour	Manufacturing overhead
Units to account for:				
Beginning WIP (w% complete)	xxx			
Started in the period	xxx			
Total units to account for	xxx			
Units accounted for/ Equivalent units				
Units completed and transferred out (100% complete)	xxx	xxx	xxx	xxx
Ending WIP (y% complete)	xxx	xxx	xxx	xxx
Total units accounted for / Total equivalent units (a)	xxx	xxx	xxx	xxx

Costs to account for :				
Beginning WIP (w% complete)	Xxx	xxx	xxx	xxx
Costs added during the period	xxx	xxx	xxx	xxx
Total cost to account for (b)	xxx	xxx	xxx	xxx
Equivalent unit cost (b) ÷ (a)	r+s+t	r	S	t
Cost reconciliation / Cost accounted for:				
Units completed and transferred out (l00% complete)	[(r + s + t) × number of units completed] xxx			
Ending WIP				
Direct materials (unit cost × equivalent units)		xxx		
Direct labour (unit cost × equivalent units)			xxx	
Manufacturing overheads (unit cost × equivalent units)				xxx
Total ending WIP	xxx			
Total cost accounted for	xxx			

Note: When calculating units for beginning work-in-process the percentage of completion is ignored.

FIFO method

An example of the FIFO method is given below.

	Total	Direct materials	Direct labour	Manufacturing overheads
Units to account for:				
Beginning WIP (w% complete)	xxx			
Started in the period	xxx			
Total units to account for	xxx			
Units accounted for/ Equivalent units:				
Beginning WIP (100% – w% complete)	xxx	xxx	xxx	xxx
Units started and completed in this period (100% complete)	xxx	xxx	xxx	xxx
Units transferred out (100% complete)	xxx	xxx	xxx	xxx
Ending WIP (y% complete)	xxx	xxx	xxx	xxx
Total units accounted for / Total equivalent units (a)	xxx	xxx	xxx	xxx
Cost to account for:				
Beginning WIP (w% complete)	xxx	xxx	xxx	xxx
Cost added during the period (b)	xxx	xxx	xxx	xxx
Total cost to account for	xxx	xxx	xxx	xxx
Equivalent unit cost (b) ÷ (a)	r+s+t	r	s	T
Cost reconciliation / Cost accounted for:				
Beginning WIP (w% complete)		xxx	xxx	Xxx
Beginning WIP (100% – w% complete) Direct materials		xxx		
Beginning WIP (100% – w% complete) Direct labour			xxx	
Beginning WIP (100% – w% complete) Manufacturing overheads				xxx
Total beginning WIP	xxx	xxx	xxx	xxx
Units started and completed during the period (100% complete)	**xxx**			
Units completed and transferred out	xxx			
Ending WIP:				
Direct materials (unit cost × equivalent units)		xxx		
Direct labour (unit cost × equivalent units)			xxx	

Manufacturing overheads (unit cost × equivalent units)				xxx
Total ending WIP	xxx	xxx	xxx	xxx
Total cost accounted for	xxx			

Example

The Dandrade Medical Supplies Company has three processes each managed by a department: mixing, drying and packing. In the mixing department labour and overhead costs are incurred uniformly as work progresses. Overhead cost is applied at a rate of 150 per cent of direct labour cost. Cost and other data for July 20X5 include the following for the mixing department:

Work-in-process: Beginning	
Units in progress	4 000
Stage of completion:	
Materials	10%
Labour and overhead	30%
Cost in the beginning inventory:	
Materials cost	$16 000
Labour cost	$7 200
Overhead cost	$10 800
Total cost in process	$38 000
Units started into production during the month	36 000
Units completed and transferred out to drying department	34 000
Cost added to production during the month	
Materials cost	126 000
Labour cost	176 000
Overhead cost applied	264 000
Work-in-process: Ending	
Units in progress	6 000
Stage of competition	
Materials	100%
Labour and overhead	40%

Required

1. Prepare the production report using the weighted average method.
2. Prepare the production report using FIFO method.

Solution:

1. Production report using the weighted average method

Dandrade Medical Supplies Company

Production Report: Weighted Average Method

	Total	Direct materials	Direct labour	Manufacturing overhead
Units to account for:				
Beginning WIP	4 000			
Started in the period	36 000			
Total units to account for	40 000			
Units accounted for/ Equivalent units:				
Units completed and transferred out (100% complete)	34 000	34 000	34 000	34 000
Ending WIP (Materials100 % complete and labour and overhead 40 % complete.)	6 000	100% complete 6 000	40% complete (6000 × 40%) 2 400	40% complete (6000 × 40%) 2 400
Total units accounted for / Total equivalent units (a)	40 000	40 000	36 400	36 400

Cost to account for:				
Beginning WIP (w% complete)	34 000	16 000	7 200	10 800
Cost added during the period	566 000	126 000	176 000	264 000
Total cost to account for (b)	600 000	142 000	183 200	274 800
Equivalent unit cost (b) ÷ (a)*	(3.55 + 5.033 + 7.55) $16.13	(142 000 ÷ 40000) $3.55	(183 200 ÷ 36400) $5.03	(274800 ÷ 36 400) $7.55
Cost reconciliation /Cost accounted for				
Units completed and transferred out (100% complete)	($16. 13 × 34 000 equivalent units) 548 420			
Ending WIP				
Direct materials (unit cost × equivalent units)		($3.55 × 6000 equivalent units) 21 300		
Direct labour (40% complete)			($5.03 × 2400 equivalent units) 12 160	
Manufacturing overheads (unit cost × equivalent units)				($7.55 × 2400 equivalent units) 18 120
Total ending WIP	51 580	21 300	12 160	18 120
Total cost accounted for	600 000			

*Figures rounded

2. Production report using the FIFO method

Dandrade Medical Supplies Company
Production Report: FIFO

	Total	Direct materials	Direct labour	Manufacturing overhead
Units to account for				
Beginning WIP (30% complete)	4 000			
Started in the period	36 000			
Total units to account for	40 000			
Units accounted for/ Equivalent units				
Beginning WIP	6 000	[(100 – 10) % to complete × 6000] 5 400	[(100 – 30) % to complete × 6000] 4 200	[(100 – 30) % to complete × 6000] 4 200
Units completed in this period (100% Complete)	28 000	28 000	28 000	28 000
Units transferred out (100% complete)	34 000	33 400	32 200	32 200

		(100 % complete)	(40% complete × 6000 units)	(40%complete × 6000 units)
Ending WIP	6 000	6 000	2 400	2 400
Total units accounted for / Total equivalent units (a)	40 000	39 400	34 600	34 600
Cost to account for :				
Beginning WIP (w% complete)	$34 000	$16 000	$7 200	$10 800
Cost added during the period (b)	$566 000	$126 000	$176 000	$264 000
Total cost to account for	$600 000	$142 000	$183 200	$274 800
Equivalent unit cost (b) ÷ (a)	(3.198 + 5.087 + 7.63) $15.915	(126 000 ÷ 39 400 equivalent units) $3.198	(176 000 ÷ 34 600 equivalent units) $5.087	(264 000 ÷ 34 600 equivalent units) $7.63
Cost reconciliation/Cost accounted for				
Beginning WIP bf		$16 000	$7 200	$10 800
Beginning WIP (100% – 10% complete) Direct materials		(5400 equivalent units × $3.198) $17 269		
Beginning WIP (100% – 30% complete) Direct labour			(4200 equivalent units × $5. 087) $21 365	
Beginning WIP (100% – w% complete) Manufacturing overheads				(4200 equivalent units × $7.63) $32 046
Total beginning WIP	104 680	$33 269	$28 565	$42 846
Units started and completed during the period (100% complete)	(28 000 equivalent units × $15.915) $445 620			
Units completed and transferred out (l00% Complete)	$550 300			
Ending WIP				
Direct materials (unit cost × equivalent units)		(6000 equivalent units × $3.198) $19 188		
Direct labour (unit cost × equivalent units)			(2400 equivalent units × $5 .087) $12 200	
Manufacturing overheads (unit cost × equivalent units)				(2400 equivalent units × $7.63) $18 312
Total ending WIP	$49 700	$19 188	$12 200	$18 312
Total cost accounted for	$600 000			

Test Your Knowledge

1. What is the definition of normal loss?   [1 mark]
2. Define equivalent units.   [1 mark]
3. The Barima-Waini Chemical Company has two departments: mixing and cooking. Production activity begins in the mixing department, then the units are transferred to the cooking department. On completion, the finished goods are stored in the warehouse. All materials are added at the beginning of the mixing process. Labour and overheads are added uniformly as work progresses. Overhead costs are added at a rate of 120 per cent of direct labour cost. The cost data for March 2020 for the Mixing department is as follows:

Work-in-process: Beginning

Units in process	30 000
Stage of completion	30%

Costs in the beginning inventory

Material costs	12 000
Labour costs	5 400
Overhead costs	8 100
Total costs in process	$25 500

Units started into production during the month	270 000
Units completed and transferred out to cooking	255 000

Costs added during the period:

Material costs	$94 500
Labour costs	132 000

Works in process, ending is 40% complete

Prepare the production report of the mixing process under:

a. Weighted average method   [17 marks]

b. FIFO method.   [23 marks]

MULTIPLE CHOICE QUESTIONS

1. Process costing industries include processes such as:

   I   printing of wedding invitations

   II   production of oil

   III   production of flour.

   (A) I

   (B) II

   (C) I and II

   (D) II and III

2. Normal loss:

   I   occurs when the actual loss is less than the normal loss

   II   is loss that occurs above the normal loss

   III   is expected wastage in usual operation conditions.

   (A) I

   (B) II

   (C) III

   (D) I and III

3. In process costing, the document used to account for units received and completed units is known as a:

   (A) Job cost sheet

   (B) Process work sheet

   (C) Standard cost card

   (D) Stock card.

The following information refers to questions 4 and 5:

Sarah manufactures Avon perfumes using a weighted average process costing system. The equivalent (EU) units produced in April were 1 000 with respect to direct materials and 800 with respect to conversion costs.

The beginning work-in-process inventory consisted of direct materials of $200 000 and conversion costs of $250 000. The cost added during April consisted of $1 000 000 in direct materials and $1 500 000 in conversion costs. Sarah uses the weighted average method.

4. What is the direct material cost per EU unit during April?

   (A) $200

   (B) $1 000

   (C) $1 200

   (D) $1 333.33

5. The conversion cost per EU is:

   (A) $312.50

   (B) $1 500

   (C) $1 875

   (D) $2 187.50

Chapter 21

Service sector costing

Objectives

At the end of this chapter you will be able to:

- identify the characteristics of service sector industries
- discuss the role of management accounting in service industries
- list different types of service industries
- distinguish the costing methods used in the service sector
- apply the traditional costing methods to service sector industries
- explain the difficulties associated with service sector costing.

Introduction

This chapter reviews the characteristics of service sector industries, the types of service industries, the role of management accounting in these industries and the costing methods used. There is also a review of how to prepare a bill for a customised service using the job costing method. And the difficulties associated with service sector costing are identified.

Characteristics of service sector industries

Service sector industries provide customised, intangible services for the organisation's internal or external customers. Some characteristics of these industries are:

- they are labour intensive
- costs per unit are usually difficult to ascertain
- services rendered cannot be stored, and
- cost of inventory (if any) is insignificant.

Types of service sector industries

Services sector industries that contribute to the economies of several countries in the Caribbean include the following businesses:

- hotels
- insurance companies
- banks and credit unions
- legal firms
- medical institutions
- beauty and spa businesses
- auto repairs and maintenance services

to name a few.

Role of management accounting in service industries

Management accounting monitors resources in service industries to identify areas that are most profitable or exhibit excessive wastage. Management can then use the information to make decisions to improve the service's profitability in the short or long term.

Difficulties associated with service sector costing

Some of the difficulties associated with service sector costing are as follows:

- The cost per unit is usually difficult to ascertain. (It is difficult to measure the value of a service. Also it depends on the customer's perception.)
- Services rendered cannot be stored (they are produced and consumed immediately). As such, they fall into perishable, intangible and heterogeneous categories.

Determining cost driver per unit

A characteristic of service sector industries is that they are labour intensive. You should note that the costs of materials, direct or indirect, are either small or non-existent. Therefore, direct labour is the largest contributor to the total operating costs.

Unlike the manufacturing sector, in service sector industries it is very difficult to determine the cost driver per unit, due to the nature of services. The cost driver per unit is:

- differentiated or heterogeneous – highly customised to the client's needs
- inseparable – must be delivered with the client present
- perishable – is consumed immediately by the client
- intangible – cannot be touched.

Some examples of service sector industries and their suggested activity / cost drivers are given below. Table 21.1 shows the cost drivers for external customers and Table 21.2 shows the cost drivers for an organisation's internal services.

Table 21.1 Examples of cost drivers for external customers

External customers	Cost driver per unit
Hotel	Bed nights available / bed nights occupied
School	Student hours / full time students
Hospital	Patients per day / rooms per day
Transport (fares)	Number of passengers / km travelled

Table 21.2 Examples of cost drivers for services provided to departments within an organisation

Internal	Cost driver per unit
Staff canteen	Meals provided/ number of staff
Machine maintenance	Maintenance hours provided by the service department to the department using the machine / machine hours
Computer department	Computer time provided to the department using the computer

Costing methods used in service sector industries

Service sector industries, like manufacturing industries generally, may adopt one of the following costing methods to assign their costs to services.

Job costing (Job order costing): In this method, the cost of a customised service is obtained by assigning costs to a distinct identifiable task. Service industries that may adopt this method are hospitals, accounting firms, repair shops, law firms, architectural firms, construction companies, hospitality and consulting firms.

Process costing: In this system the cost of a service is obtained by assigning costs to masses of similar units and computing the unit cost on an average basis. Industries that may adopt this method are chemical-producing companies, garment industries, bakeries, paint shops, shoe-making industries, sugar industries, retail banking, postal delivery services and credit card companies.

Activity based costing (ABC): This method is a refined system for allocating/ assigning overhead costs to services. Each activity has its own allocation base called a cost driver. Some examples of the bases and the approach in handling this method are shown in Chapter 18.

Job costing and Process costing systems are known as traditional methods in the manufacturing sector. We will now look at the application of both methods in the service sector.

Job costing in the service sector

It is important for firms to continuously monitor the costs for each job and record such information; this guides decisions made on job pricing and assists in enhancing the firm's profitability through cost planning and control. In the job costing method the direct labour and service overheads costs are monitored closely. The following steps (divided into cost accumulation and cost allocation) are generally adopted for assigning costs to jobs.

Cost accumulation:

- Identify the job that is chosen as the cost object (e.g. type of work required).
- Identify the direct cost for the job (e.g. amount of professional time required for doing the work).
- Identify indirect costs (overheads) incurred for providing services (e.g. the costs of support labour, travel, telephone/fax/computer time or photocopying).

Cost allocation

- Select the cost allocation base to be used in assigning each indirect cost to the job (this step requires that the base selected is the one which drives the indirect cost. This is shown as increases in the base increases the indirect cost).
- Identify the rate per unit of the cost allocation base used to allocate costs to the job (budgeted total indirect cost ÷ budgeted total quantity of cost allocation base).
- Compute the total overhead cost (estimated rate per unit × quantity).

Terminology

The term 'job', which is normally used in the manufacturing sector, may not be used in service sector industries; instead, terms such as 'client', 'project', 'case', 'contract', 'patient' may be used.

Example

Victoria Nursing Hospital uses a job costing system for all patients who have surgery. The hospital uses a budgeted overhead rate for allocating overheads to patient stays. In April the operating room had a budgeted allocation base of 1000 operating hours. The budgeted operating overhead costs were $66 000. Dr Rachael Trotman worked in the operating room for 4 hours in April. Other costs related to Dr Trotman's 4-hour surgery included:

	Costs ($)
Patient medicine	250
Cost of nurses' services	3 500
Cost of supplies	800

The physician's costs, which were not included in the hospital bill, were issued separately.

Required

a. Determine the overhead rate for the operating room.

b. Compute the total overhead cost of the 4-hour surgery.

c. Compute total cost of patient stay.

Solution

a. Overhead rate for the operating room = budgeting operating overhead costs/ total operating hours

$= \$66\ 000/1\ 000 = \$66$ per operating hour

b. Total overhead of the 4-hour surgery = $\$66 \times 4 = \$264$

c. Total cost of patient stay = patient medicine + cost of nurses' services + cost of supplies + total overheads

$= \$250 + \$3\ 500 + \$800 + \$264 = \$4\ 814$

Points to note:

- The cost object is the surgery.
- The direct cost for surgery is the time taken is 4 hours.
- Other related costs for the surgery are patient medicine, cost of nurses' services and cost of supplies.
- The allocation base to be used in assigning indirect costs to the job is the total operating cost.

Mark-up pricing in service sector industries

Service industries such as repair shops, for example, use a cost-based approach (mark-up percentage) to add the cost of overheads to the direct costs of labour, materials and parts as a basis for determining price. For the professional service sector such as accounting and consulting agencies, a factor representing all overhead costs is applied to the base labour costs to establish a price for the services.

Example

Akouswa Law Chambers specialises in copyright protection for authors. Raebekah, a client, approached the law firm about handling her lawsuit against Tiffany, who she believes stole a plot from one of her books for a mini television series.

Akouswa Law Chambers estimated that the case would require 500 professional labour hours. The Chambers accountant estimated the following direct costs:

	Costs ($)
Direct professional labour cost (500 hours)	75 000
Direct support labour	20 000
Fringe benefits for direct labour	15 000
Photocopying	1 000
Telephone calls	1 000
Total direct costs	112 000

Additional information:

Total overheads for last year $450 000

Two law partners worked 5 000 professional labour hours.

The law firm's policy is to mark-up costs by 20% for the estimated price.

Required:

a. Compute the total overhead costs.

b. Compute the estimated profit.

c. Compute the estimated selling price.

Solution

Budgeted overhead rate:

Total overhead ÷ Total professional labour hours = $450 000 ÷ 5 000 = $90 per hour

Estimated overhead cost for the case: $90 × 500 = $45 000

	Costs ($)
Direct professional labour cost (500 hours)	75 000
Direct support labour	20 000
Fringe benefits for direct labour	15 000
Photocopying	1 000
Telephone calls	1 000
Total direct costs	112 000
Estimated overhead cost ($90 × 500)	45 000
Total cost	157 000
Mark-up ($157 000 × 20%)	31 400
Total estimated selling price	188 400

Note the following:

- The calculation of the estimated overhead rate (Total budgeted overhead costs ÷ Total number of professional hours)
- The calculation of the overhead cost for the case (OAR × number of professional hours for the case)
- The total estimated cost (total direct cost + estimated overhead cost)
- Calculation of mark-up (mark-up policy × total estimated cost for the job)

Process costing method in the service sector

The cost of services in this method is obtained by assigning costs to lots of units and then computing the unit cost on an average basis.

Example

FCB loans department performs several functions in addition to processing the HDC starter home loan applications. It is estimated that 25% of the overhead costs of the loans department apply to processing home loan applications. FCB provided the following information:

Cost of monthly staff working on the application forms for home starter loans:

4 employees @ $20 000 = $80 000

Monthly overhead costs for the loans department:

	Costs ($)
Loans' manager's salary	5 000
Telephone expenses	750
Depreciation of building	2 800
Legal fees	2 400
Advertising	400
General expenses	650
Total overheads	12 000

Additional information

One hundred starter home loan application forms are processed each month.

Required

a. Compute the cost of processing the starter home loan application.

b. Compute the total processing cost per starter home application.

Solution

a. Cost of processing the starter home application:

Direct professional labour cost (4 × $20 000)	80 000
Service overhead cost (25% × $12 000)	3 000
Total processing cost per month	83 000

b. Total processing cost per home starter loan application:

Total processing cost per month ÷ Number of applications processed per month

83 000 ÷ 100 = $830 per home starter loan application

Test Your Knowledge

1. The table below lists several different services. You are required to tick the appropriate boxes to identify the costing method. (Hint: Is it Job or Process?)

   [6 marks]

Industry	Job	Process
Law firm		
Garment industry		
Construction firm		
Chemical production firm		
Consulting agency		
Hospital		

2. Alleeyah requested a fixed price quotation from Rachel's Accounting firm. The information provided was as follows:

	Costs ($)
Direct professional labour	20 000
Direct support labour	10 000
Fringe benefits	13 000
Photocopying	2 000
Telephone	2 000
Computer	6 000

   Additional information

   Overhead is allocated at the rate of 10% of direct professional labour

   Policy fee is quoted at 10% above the total cost

   Required:

   Prepare Alleeyah's quotation showing the total to be paid to Rachel's Accounting firm.

   [6 marks]

MULTIPLE CHOICE QUESTIONS

1. Management accounting monitors resources in service sector industries to identify:

    I   profitable areas

    II exhibit wastage

    III inventory collected

    (A) I only

    (B) II

    (C) I and II

    (D) II and III

2. The cost driver per unit for external customers in service sector industries is:

    I   number of full-time students

    II number of meals provided

    III patients per day

    (A) I only

    (B) I and II

    (C) I and III

    (D) II and III

3. The costing method(s) used in a service sector industry to assign costs to a distinct identifiable task is known as:

    (A) Job costing

    (B) Process costing

    (C) Marginal and absorption costing

    (D) Job and process costing

4. Which of the following service sector industries use the mark-up percentage approach as a basis for determining price?

    I   accounting agencies

    II consulting agencies

    III repair shops

    (A) I

    (B) II

    (C) I and II

    (D) I, II and III

Use the statement below to answer questions 5 and 6.

Zaria is the owner and general practitioner of a private hospital, which handles accident and emergency cases only. The budgeted operating base for the month of March is 1500 hours. On 30 March the accident surgical room was used for 6 hours. The total budgeted overhead costs for March is $150 000.

5. The overhead rate for the use of the accident surgical room is:

    (A) $100

    (B) $250

    (C) $600

    (D) $1500

6. The total overhead cost for the time used on 30 March is:

    (A) $100

    (B) $600

    (C) $1500

    (D) $3600

7. Categories used to identify the difficulties associated with service sector costing are:

    I   perishable or heterogeneous

    II is produced and consumed simultaneously

    III intangible or homogeneous

    (A) I

    (B) I and II

    (C) I and III

    (D) II and III

Chapter 22

Marginal costing vs. Absorption costing techniques

A comparison of marginal and absorption costing is set out in Table 22.1.

Table 22.1 Comparing absorption costing to marginal costing

	Absorption costing, total costing or full costing	Marginal costing or variable costing
Product costs (capitalised as inventory until expensed as cost of goods sold)	• Direct materials • Direct labour • Variable manufacturing overhead • Fixed manufacturing overhead	• Direct materials • Direct labour • Variable manufacturing overhead
Period costs (expensed in the period they are incurred)	• Variable non-manufacturing overhead • Fixed non-manufacturing overhead	• Fixed manufacturing overhead • Variance non-manufacturing overhead • Fixed non-manufacturing overhead
Focus	External reporting: required by Generally Accepted Accounting Principles (GAAP)	Internal reporting only: used by managers in the ongoing decision-making to meet the firm's objectives
Income statement format	Conventional income statement for external reporting	Contribution margin statement
Major difference	Fixed manufacturing overheads are part of product or inventoriable costs	Fixed manufacturing overhead is considered period cost and forms part of the firm's expenses

Marginal costing: contribution margin statement detailed format – for internal use only

Jays Sports Company Ltd
Income Statement (Variable Costing)
For the period ended.........

	Total $	Total $	Unit $	Unit $
Sales		xxxx		x
Less: **Variable cost**				
Cost of goods sold				
Opening inventory	xxxx			
Add: Cost of goods manufactured	xxxx			
Cost of goods available for sale	xxxx			
Less: closing inventory	(xxxx)			
Cost of goods sold	xxxx		x	
Add: variable non-manufacturing	xxxx		x	
Total variable cost		(xxxx)		(x)
Contribution margin		xxxx		x
Less: fixed costs				
Fixed manufacturing overheads	xxxx			
Add: fixed non-manufacturing overheads	xxxx			
Total fixed costs		(xxxx)		
Net income		xxxx		

Absorption costing: income statement detailed format – for external reporting

Jays Sports Company Ltd
Income Statement
For the period ended.....

	Total $	Total $
Sales		xxxx
Cost of goods sold		
Opening inventory	xxxx	
Add: cost of goods manufactured	xxxx	
Cost of goods available for sale	xxxx	
Less: closing inventory	(xxxx)	
Cost of goods sold		(xxxx)
Gross profit		xxxx
Less: expenses		
Variable non-manufacturing overheads	xxxx	
Add: fixed non-manufacturing overheads	xxxx	
Total expenses		(xxxx)
Net income		xxxx

Marginal costing: contribution margin statement summary format – for internal use only

Jays Sports Company Ltd
Income Statement (Marginal Costing)
For the period ended.......

	Total		Unit
Sales	xxxx		x
Less: total variable cost	(xxxx)		(x)
Contribution margin	xxxx		x
Less: total fixed cost	(xxxx)		
Net income	xxxx		

Absorption costing: income statement summary format – for external reporting

Jays Sports Company Ltd
Income Statement (Absorption Costing)
For the period ended.......

	Total		Unit
Sales	xxxx		x
Less: cost of goods sold	(xxxx)		(x)
Gross profit	xxxx		x
Less: Expenses	(xxxx)		
Net income	xxxx		

Reconciliation of net income: absorption costing vs. marginal costing

Example 1
Jays Sports Company Ltd
Reconciliation of Net Incomes Statement

Net income: Marginal costing income statement	xxx
Add: Fixed manufacturing overhead in closing inventory (closing inventory absorption costing less closing inventory marginal costing)	xxx
	xxx

Less: Fixed manufacturing overhead in closing inventory (opening inventory absorption costing less opening inventory marginal costing)	(xxx)
Net income: absorption costing	xxx

Will the net income under absorption costing be higher, lower or the same as marginal costing?

1. If units produced > units sold then,
   absorption costing net income > marginal costing net income
2. If units produced < unit sold then,
   absorption costing net income < marginal costing net income
3. If units produced = units sold then,
   absorption costing net income = marginal costing net income

Example 2

Sambrano Company manufactures guitars and supplied the following information at 31 December 2016.

Opening inventory was 300 units totalling $2 745 under absorption costing and $2 250 under marginal costing.

Production: 1 000 guitars	Direct materials: $12 075
Direct labour: $8 625	Variable manufacturing overheads: $3 450
Fixed manufacturing overheads: $2 760	Variable non-manufacturing overheads $1 725
Fixed non-manufacturing overheads:	Sales 1 200 guitars at $70 per guitar $5 520

Required:

a. What is the unit cost of production under marginal costing and absorption costing?
b. Prepare a marginal costing income statement.
c. Prepare an absorption costing income statement.
d. Reconcile the profits of the two statements.

Solution

a. Calculation of the unit cost of production under marginal costing and absorption costing

	Marginal costing	Absorption costing
Total direct materials	12 075	12 075
Total direct labour	8 625	8 625
Total variable manufacturing overhead	3 450	3 450
Total fixed manufacturing overhead	–	2 760
Total cost of production	24 150	26 910
Unit cost of production	$24 150/1 000 guitars = $24.15 per guitar	$26 910/1 000 guitars = $26.91

b. Marginal costing income statement

Sambrano Company
Income Statement (Marginal Costing)
For the year ended 31 December 2016

Sales (1200 guitars × $70)		84 000
Total variable costs		
Opening inventory	2 250	
Total cost of production	24 150	
Cost of goods available for sale	26 400	
Less: Closing inventory (300 + 1000 – 1200) guitars (100 units × $24.15)	(2 415)	

Cost of goods sold	23 985	
Add: Total non-variable non-manufacturing overhead	1 725	
Total variable costs		**(25 710)**
Contribution margin		**58 290**
Less: Total fixed costs		
Total Fixed manufacturing overheads	2 760	
Total Fixed non-manufacturing overheads	5 520	
Total fixed costs		**(8 280)**
Net income		**$50 010**

c. **Absorption** costing income statement

Sambrano Company

Income Statement (Absorption Costing)

For the year ended 31 December 2016

Sales (1 200 guitars × $70)		**84 000**
Cost of goods sold		
Opening inventory	2 745	
Total cost of production	26 910	
Cost of goods available for sale	29 655	
Less: Closing inventory (300 + 1000 – 1200) guitars 100 guitars × $26.91	(2 691)	
Cost of goods sold		**(26 964)**
Gross profit		**57 036**
Less: Expenses		
Total variable non-manufacturing overheads	1 725	
Total Fixed non-manufacturing overheads	5 520	
Total expenses		**(7 245)**
Net income		**$ 49 791**

d. Reconciling profits

Sambrano Company

Net Income Reconciliation Statement

For the year ended 31 December 2016

Net income: Marginal costing	50 010
Add: Fixed manufacturing overhead in closing inventory ($2 691 – $2 415)	276
	50 286
Less: Fixed manufacturing overhead in opening inventory ($2 745 – $2 250)	(495)
Net income: Absorption costing	49 791

Test Your Knowledge

1. Which of the items listed below make up the total cost of production under absorption costing?
   a. fixed non-manufacturing overhead
   b. variable manufacturing overhead
   c. direct materials
   d. variable non-manufacturing overhead
   e. direct labour
   f. fixed manufacturing overhead.   [4 marks]

2. Which of the items listed below make up the total cost of production under marginal costing?
   a. fixed non-manufacturing overhead
   b. variable manufacturing overhead
   c. direct materials
   d. variable non-manufacturing overhead
   e. direct labour
   f. fixed manufacturing overhead. **[3 marks]**

3. Copy and complete the following equations
   a. Sales – Total variable cost = _____
   b. Net Income + Total fixed cost = _____
   c. Gross profit = _____ + _____
   d. Gross profit – _____ = Net Income **[5 marks]**

4. Neru Manufacturing Company provided the following income statement for the month ended 31 October 2016.

Absorption Costing Income Statement

	$	$
Sales		1 800 000
Less: Cost of goods sold		
Variable production costs	450 000	
Fixed Production costs	900 000	
Total production costs	1 250 000	
Less: Closing inventory	337 500	
		912 500
Gross profit		887 500
Less: Non-production costs		
Variable administration and selling expenses	135 000	
Fixed administration and selling expenses	150 000	
		285 000
Income from operations		$ 670 000

Additional information:
   i. Revenues and costs per unit:
      Sales per unit $60
      Variable production $15
      Variable selling $ 6
   ii. There was no opening inventory
   iii. Units produced 30 000 units
   iv. Units sold 22 500 units

   a. Prepare the marginal costing income statement for the month of October 2016. **[10 marks]**
   b. Reconcile the net incomes of the absorption costing and marginal costing approaches. **[5 marks]**

MULTIPLE CHOICE QUESTIONS

1. Absorption costing is also known as:

    I   Full

    II Total

    III Marginal.

    (A) I

    (B) II

    (C) I and II

    (D) I and III

2. Marginal or variable costing product costs are:

    I   fixed manufacturing overhead

    II direct material and direct labour

    III variable manufacturing overhead.

    (A) I

    (B) II

    (C) I and II

    (D) II and III

    The following information refers to questions 3 and 4:

    Kirk P manufactures a single product. He has provided the following data for the month of January.

	$	$
Selling price		200
Units in beginning inventory		0
Units produced		8 500
Units sold		8 400
Units in ending inventory		100
Variable cost per unit:		
Direct material	30	
Direct labour	50	
Variable manufacturing overhead	5	
Variable selling and administration	7	
Fixed cost:		
Fixed manufacturing overhead		200 000
Fixed selling and administration overhead		100 000

3. Using the variable costing method, the unit product cost for the month is:

    (A) $85

    (B) $92

    (C) $108.52

    (D) $108.80

4. Using the absorption costing method, the unit product cost for the month is:

    (A) $0.85

    (B) $0.92

    (C) $108.53

    (D) $108.80

5. What is the major difference between the cost of production under marginal costing as against absorption costing methods:

    (A) fixed selling and administration costs

    (B) variable selling and administration costs

    (C) variable manufacturing overhead

    (D) fixed manufacturing overhead.

Chapter 23   Budgeting

Profit planning is accomplished through the preparation of a number of budgets. Planning is the key to good management. This chapter reviews the budgeting process, the steps in preparing a master budget and subsidiary schedules, and how the budget can be used as an element of coordination and control in organisations.

A budget is a future financial plan expressed in quantitative terms. It is the process of formulating an organisation's plan.

Purpose/objectives of budgeting

Budgeting serves many purposes in an organisation and includes the following:

- serves to motivate staff in achieving the goals and objectives of the business
- facilitates the communication of management's plans throughout the organisation
- facilitates the allocation of resources to parts of the organisation where they can be used effectively
- provides authority for action
- integrates the goals and objectives of departments by facilitating the coordination and communication of the activities of businesses
- assists management with their planning functions
- uncovers bottlenecks in an organisation's operations and alerting management of resource constraints
- provides data/references as benchmarks from which comparisons can be made.

Budgeting process

The budgeting process starts with the collection of data from the various departments within an organisation and culminates in the preparation of budgets. The process includes:

- the formation of a budget committee
- the determination of the budget period
- specification of budget guidelines
- preparation of the initial budget proposal
- budget negotiation, review, and approval
- budget revision.

The preparation and implementation of budgets vary in organisations depending on whether the operations are centralised, decentralised, or a combination of both. The common styles used in the preparation of budgets are:

- imposed (top-bottom)
- self-imposed (bottom-up or participative), or
- negotiated.

Budgetary control

This is a system that uses the budgets for planning and controlling a firm's business activities. This is done periodically by comparing a firm's actual results with its budgeted results, then taking corrective action to achieve the required targets. The system just described is one of the functions of the budget committee.

Budget committee

The budget committee is made up of a group of key managerial persons from each department within an organisation whose job is to coordinate and review their departmental budgets. Figure 23.1 highlights the functions the budget committee performs:

Figure 23.1 Functions of the budget committee

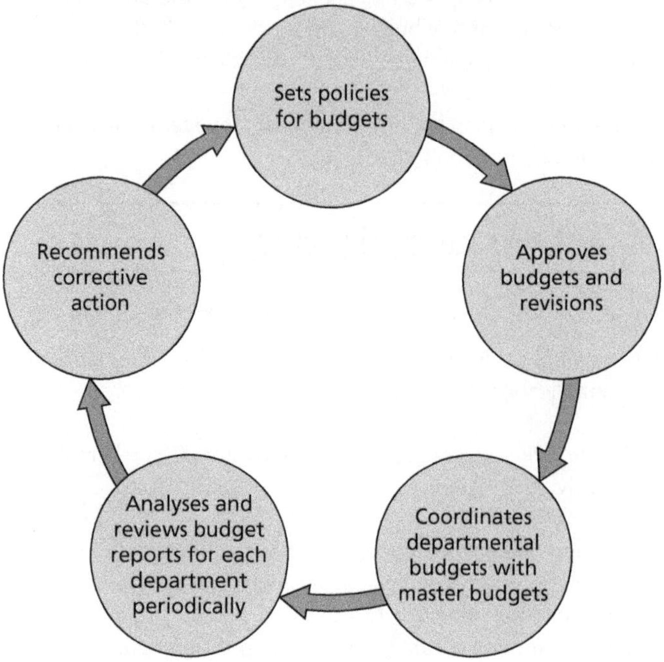

Key points to note

- A budget is a plan of action used in short-term planning and controlling of a firm's business activities.
- The purposes of budgeting are uncovering bottlenecks; providing authority for action; assisting management with their planning functions; serving to motivate staff to achieve the goals and objectives of the business; and facilitating the allocation of resources to parts of the organisation where they can be used most effectively.
- The budget styles are imposed, self-imposed or negotiated.
- Budgetary control compares actual result with budgeted results and takes corrective action.
- Budget committee is a group of key persons from each department within a firm whose job is to coordinate and review departmental budgets.

Test Your Knowledge

1. List three purposes of budgeting.   **[3 marks]**
2. What are the functions of a budget committee?   **[4 marks]**
3. What is the budgeting process?   **[5 marks]**

Preparation of budgets

Budgets are commonly prepared for a period of time known as a budget period. This period normally coincides with the financial period of the business. The period is broken down into weeks, months or quarters, based on the type of budgets. In most organisations, a comprehensive set of budgets or schedules covering all aspects of its operations are prepared for a specific period. These comprehensive budgets or plans are called a master budget or profit plan.

Master budget

A master budget is a comprehensive set, made up of budgets, schedules and budgeted financial statements of an organisation. It sets the targets for sales, production, distribution and financing activities and ends with budgeted financial statements. Figure 23.2 highlights the sequence in the preparation of the master budget and clearly illustrates the interrelationship.

Figure 23.2 Sequence/steps in the preparation of the master budget

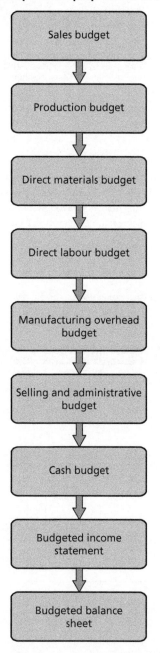

Sales budget and cash collection schedule

The sales budget shows the expected sales for the period. It is expressed in both dollars and units of the product for sale. The sales budget starts the budgeting process in the master budget preparation. It is the key to the entire budgeting process. The budget determines the inventory levels, purchases and operating expenses. Thus, when the process continues, the production budget becomes the key factor in the determination of the other budgets such as the direct materials budget, the direct labour budget and the manufacturing budgets. Then these budgets, in turn, are needed to construct a cash budget. It is essential therefore, that organisations prepare accurate and reliable sales budgets.

In some organisations, the sales budget is followed by the preparation of a cash collection schedule. This schedule is needed to prepare the cash budget. Expected receipts consist of collections on credit to customers from the previous period and both cash and credit sales collections made in the current budget period. The following example illustrates the preparation of the sales budget and the cash collection schedule

Example

Alfred Ltd., located in Basseterre, Montserrat has budgeted the following unit sales:

2014	Units
September	40 000
October	70 000
November	90 000
December	60 000

Additional information:

1. The company's single product sells for $20 per unit.

2. Sales are collected in the following pattern: 75 per cent in the month the sales are made, and the remaining 25 per cent in the following month. The balance sheet for the last accounting period showed $70 000 in accounts receivable was still outstanding, all of which will be collected in September 2014.

Required:

Prepare:

a. a sales budget

b. a schedule of expected cash collections.

Solution

a. Sales budget

	September	October	November	December	Total
Budgeted sales in units	40 000	70 000	90 000	60 000	260 000
Selling price per unit	X $20	X $20	X $20	X $20	X $20
Budgeted sales	$800 000	1 400 000	1 800 000	1 200 000	5 200 000

b. Cash collection schedule

	September	October	November	December	Total
Accounts receivable	$70 000				70 000
Sales for September: 800 000 × 75%, 25%	600 000	200 000			800 000
Sales for October: 1 400 000 × 75%, 25%		1 050 000	350 000		1 400 000
Sales for November: 1 800 000 × 75%, 25%			1 350 000	450 000	1 800 000
Sales for December: 1 200 000 × 75%				900 000	900 000
	$670 000	1 250 000	1 700 000	1 350 000	4 970 000

Don't forget

- Check for unit selling price.
- Cross-check totals both in the sales budget and cash collection schedule.
- Read properly for terms of payments.
- Look out for outstanding accounts receivable.

Test Your Knowledge

Ingrid Step has the following budgeted sales in units for the next four months:

2014	Units
January	30 000
February	45 000
March	60 000
April	50 000

Additional information:

1. Ingrid Step sells her single product for $15 per unit.

2. Sales are collected in the following pattern: 20 per cent in the month sales are made and the remaining 80 per cent in the following month. The balance sheet from the last financial year showed $40 000 in accounts receivable, all of which will be collected in January 2014.

Required: Prepare:

a. A sales budget   [6 marks]

b. A schedule of expected cash collections.   [3 marks]

Production budget

The production budget is prepared after the sales budget. It is important that sufficient goods are available to meet the sales needs and provide for the desired ending inventory. A portion of these goods already exist in the beginning inventory and the remainder will have to be produced by the firm. The production budget lists the number of units that must be produced each period, based on the expected sale and the firm's inventory policy. To determine the production needs the following formula is used:

   Production budget = expected sales (units) + desired ending inventory (units) – beginning inventory (units)

Example

Alfred Ltd., located in Basseterre, Montserrat has budgeted the following unit sales:

2014	Units
September	40 000
October	70 000
November	90 000
December	60 000

Additional information:

1. The finished goods inventory on hand in August 2014 was 10 000 units.

2. It is the company's policy to maintain a finished good inventory at the end of the month equal to 10 per cent of the next month's anticipated sales.

Required

Prepare a production budget for the first quarter (Hint: the first three months.)

Solution

	September	October	November	Quarter
Expected sales	40 000	70 000	90 000	200 000
Desired ending inventory (equal to 10% of next month sales)	7 000	9 000	6 000	6 000
Total required units	47 000	79 000	96 000	206 000
Less beginning finished goods	10 000	7 000	9 000	10 000
Required production units	37 000	72 000	87 000	196 000

Don't forget

1. Remember the formula for the production budget (when examined it is the reverse of the trading account format, for example, add the ending inventory and deduct the opening inventory).

2. Always start the budget for the sales in units and not the dollar value.

3. Look out for the company's policy for maintaining the finished goods inventory at the end.

Test Your Knowledge

Forbes Company budgeted sales for the next four months are follows:

	Sales in units
July	30 000
August	45 000
September	60 000
October	50 000

Additional information:

1. The end of the month inventories of finished goods must be equal to 10 per cent of the next month's sales.

2. The ending inventory at the end of June was 3000 units.

Required: Prepare a production budget for the first three months, showing the number of units to be produced each month and for the three months in total.   **[18 marks]**

Direct (raw) materials purchases budget and expected schedule of expected cash disbursements for raw materials

The direct materials purchases budget will be prepared based on goods produced. The budget details the raw materials that must be purchased to fulfil the production budget and to provide adequate inventories. This budget is shown in units or dollars. The formula for the direct materials budget is:

Production requirements (units) + desired ending inventory (units) – beginning inventory (units)

The direct materials budget is usually accompanied by a schedule of expected cash disbursements for raw materials. This computation is needed to prepare the cash budget. The schedule consists of payments for purchases on account in the previous period plus any payments for purchases in the current budget period.

Example

Destra manufactures compact discs (CDs). The budgeted sales in units in 2014 are as follows:

April	20 000
May	12 000
June	18 000
July	16 000
August	20 000
September	30 000

Additional information:

1. The company requires an ending inventory of finished units on hand at the end of each month equal to 35 per cent of the budgeted sales for the next month. The requirement was met at the end of the last financial year, in that the company had 10 000 units on hand to start the New Year.

2. Three pounds of raw material are required to complete one unit of product.

3. The company requires an ending inventory of raw materials on hand at the end of each month equal to 10 per cent of the production needs. This requirement was met at the end of the previous financial year; in that the company had 20 000 pounds of raw materials on hand to start the New Year.

4. The raw material costs $0.70 per pound. Purchases of raw materials are paid for in the following pattern: 60 per cent is paid in the month purchases are made, and the remaining 40 per cent is paid in the following month. The company's balance sheet at the end of the last financial year showed $50 000 in accounts payable for raw materials, all of which will be paid in the first month of the year.

Destra manufactures compact discs (CDs). The budgeted sales in units in 2014 are as follows:

April	20 000
May	12 000
June	18 000
July	16 000
August	20 000
September	30 000

Additional information:

1. The company requires an ending inventory of finished units on hand at the end of each month equal to 35 per cent of the budgeted sales for the next month. The requirement was met at the end of the last financial year, in that the company had 10 000 units on hand to start the New Year.

2. 3 pounds of raw material are required to complete one unit of product.

3. The company requires an ending inventory of raw materials on hand at the end of each month equal to 10 per cent of the production needs. This requirement was met at the end of the previous financial year; in that the company had 20 000 pounds of raw materials on hand to start the New Year.

4. The raw material costs $0.70 per pound. Purchases of raw materials are paid for in the following pattern: 60 per cent is paid in the month purchases are made, and the remaining 40 per cent is paid in the following month. The company's balance sheet at the end of the last financial year showed $50 000 in accounts payable for raw materials, all of which will be paid in the first month of the year.

Required

Prepare:

a. a production budget (for the first 4 months)

b. a direct materials budget

c. an expected cash disbursements schedule.

Solution

a. Production budget

	April	May	June	July	Year	August	September
Budgeted sales in units	20 000	12 000	18 000	16 000	66 000	20 000	30 000
Add desired inventory	4 200	6 300	5 600	5 600	5 600	10 500	
Total needs	24 200	18 300	23 600	21 600	71 600	30 500	
Less beginning inventory	10 000	4 200	6 300	5 600	10 000	5 600	
Units to be produced	14 200	14 100	17 300	16 000	61 600	24 900	

b. Direct materials budget

	April	May	June	July	Year	August
Units to be produced	14 200	14 100	17 300	16 000	61 600	24 900
Raw materials needed per pound	× 3	× 3	× 3	× 3	× 3	× 3
Production needs (pounds)	42 600	42 300	51 900	48 000	184 800	74 700
Add desired ending inventory (pounds)	4 230	5 190	4 800	7 470	7 470	

Total needs (pounds)	46 830	47 490	56 700	55 470	192 270	
Less beginning inventory (pounds)	20 000	4 230	5 190	4 800	20 000	
Raw materials to be purchased (pounds)	26 830	43 260	51 510	50 940	172 270	

c. Expected cash disbursements schedule

	April	May	June	July	Total
Cost of raw materials to be purchased at $0.70 per pound	$18 781	$30 282	$36 057	$35 658	$120 589
Accounts payable beginning balance	50 000.00				50 000.00
April purchases: $18 781 × 60%, 40%	11 268.60	7 512.40			18 781.00
May purchases: $30 282 × 60%, 40%		18 169.20	12 112.80		30 282.00
June purchases: $36 057 × 60%, 40%			21 634.20	14 422.80	36 057.00
July purchases: $35 658 × 60%				21 394.80	21 394.80
Total cash payments	61 268.60	25 681.60	33 747.00	35 817.60	156 514.80

Keys points to note

1. Remember the formula for the direct materials budget (when examined it is the reverse of the trading account format; for example, add the ending inventory and deduct the opening inventory).
2. Always start the budget with the units to be produced.
3. Look out for the company's policy for maintaining the finished goods inventory at the end.
4. Remember to multiply the units produced by the pounds of raw material needed to complete one unit of product.
5. Remember to multiply the cost of a product by the total cost of raw materials to be purchased.
6. Cross-check your total both in the materials purchases budget and cash disbursements schedule.
7. Read your question properly for terms of payments.
8. Look out for outstanding accounts payable.

Cash budget

A cash budget is prepared for short periods of time to the expected flow of cash during the budgeted period. Information obtained in the cash budget is useful in making decisions such as the need for external financing during critical cash flow traps in an organisation.

To prepare the cash budget, the opening cash balance, cash receipts and cash payments must be known and shown separately in the document. Important points to remember when preparing this document are:

- Record only cash paid and received.
- Exclude non-cash items such as depreciation and provision (allowance) for doubtful debts.
- Include capital expenditure payments such as non-current (fixed/tangible) assets.

Preparation of the cash budget

The cash budget comprises the following sections:

- cash receipts
- cash payments
- the cash excess or deficiency section, and
- financing.

The cash receipts include all estimated cash receipts from cash sales and receipts from accounts receivables. Other receipts may include interest income, rental income, dividends, and sale of investments, non-current assets or capital stocks.

Cash payments include all estimated cash payments such as direct materials, direct labour, and manufacturing, selling and administrative expenses paid during the budget period. Other payments include income taxes, dividends, investments and the purchase of non-current assets.

The financing section contains cash receipts from financing activities such as investment by owners, receipt of loans from creditors and cash payments made by the firm to reduce loan payments, interest paid on loans and other creditors. Whenever there is a cash flow deficit (cash trap), arrangement is estimated for temporary financing, and is reflected in this section as well.

Format of cash budget

The format for the cash budget is shown below.

	Month	Month	Month	Total
Beginning cash balance	xxxx	xxxx	xxxx	xxxx
Add: Receipts				
Cash sales	xxxx	xxxx	xxxx	xxxx
Credit sales	xxxx	xxxx	xxxx	xxxx
Other receipts (itemise)	xxxx	xxxx	xxxx	xxxx
Total cash available	xxxx	xxxx	xxxx	xxxx
Less: Payments				
Raw materials	xxxx	xxxx	xxxx	xxxx
Direct labour	xxxx	xxxx	xxxx	xxxx
Manufacturing cost (excluding depreciation)	xxxx	xxxx	xxxx	xxxx
Other payments (itemise)				
Total cash payments	xxxx	xxxx	xxxx	xxxx
Excess (deficiency) of receipts over payments	xxxx	xxxx	xxxx	xxxx
Financing				
Loan	xxxx	xxxx	xxxx	xxxx
Loan payment	xxxx	xxxx	xxxx	xxxx
Interest	xxxx	xxxx	xxxx	xxxx
Ending cash balance	xxxx	xxxx	xxxx	xxxx

Test Your Knowledge

Canute Landscaping Company needs a cash budget for the month May 2014. The company's management accountant has provided you with the following information:

1. The 1 May 2014 cash balance is expected to be $24 000.

2. All sales are on account. Credit sales are collected over a 3-month period: 60 per cent in the month of sale and 40 per cent in the month following the sale. Actual sales for March and April were $100 000 and $80 000, respectively. May's sales are budgeted at $100 000.

3. Investments are expected to be sold for $40 000 during the month of May.

4. The controller estimates that direct materials totalling $56 000 will be purchased in May. Fifty per cent of a month's direct materials purchases are paid in the month of purchase with the remaining 50 per cent paid in the following month. Accounts payable for April purchases total $20 000 and will be paid in May.

5. During May, direct labour costs are estimated to be $28 000.

6. Manufacturing overhead is estimated to be 50 per cent of direct labour costs. Further, the management accountant estimates that approximately 10 per cent of the manufacturing overhead is depreciation on the factory building and equipment.

7. Selling and administrative expenses are budgeted at $34 000 for May. Of this amount, $16 000 is for depreciation.

8. During May, Canute Landscaping Company plans to buy a new brush cutter costing $20 000. The company will pay cash for the brush cutter.

9. Canute Landscaping Company owes $7 000 in income tax, which must be paid in May.

10. Canute Landscaping Company must maintain a minimum cash balance of $15 000. To bolster the cash position, as needed, an open line of credit is available from the bank.

Required: Prepare the following:

a. A schedule of cash collections   **[4 marks]**

b. A schedule of cash payments for raw materials   **[4 marks]**

c. A cash budget for the month of May. Indicate in the financing section any borrowing that will be necessary during the month.   **[10 marks]**

MULTIPLE CHOICE QUESTIONS

1. The budgeting objectives include:

   I   Motivate staff in achieving goals.

   II Uncover bottlenecks in the operations of a firm.

   III Provide data for benchmarks.

   (A) I

   (B) II

   (C) I and II

   (D) I, II and III

2. The budgeting process include:

   I   preparation of budgets

   II collection of data from various departments

   III collection of data from owner.

   (A) I

   (B) II

   (C) I and II

   (D) II and III

3. The budget committee:

   I   sets policies for budgets

   II analyses and reviews budget reports

   III approves budgets.

   (A) I

   (B) II

   (C) I and II

   (D) I, II and III

4. Ingrid has budgeted sales of 30 000 units in April, 40 000 units in May and 60 000 units in June. Her company has 6 000 units on hand on 1 April. Assume that Ingrid's company requires an ending inventory equal to 20 per cent of the following month's sales, then her production during May should be equal to:

   (A) 32 000 units

   (B) 36 000 units

   (C) 40 000 units

   (D) 44 000 units

5. In budgeting, schedules are prepared after the sales budget and materials purchases budgets. Which of the following schedules will be prepared after the sales budget?

   (A) expected cash collections

   (B) expected cash disbursement

   (C) expected manufacturing overhead

   (D) cash budget.

6. In the budgeting process, there are steps for preparing the master budget. Which of the following budgets will be prepared first?

   (A) production

   (B) sales

   (C) direct materials

   (D) cash.

Chapter 24

Standard costing and variances

On a daily basis, managers make decisions in controlling costs and optimising outputs. Some of the more critical decisions relate to acquiring inputs in terms of prices paid (for example, the lowest possible price) for them and the quantities used (that is, the minimum quantity to be used) in producing a good or service. Standard costing allows a business to plan its cost according to the level that favours management in optimal usage of resources and minimum price.

This chapter reviews the difference between standards and budgets, looks at standard costing as a process and the advantages and disadvantages of standard costing. Furthermore, it reviews the difference between flexible and static budgets; looks at the types of standards, variances and the sub-variances; and, lastly, the reasons for and significance of variances.

Difference between standards and budgets

Standards ensure that the overall quality of a product is high. In concept, it is essentially the same as budgets; both predetermined costs contribute to management planning and control. The difference lies in the way the terms are expressed; for example, a standard is the budgeted cost (process cost) per unit of product. In other words, in standard costing, a budget is prepared for each unit (each process) instead of just for each particular department.

Standard costing system

A standard costing system is a product costing system that determines product cost by using standards or norms for quantities and prices of the various components. These standards are compared against actual costs for cost control purposes. A standard cost is an estimated or budgeted cost (benchmark) to produce a single unit of product or perform a single service.

Standard costing oversees each individual cost component that makes up an entire budget. Standards costs are planned unit costs of products, components or services produced in a period. These costs offer a number of advantages to an organisation. These advantages will only be realised when standard costs are carefully established and used prudently. Table 24.1 lists the advantages and disadvantages of standard costing.

Objectives

At the end of this chapter you will be able to:
- define standard costing
- discuss its advantages and disadvantages
- explain the role of personnel in the standard-setting process
- discuss how standards are set in any organisation
- define ideal and practical standards
- define variance analysis
- calculate various variances in a manufacturing environment
- prepare accounting entries for variances.

Table 24.1 Advantages and disadvantages of standard costing

Advantages of standard costing	Disadvantages of standard costing
1. Management can focus on problem areas.	1. Standards are loosely determined as too vigorous; tight standards may be ineffective.
2. Problems can be spotted on time and remedial actions taken promptly.	2. Standards which are changed constantly produce elastic criteria.
3. Standards can be used to motivate employees to performance improvement.	3. It is difficult in practice to assign responsibility for variances to specific individuals.
4. Standards are yard-sticks for measuring efficiency and are predetermined costs for control purposes.	4. Too much attention is focused on the 'exception' resulting in insufficient time given to setting realistic standards.
5. Standard costs facilitate cash planning and inventory planning.	5. Difficulty in determining which variances are 'material' or significant in amount.
6. Useful in setting selling prices.	

Test Your Knowledge

1. What is the difference between budgets and standards? **[4 marks]**
2. Explain the use of standard costing. **[4 marks]**
3. Give three advantages and three disadvantages of standards costing. **[6 marks]**

Setting standard costs

Setting standard costs requires the combined thinking and expertise of all persons in an organisation who have responsibility over prices and quantities of inputs. In a manufacturing company environment, this would include the managerial accounting personnel, the purchasing staff, the industrial engineers, production supervisors, line managers and the production workers. The roles of personnel involved in the standard setting process are given in Table 24.2.

Table 24.2 Personnel role in the standard setting process

Personnel	Role/tasks
Management consult purchasing agents, product managers, quality control engineers and production supervisors	Determines the standard cost of direct materials
Payroll department will furnish information on pay rate	Setting the standard cost for direct labour
Managerial accountant	Provides important input into the standard setting process. Accumulates historical cost data to determine how costs responds to changes in activity levels
Industrial engineer	Determines labour time requirements. For example, the standard time should include allowances for coffee breaks, workers' personal needs, clean-ups and machine downtime

Producing standard costs

The types of information required (and source) to produce standard costs are:

1. Direct materials (types, quantities and price); document – bill of materials
2. Direct labour (grades, number and rates of pay); document – wages records
3. Variable overhead (the total variable overhead costs analysed into various categories such as employee and general costs)
4. Fixed overhead (the total overhead analysed into various categories such as employee costs, building costs and general administration expenses).

Setting direct materials standards

The standards set for direct raw material are price and quantity. The direct materials price standard is the cost per unit of direct materials that should be incurred. This standard is based on current purchase prices at times. The standard price per unit for materials purchased reflects the final cost, net of discounts taken and handling charges. In addition, the price reflects the grade (namely good quality), quantity and method of delivery. The information for setting standard price can be prepared as shown below:

Purchase price (indicate grade)	x
Freight (indicate type and from where)	x
Receiving and handling	x
Less purchase discount	(x)
Total cost	x
Units (divided)	(÷) x
Standard price per pound	x

The standard quantity per unit for direct materials reflects the amount of material going into each unit of finished product including allowances for unavoidable waste, spoilages and other normal inefficiencies. In setting the standard, management considers both the quality and quantity of materials required to make products. This standard is expressed as a physical measure such as pounds, barrels or board feet. The documentation prepared should contain some of the information below:

Material requirements as specified in the bill of materials in pounds	x
Allowance for waste and spoilage in pounds	x
Allowance for rejects in pounds	x
Standard quantity in pounds	x

When the price and quantity standards have been set the standard cost of materials per unit of the finished product will be computed and entered in the standard cost card. The information should be shown in the cost card as follows:

X pounds per unit × $ per pound = $ per unit

Example

Kimberly was given the task to prepare a price and quantity standard for the raw materials, tamarind, used in the production of their product, tamarind sauce. The standard prices per unit for the materials are follows:

	$
Purchase price (case of 2000 kg)	5 000
Freight in	500
Cost of receiving and handling	100
Purchase discounts	200
Tamarind required to produce 1 kg of tamarind sauce	3.5
Allowance for waste and spoilage	0.5

Required

Prepare:

a. The document for the standard price for 1 kg of tamarind.

b. The document for total standard quantity required for the production of tamarind sauce.

c. Calculate the standard cost per kg for the tamarind sauce.

Solution

a. The standard price for 1 kg of tamarind:

Purchase price (case of 2 000 kg)	$5 000
Freight in	500
Receiving and handling	100
Purchase discounts	(200)
Total cost	5 400
Units	(÷2 000)
Unit cost	$2.70

b. The total standard quantity required for the production of tamarind sauce:

Tamarind required to produce 1 kg of tamarind sauce	3.5
Allowance for waste and spoilage	0.5
Total standard quantity required	4.0

c. The standard cost per kg for the tamarind sauce:

The standard cost = 4.0 kg × $2.70 per kg = $10.80 per kg of tamarind

Setting direct labour standards

Direct labour price and quantity standards are expressed as labour rate and labour hours. Direct labour price standard is the rate per hour that should be incurred for direct labour. This standard is based on current wage rates, adjusted for anticipated changes such as cost of living allowance (COLA). The standard labour rate per hour would include not only wages earned, but also employer payroll taxes, an allowance for fringe benefits such as paid holidays and vacations and other labour costs. A company determining the standard rate per hour should include the following:

	$
Basic wage rate per hour	x
Income tax (PAYE)	x
NIS/Social Security	x
Fringe benefits	x
Total cost per worker	x
Divided by total hours per week	(÷)x
Standard rate per direct labour hour	x

Standard hours per unit

This is the determination of the standard direct labour time (quantity or efficiency) required to make one unit of product especially in labour-intensive companies. The standard time should include allowances for coffee breaks, employees' personal washroom breaks, clean-ups and machine setup and machine breakdown. The documentation when prepared should contain the following:

Basic labour, time per unit in hours	x
Allowance for breaks and personal needs	x
Allowance for clean-up and preparation	x
Allowance for machine breakdowns	x
Allowance for rejects (or spoilage)	x
Standard labour hours per unit of product	x

Example

Joy Saw is preparing a rate and quantity standard for the company's direct labour, required for production of their product, tamarind sauce. The payroll clerk, Frank Simm, provided Joy with the following information:

Basic wages for 40-hour week	$700
NIS/Social Security (the employer's portion)	$50
Fringe benefits	$200
Allowance for machine breakdowns	$3.0
Allowance for clean-up and preparation	$1.0
Allowance for spoilage	$0.5
Allowance for breaks and personal needs	$2.0
Total production	600kg

Required

Prepare:

a. The document for the standard rate per direct labour hour

b. The document for standard hours (per kg)

c. Calculate the standard cost (per kg) for the tamarind sauce.

Solution

a. The standard rate per direct labour hour:

	$
Basic wage for 40-hour week	700
NIS/Social Security (employer's portion)	50
Fringe benefits	200
Total cost per worker	950
Hours per week	(÷ 40)
Standard rate per direct labour hour	$23.75

b. Standard hours (per kg):

Basic labour time per week	40
Allowance for machine breakdowns	3.0
Allowance for clean-up and preparation	1.0
Allowance for spoilage	0.5
Allowance for breaks and personal needs	2.0
Total hours	46.5
Total production	(÷ 600)
Standard hours (per kg)	0.08

c. The standard cost (per kg) for the tamarind sauce:

The standard cost = 0.08 hour per kg × $23.75 = $1.90 per kg of tamarind sauce

Setting manufacturing overhead standards

A predetermined overhead rate is used to set manufacturing overhead standards. This rate is determined by dividing budgeted overhead costs by an expected standard activity base such as standard machine hours and standard direct labour hours.

Total standard cost per unit

The total standard cost per unit is the sum of the standard costs of direct materials, direct labour and manufacturing overheads. The information will be shown as follows on a standard cost card:

Standard cost card

Inputs	Standard quantity or hours	Standard price or rate $	Standard cost (standard quantity or hours × standard price or rate) $
Direct materials	X pounds	x	x
Direct labour	X hours	x	x
Variable manufacturing overhead	X hours	x	x
Total standard cost per unit ($)			x

Key point to note

A standard cost card is prepared for each product. The card is used as a basis to determine variances from standards.

The setting of price and quantity standards requires the experience of key managerial persons who have key roles in the production of goods/services (that is, responsibility over input prices and over the effective use of inputs). From your previous knowledge, you will be aware that there are two types of manufacturing overheads (variable and fixed). Variable standards are set using the input-output relations used in direct materials and direct labour. Fixed overhead variances focus more on the effective use (that is, the capacity, volume, efficiency and productivity).

Test Your Knowledge

1. Design a table and identify personnel in organisations and their roles in setting direct labour, direct material and overhead standards. **[15 marks]**

2. What is a standard cost card? **[1 mark]**

3. Identify three main elements used to construct a price and quantity standard for a company's raw materials used in the production of a product. **[6 marks]**

4. Name the two types of manufacturing overheads. **[2 marks]**

Types of standards

1. Ideal standard is a standard which is attainable under the most favourable conditions and where no allowance is made for normal losses, wastage and machine breakdowns or work interruptions. The major problem, however, is that employees may not strive to meet the standard because they are demotivated.

2. Practical standard is stringent but attainable. The standards allow for normal machine downtime and employee rest period. This is where the overall lowest price is used for costing and allows for normal inefficiencies or delays in production. When these standards are used by companies, they provide positive motivation to their employees.

Difference between static budgets and flexible budgets

A static budget is a budget prepared at the beginning of a budget period for a single planned output. A flexible budget is a series of static budgets at different levels of activity adjusted (flexed) to recognise the actual output level for a budgeted period. This particular type of budget gives managers a clearer picture into the causes of variances in static budgets.

Example of static budget

The information below relates to the CornPone Company located in Jamaica. The company usually produces 10 000 units per annum.

	$
Sales price	25 per unit
Variable costs:	
Manufacturing	10 per unit
Administrative	3 per unit
Selling	2 per unit
Fixed costs:	
Manufacturing	70 000
Administrative	10 000

Required

Prepare a static budget

CornPone Static budget

Units		10 000
Sales		$250 000
Variable costs:		
Manufacturing	$100 000	
Administrative	$ 30 000	
Selling	$20 000	
Total variable costs		$150 000
Contribution margin		$100 000
Fixed costs:		
Manufacturing	$70 000	
Administrative	$10 000	
Total fixed costs		$80 000
Operating income		$20 000

Flexible budget

Steps in constructing a flexible budget are set out below:

1. Identify the actual quantity of output.
2. Calculate the flexible budget revenues based on the budgeted selling price and actual quantity of output.
3. Calculate the flexible budget for costs based on budgeted variable costs per output unit, actual quantity of output, and the budgeted fixed costs.

Example of flexible budget

Cornpone has requested that you prepare a flexible budget for the coming year using the information given below. The company has estimated the production level to be somewhere between 9 000 and 11 000 units.

Required

You are required to prepare a flexible budget for possible sales or production levels of 9 000, 10 000 and 11 000 units.

Sales price	$25 per unit
Variable costs:	
Manufacturing	$10 per unit
Administrative	$3 per unit
Selling	$2 per unit
Fixed costs:	
Manufacturing	$70 000
Administrative	$10 000

Solution

Units		9 000		10 000		11 000
Sales		$225 000		$250 000		$275 000
Variable costs:						
Manufacturing	90 000		100 000		110 000	
Administrative	27 000		30 000		33 000	
Selling	18 000		20 000		22 000	
Total variable costs		135 000		150 000		165 000
Contribution margin		90 000		100 000		110 000
Fixed costs:						
Manufacturing	70 000		70 000		70 000	
Administrative	10 000		10 000		10 000	
Total fixed costs		80 000		80 000		80 000
Operating income		10 000		20 000		30 000

Key points to note

- The changes in income resulted from the different production and sales level.
- The changes in income were not in direct proportion, owing to fixed and variable cost differences.
- In a situation such as this, you need to evaluate the performance of the company to determine whether there is efficient use of resources.

Test Your Knowledge

1. Distinguish between ideal and practical standards. **[4 marks]**
2. What is a flexible budget, and how does it differ from a static budget? **[4 marks]**

Variance analysis

In most firms, managers separate price considerations from quantity considerations in the control of costs. The latter gives a clearer picture as to the personnel who are solely responsible for price or quantity considerations (known as responsibility accounting). This separation distinguishes between price and quantity and provides a base for variance analysis. Variance analysis is the evaluation of performance by means of variances, where timely reporting should maximise the opportunity for managerial action.

Key points to note

1. Price variance and quantity variance can be computed for all three variable cost elements – direct materials, direct labour and variable manufacturing overhead.
2. Variance analysis measures the actual quantity of direct materials, direct labour, and variable manufacturing overhead used (in some textbooks referred to as the inputs) with standard quantity or standard hours allowed in the manufacturing of a product (known as outputs in textbooks). The output represents the good production for a period. Examples of output are the amount of direct materials, direct labour or variable manufacturing overhead that could have been used to produce the actual output of the period. These amounts might be more or less depending on the operations.

Variances and sub-variances

Now that you have reviewed the model, this chapter will examine the variances.

Variance is the difference between actual prices and quantities and standard prices and quantities. These variances may either be favourable or unfavourable.

The price and quantity variances are:

- Direct material: Total = Price and usage (materials quantity)
- Direct labour: Total = Rate and efficiency
- Variable production overhead: Total = Expenditure (spending) and efficiency
- Fixed production overhead: Total = Expenditure and volume

Formulae used to calculate variances

Material variances (price and usage)

1. Price = (actual price per unit – standard price per unit) × total actual quantity used

    Or   AQ (SP – AP)

    Or   AQp (AP – SP) [used if purchased during the period]

2. Usage = (total actual quantity used – standard quantity for actual production) × standard price

    Or   SP (SQ – AQ)

3. Total = actual quantity used × (actual price per unit – standard price per unit) – standard price per unit × (actual quantity used – standard quantity for actual production)

Causes of materials variances

1. **Price paid for raw materials:**
    a. **Internal:**
        i.   delivery method used
        ii.   availability of quantity
        iii. availability of cash discounts
        iv.   quality of the materials requested
        v.   rush order forces the company to pay a higher price for materials.
    b. **External:**
        i.   Prices may rise faster than expected, for example oil price increases.
2. **Materials quantity used:**
    a. inexperienced workers
    b. faulty machinery or carelessness
    c. inferior quality.

Labour variances (wage rate and efficiency)

1. Rate = (actual hourly rate per unit – standard hourly rate per unit) × total actual hours worked

    Or   AH (SR – AR)

2. Efficiency = (total actual hours worked – standard hours for actual production) × standard hourly rate

    Or   SR (SH – AH)

3. Total = (actual hourly rate per unit × actual hours) – (standard hourly rate per unit × standard hours for actual production)

Causes of labour variances

1. **Labour price variance:**
    a. paying workers higher wages than expected
    b. misallocation of workers (such as using skilled workers instead of unskilled, or the reverse).
2. **Labour efficiency:**
    a. poor training of workers
    b. worker fatigue
    c. faulty machinery or carelessness.

Variable overhead variances (expenditure [spending] and efficiency)

1. Expenditure(spending) = (actual variable overhead expenditure rate per unit – variable production overhead absorption rate) × actual hours worked

    Or   AQ (AVOR – SVOR)

2. Efficiency = (standard hours for actual production – actual hours worked) × variable production overhead absorption rate

    Or   SVOR (AQ – SQ)

3. Total = (actual variable overhead) – (standard hours for actual production) × variable production overhead absorption rate

Example

Sherrain Company produces a single product. Variable manufacturing overhead is applied to products on the basis of direct labour hours. The standard costs for one of product are as follows:

	$
Direct material: 5 ounces at $0.60 per ounce	3.00
Direct labour: 1.9 hours at $10 per hour	19.00
Variable manufacturing overhead: 1.9 at $5 per hour	9.50
Total standard variable cost per unit	31.50

During January 2500 units were produced. The costs associated with January were as follows:

	$
Materials purchased: 18 000 ounces at $0.70	12 600
Materials used in production: 15 000 ounces	–
Direct labour: 3 500 hours at $9.50	33 250
Variable manufacturing overhead costs incurred	25 000

Required

Compute the materials, labour and variable manufacturing overhead variances and indicate for each whether it is favourable (F) or unfavourable (U).

Solution

1. Materials price variance: AQ (AP – SP)
   15 000 ounces (0.70 – 0.60) = $1 500 (U)

2. Materials quantity variance: SP (AQ – SQ)
   0.60 (15 000 – [2 500 × 5]) = $2 500 (U)

3. Labour rate variance: AH (AR – SR)
   3 500 hours ($9.50 – $10.00) = $1 750 (F)

4. Labour efficiency variance = SR (AH – SH)
   $10 (3 500 – [2 500 ×1.9]) = $12 500 (F)

5. Variable overhead spending variance = AH (AR – SR)
   3 500 ([25 000 ÷ 3 500] – 5.00) = $7 500 (U)

6. Variable overhead efficiency variance = SR (AH – SH)
   5(3 500 – 4 750) = $6 250 (F)

Test Your Knowledge

1.   What is meant by the term variance?   [1 mark]

2.   An examination of the cost records of Boom Champion CD Company reveals that the materials price variance is favourable but the materials quantity variance is unfavourable by a substantial amount. What might this indicate?   [4 marks]

3. Sacha Cosmetics produces a make-up called Fancy. The direct materials and direct labour standards for one sachet of Fancy are given below:

	Standard quantity or hours	Standard price or rate	Standard cost
Direct materials	7.2 ounces	$2.50 per ounce	$18
Direct labour	0.4 hours	$10 per hour	$4

Recently, the following activity was recorded:

- 20 000 ounces of material were purchased at a cost of $2.40 per ounce.
- All of the material was used to produce 2 500 sachets of Fancy.
- 900 hours of direct labour time were recorded at a total labour cost of $10 800.

Required:

a. Compute the direct materials price and quantity variances for the month. **[6 marks]**

b. Compute the direct labour rate and efficiency variances for the month. **[6 marks]**

Fixed overhead variances (expenditure, capacity, productivity and volume)

1. Expenditure (spending or fixed overhead flexible budget) = (actual expenditure – total budgeted expenditure)
2. Efficiency = (standard hours of production – actual hours worked) × fixed absorption rate
3. Productivity (denominator or output level) = (actual hours worked (denominator hours) – standard hours for actual production) × fixed overhead absorption rate
4. Volume = budgeted expenditure – (actual hours for production × fixed absorption rate)
5. Total = (actual overhead) – (standard hours of production) × fixed overhead absorption rate

Causes of manufacturing overhead variances

Causes of manufacturing overhead variances include:

1. higher than expected use of indirect materials, indirect labour and factory supplies
2. increases in indirect manufacturing costs such as fuel and maintenance costs
3. inefficient use of direct labour or machine breakdowns
4. lack of sales orders.

Accounting entries for variances

The rules are as follows:

1. Open an account for each type of variance.
2. Debit adverse variances.
3. Credit favourable variances.

Test Your Knowledge

1. Identify two fixed overhead variances. **[2 marks]**
2. Identify three causes of manufacturing overhead variances. **[3 marks]**
3. Give the formula for fixed overhead efficiency variance. **[3 marks]**
4. List the accounting rules for variances. **[3 marks]**

MULTIPLE CHOICE QUESTIONS

1. In a standard setting process exercise, industrial engineers:

   (A) determine the standard cost of direct materials

   (B) set the standard cost for direct labour

   (C) determine labour time requirements

   (D) accumulate data to determine how costs responds to changes in activity level.

2. The information used for setting the standard price for direct materials are:

   I   number and rates of pay

   II freight and purchases discount

   III purchase price, receiving and handling.

   (A) I

   (B) II

   (C) I and II

   (D) II and III

3. The information used for setting the direct labour time is:

   I   basic labour time per unit

   II fringe benefits

   III allowance for breaks and personal needs.

   (A) I

   (B) II

   (C) I and II

   (D) I and III

4. Which of the following documents is used to determine variances in a standard costing system?

   (A) Production cost report

   (B) Standard cost card

   (C) Job cost card

   (D) Stock card.

5. A company determines the standard for the use of materials in its operations without considering normal wastage and its labour with idle time in the making of its products. This is an example of:

   (A) ideal standards

   (B) minimum standards

   (C) practical standards SR(SH_AH)

   (D) variable standards.

6. The formula for the labour efficiency variance is:

   (A) (standard rate × standard hours) – (actual rate × actual hours)

   (B) (standard rate × actual hours) – (actual rate × actual hours)

   (C) (standard rate × standard hours) – (standard rate × actual hours)

   (D) (actual rate × standard hours) – (actual rate × actual hours)

Chapter 25

Cost volume profit (CVP) analysis

Objectives

At the end of this chapter you will be able to:

- discuss the role of CVP analysis
- outline the assumptions of CVP analysis
- calculate:
  - contribution margin unit value, total value and ratio
  - break-even point in units and dollars
  - required units and revenue to make a desired profit
- construct a CVP graph
- calculate the margin of safety in units, revenue and as a ratio
- discuss sensitivity analysis.

Cost volume profit (CVP) analysis is a management accounting tool used to evaluate the shifts in costs and volume and their resulting effects on profits. In evaluating the shifts, managers focus on interactions between elements such as prices of products, volume or level of activity, per unit variable costs, total fixed costs and mix of products sold.

CVP analysis facilitates planning, control and is a key factor in decision-making. Decisions include choice of product lines, pricing of products and services, marketing strategies and utilisation of revenue-generating production facilities.

This chapter reviews cost behaviour analysis first because it is a prerequisite to understand how costs behave in CVP. In addition, the five basic components of CVP analysis and the underlying assumptions of each are reviewed. Furthermore, the CVP income statement, concepts used in cost volume profit analysis, computing break-even point and using graphs to calculate the break-even point are also reviewed.

Cost behaviour analysis

Cost behaviour analysis studies how specific costs respond to changes in the level of business activity. The starting point in cost behaviour analysis is measuring the key business activities. You learnt in Chapter 13 about some of the key activity levels and of the changes in the level or volume of activity. The chapter indicated that the key activity levels should be correlated with changes in costs. Costs are classified into three categories: variable, fixed or mixed. The concepts of each will now be reviewed.

Variable costs

Variable costs are costs that vary in total directly and change in proportion to the activity level, that is, if the level increases by a percentage, the total variable costs will also increase by that percentage. Examples of variable costs include direct materials and direct labour for a manufacturer; cost of goods sold, sales commission, and freight-out for a merchandiser. Variable cost per unit is assumed to remain constant within the relevant range.

Fixed costs

Fixed costs are costs that remain the same (within the relevant range) in total regardless of changes in the activity level. Examples include property taxes, selling and administrative expenses, fixed factory overhead, insurance, rent, supervisory salaries and depreciation on buildings and equipment. An important concept to remember for fixed cost is that because it remains constant as activity changes, the fixed cost per unit varies inversely with activity.

Remember also that a lot of manufacturing firms now use more technology (fixed costs such as automation) and make less use of employee labour (variable costs). The change in use in each case results in depreciation and lease charges (fixed costs) increasing, and direct labour costs (variable costs) decreasing.

Relevant range (normal or practical range)

Relevant range is the range over which a company expects to operate during a year (or short term). The relevant range is the range of activity over which a variable cost remains constant on a per-unit basis and a fixed cost remains constant in total.

Mixed costs (semi-variable costs)

Mixed costs are costs that contain both variable and fixed elements. These costs change in total but not proportionately with changes in the activity level. Mixed costs must be classified into fixed and variable elements before they can be used in CVP analysis. The approach used by most firms to determine (classify) variable and fixed cost is the high-low method. This method uses the total costs incurred at the high and low levels of activity. The difference in costs between the high and low levels represents variable costs.

Test Your Knowledge

Required: Copy the table and classify the costs of items 1–7 under the headings: Fixed, Variable and Mixed.

1	Telephone bill based on a monthly rental of $26 plus different per calls made
2	Depreciation on factory machinery using straight line method
3	Production manager's salary
4	Direct material
5	Sales manager's commission
6	Direct labour
7	Rental cost on a warehouse

[7 marks]

CVP analysis

CVP analysis considers the effects (interrelationships) among five basic components: volume or activity, unit selling prices, variable cost per unit, total fixed costs and sales mix. The following assumptions underlie each CVP analysis.

1. The behaviour of costs and revenues are linear throughout the relevant range of volume, and they can be divided into variable and fixed elements (using the high-low method for mixed costs). The variable element is constant per unit, and the fixed element is constant in total over the entire relevant range.

2. Selling price is constant throughout the entire relevant range. The price of a product or service will not change as volume changes. Changes in activity are the only factors that affect costs.

3. In manufacturing companies, inventories do not change. The number of units produced equals the number of units sold.

4. When more than one type of product is sold, the sales mix will remain constant (that is, the percentage that each product represents of total sales will stay the same).

5. Changes in the level of revenues and costs arise only because of changes in the number of products units produced and sold.

6. Efficiency will remain constant; that is, during the period there are no productivity gains or losses.

CVP (variable costing) income statement

Earlier in this chapter, it was indicated that CVP is very important for internal decision-making. Therefore, you need to remember that accounting information for internal use should be reported in a CVP income statement format. The CVP income statement classifies cost as variable and fixed and computes a contribution margin. Contribution margin is the amount of revenue remaining after deducting variable costs. It is often stated both as a total amount and on a per unit basis. The CVP income statement should be reported in the following format:

	Total $	Per unit $
Sales (quantity of items)	x	$x
Variable costs	(x)	(x)
Contribution margin	X	x
Fixed costs	(x)	
Net income	X	

Don't forget

1. Sales, variable expenses and contribution margin are expressed on a per unit basis.
2. Fixed costs are deducted from the total column only.

Example

Briana Software Company data for accounting apps made are as follows:

Unit selling price of accounting apps	$600
Unit variable costs	$400
Total monthly fixed costs	$250 000
Units sold	2 000

Solution

Briana Software Company
CVP (Variable costing) Income Statement
For the month ended 31 December 2015

	Total $	Per unit $
Sales (2 000 accounting apps)	1 200 000	$600
Variable costs	(800 000)	(400)
Contribution margin	400 000	200
Fixed costs	(250 000)	
Net income	150 000	

Test Your Knowledge

Torres Video Company data for Riddim DVDs made for the 2015 Carnival are as follows:

Unit selling price of Riddim DVDs	$1 000
Unit variable costs	$600
Total monthly fixed costs	$200 000
Units sold	3 000

Required: Prepare a CVP (variable costing) income statement for Torres Video Company.   **[8 marks]**

Concepts/computations used in CVP

Operating income

1. Operating income = Total revenues from operations – (cost of goods sold + operating costs)
2. Net income = Operating income – income taxes

Contribution

Contribution is the difference between selling price and variable cost (which is the amount remaining after the deduction of variable costs). It is computed as follows:

Contribution = Sales – variable costs

Contribution margin per unit

Contribution margin per unit = Unit selling price – unit variable costs

Contribution margin ratio

Contribution margin ratio = Contribution margin per unit ÷ unit selling price

Computing break-even point

Break-even analysis

Break-even analysis is the process of finding break-even point. This analysis is useful in helping managers in making decisions such as whether to introduce new product lines, change sales prices on established products, or enter new market areas.

Break-even point

Break-even point is the level of activity at which total revenues equal total costs (both fixed and variable) and net income is zero. Break-even point can be computed from a mathematical equation, using contribution margin, or derived from a cost volume graph. The break-even point can be expressed either in sales units or sales dollars.

Mathematical equation (equation method or income statement approach)

This method represents the contribution approach (variable costing) income statement and shows the relationships among revenue, fixed cost, variable cost, volume and profit. The formula to express break-even point is as follows:

- Sales (x) − (variable expenses (x) − fixed expenses) = Net income

When rearranged the above equation produces the following expression (causing break-even profit to be zero):

- Sales = (variable expenses + fixed expenses) + operating profits

The formula for the sales break-even point in dollars is:

- Break even in units × unit selling price

Example

Sound off Company had fixed expenses of $40 000 per month and each boom boom box has a selling price of $3 000. The variable expenses are $1 500 per boom boom box.

Required

Compute:

a. Break-even point in units
b. Break-even point in sales
c. Using the above information prepare a variable costing income statement.

Solution

a. Break-even point in units
   Sales = (variable expenses + fixed expenses) + operating profits
   $3 000x = $1 500x + $40 000 + 0
   1 500x = $40 000
   X = 26.67 boom boom boxes

b. Break-even point in sales
   Break-even units × unit selling price
   26.67 boom boom boxes × $3 000 = $80 000

c. Variable costing income statement

Sound off Company

Income Statement

	$
Sales (27 × $3 000)	80 000
Variable cost (27 × $1 500)	(40 000)
Contribution	40 000
Fixed costs	40 000
Net profit	0

Key points to note

Remember that:

1. Sales represent the selling price per unit.
2. X represents the number of units sold or to be sold.
3. Fixed costs represent total fixed cost.
4. Variable costs represent variable cost per unit.
5. The variable costing income statement net profit is also zero.
6. The break-even point in sales may also be computed directly once the percentage relationship between variable expenses and sales are known. For example:

   Sales = variable expenses + fixed expenses + operating profit

   $X = S\%X + \text{fixed expenses} + 0$

   $X - S\%X = \text{fixed expenses}$

   $CM\%X = \text{fixed expenses}$

   $X = \text{fixed expenses} \div CM$ and VC%.

7. The break even in units sold can also be computed as follows:

   Break even in sales ÷ selling price per unit

Test Your Knowledge

Natalie Marc has fixed expenses of $30 000 per month and each chemical product has a selling price of $5000 and variable expenses are $2500 per chemical product.

Required:

1. Compute:
   a. Break even in units
   b. Break-even point in sales dollars.   [6 marks]
2. Prepare a CVP (variable costing) income statement.   [8 marks]

Contribution margin (unit contribution approach) technique

This approach centres on the idea that each unit sold provides a certain amount of contribution margin to cover fixed costs. The formula to calculate the break-even point in units is:

- Fixed expenses ÷ unit contribution margin (which is selling price – variable cost)

The formula to calculate break-even point in total sales dollars is:

- Fixed expenses ÷ contribution margin ratio (which is contribution margin per unit ÷ selling price per unit × 100)

Example			

C and D Enterprises manufacture and sell Galaxy mobile phones. The company's income statement for January 2015 is given below:

	Total $	Per unit $	Per cent
Sales (20 000 units)	1 200 000	60	100
Less variable expenses	900 000	45	??
Contribution margin	300 000	15	??
Less fixed expenses	240 000		
Net income	60 000		

Required

Compute the following:

a. Unit contribution margin ratio
b. Variable expense ratio
c. Break-even point in both units and sales dollars. Use the contribution margin technique.

Solution

a. Contribution margin (unit) ÷ selling price (unit) × 100 = 15 ÷ 60 × 100 = 25%

b. Variable expense (unit) ÷ selling price (unit) × 100 = 45 ÷ 60 × 100 = 75%

c. Units: fixed costs ÷ contribution margin per unit = 240 000 ÷ 15 = 16 000 units
   Dollars: fixed costs ÷ contribution margin ratio = 240 000 ÷ 25% = $960 000

Test Your Knowledge

Susan Company manufactures and sells a single product. The company's sales and expenses for February 2015 were as follows:

	Total $	Per unit $
Sales	600 000	40
Less variable expenses	420 000	28
Contribution margin	180 000	12
Less fixed expenses	150 000	
Net income	30 000	

Required: Using the contribution margin technique, compute the break-even point in both units and sales dollars.   **[6 marks]**

Graphs for calculating the break-even point

The break-even graph (CVP graph)

The break-even graph (CVP graph) also shows costs, volume and profits. The labelled CVP graph below (Figure 25.1) illustrates sales volume recorded along the horizontal axis. This axis should extend to the maximum level of expected sales. Both total revenues (sales) and total costs (fixed and variable) are recorded on the vertical axis.

Figure 25.1 Break-even graph (CVP graph)

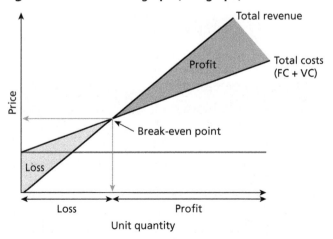

Steps for constructing a CVP graph

The steps for constructing a CVP graph are as follows:

1. Plot the total revenue line, starting at the zero activity level. Note that the revenue line is assumed to be linear throughout the full range of activity.
2. Plot the total fixed cost using a horizontal line. The fixed cost is the same at every level of activity.
3. Plot the total cost line. This starts at the fixed-cost line at zero activity. It increases by the variable cost at each level of activity. On the graph, the amount of the variable cost can be derived from the difference between the total cost and fixed cost lines at each level of activity.
4. Determine the break-even point from the intersection of the total cost line and the total revenue line. The break-even point in dollars is found by drawing a horizontal line from the break-even point to the vertical axis. The break-even point in units is found by drawing a vertical line from the break-even point to the horizontal axis.

Key points to note

1. The anticipated profit or loss at any given level of sales is measured by the vertical distance between the total revenue line (sales) and the total expenses line (variable expenses and fixed expenses).
2. The break-even point is where the total revenue and total expenses lines cross.
3. A CVP graph is useful because the effects of a change in any element in the CVP analysis can be quickly seen.

Profit graph

Profit focuses more directly on how profit changes with changes in volume. The profit graph is constructed in two steps. These steps are:

1. Locate total fixed expenses on the vertical axis, assuming zero level of activity. This point will be in the loss area.
2. Plot a point representing expected profit or loss at any chosen level of sales. After the point is plotted, draw a line through it back to the point on the vertical axis. This represents total fixed expenses. The break-even point is where the profit line crosses the break-even line.

Figure 25.2 Chart comparing total cost to total revenue

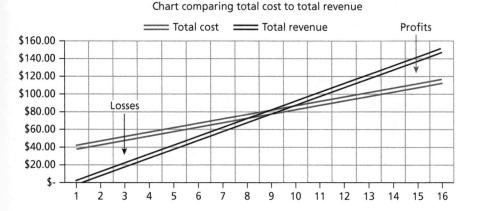

Key points to note

1. The vertical distance between the two lines represents the expected profit or loss at any given level of sales volume.
2. The vertical distance can be translated directly into dollars by referring to the profit and loss figures on the vertical axis.

Margin of safety

The margin of safety is the excess of budgeted (or actual) sales over break-even volume of sales. It states the amount by which sales can drop before losses begin to be incurred. The formula for margin of safety in dollars is as follows:

- Total sales – break-even sales

Margin of safety can also be expressed in percentage form. The percentage is obtained by:

- Margin of safety in dollars ÷ sales × 100

Example

Sound off Company
Income statement

	$
Sales (27 × $3 000)	80 000
Variable cost (27 × $1 500)	(40 000)
Contribution	40 000
Fixed costs	40 000
Net profit	0

Assume that Sound off Company actual (budgeted) sales for the Galaxy mobile phones is $150 000.

Required

You are required to compute:

1. Margin of safety in dollars
2. Margin of safety ratio.

Solution

1. Margin of safety in dollars = Actual sales – break-even sales = $150 000 – 80 000 = $70 000
2. Margin of safety ratio = Margin of safety in dollars ÷ actual sales × 100 = $70 000 ÷ $150 000 × 100 = 46.7%

Target net income (profit or target net profit analysis)

This is the income objective firms set for individual product lines. It indicates the sales necessary to achieve a specified level of income. The three approaches (equation method, contribution margin method and through graphic presentations) can be used to determine the required sales (either in sales units or sales dollars).

Equation method

The formula for this method has an amount for target net income added to the equation. Required sales are determined as follows:

- Variable costs + fixed costs + target net income

Example

Sound off Company had fixed expenses of $40 000 per month and each boom boom box has a selling price of $3 000. The variable expenses are $1 500 per boom boom box.

Required

Assuming that Sound off Company target net income is $120 000, compute:

a. Units of the target net income
b. Sales revenue for target net income.

Solution

a. Units of the target net income
$3 000 x = $1 500x + $40 000 + $120 000
$1 500 x = $160 000
X = 106.667 units

b. Sales revenue for target net income
107 × $3 000 = $321 000

Contribution margin technique

The sales required to meet a target net income can be computed in either units or dollars. The formula using the contribution margin per unit is as follows:
- (Fixed costs + target net income) ÷ contribution margin per unit

The formula for the contribution margin ratio is:
- (Fixed costs + target net income) ÷ contribution margin ratio

Example

C and D Enterprises manufacture and sell Galaxy mobile phones. The company's income statement for January 2015 is given below:

	Total $	Per unit $	Per cent
Sales (20 000 units)	1 200 000	60	100
Less variable expenses	900 000	45	??
Contribution margin	300 000	15	??
Less fixed expenses	240 000		
Net income	60 000		

Required

Compute the following:

1. Unit contribution margin ratio
2. Variable expense ratio
3. Break-even point in both units and sales dollars. Use the contribution margin technique
4. Assuming that the C and D Enterprises target net income is $100 000, determine the required sales in both units and sales dollars.

Solution

1. Contribution margin (unit) ÷ selling price (unit) × 100 = 15 ÷ 60 × 100 = 25%
2. Variable expense (unit) ÷ selling price (unit) × 100 = 45 ÷ 60 × 100 = 75%
3. Units: fixed costs ÷ contribution margin per unit = 240 000 ÷ 15 = 16 000 units
    Dollars: fixed costs ÷ contribution margin ratio = 240 000 ÷ 25% = $960 000
4. Units: fixed costs + target net income ÷ contribution margin per unit =
    240 000 + 100 000 ÷ 15 = 22 667 units
    Dollars: fixed costs + target net income ÷ contribution margin ratio =
    240 000 + 100 000 ÷ 25% = $1 360 000

Graphic presentation

The required sales to meet the target net income on a graph are shown as the distance between the sales line and the total cost line. Figure 25.3 shows the distance.

Figure 25.3 Graph to show required sales to meet the target net income

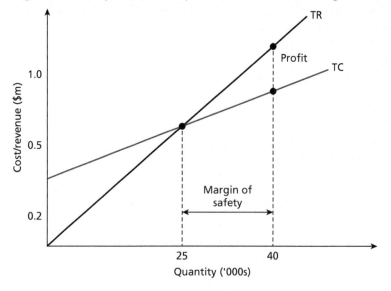

Key point to note

- Required sales are found by analysing the differences between the two lines until the desired net income is found.

Sensitivity analysis (incremental analysis)

The break-even point may increase or decrease, depending on particular changes that occur in the revenue and cost factors. The changes are evaluated, including the focus on factors that differ from one course of action or decision to another. Listed below are particular changes:

1. If there is an increase in total fixed cost or a decrease in unit contribution margin, the break-even point will increase.
2. Reductions in selling price, an increase in variable unit cost or a combination of the two would cause a decrease in contribution margin.
3. If there is a decrease in total fixed cost or an increase in unit contribution margin, the break-even point will decrease.
4. Any factor that causes a change in the break-even point will also cause a shift in total profits or losses at any activity level.

MULTIPLE CHOICE QUESTIONS

1. CVP is used to evaluate shift:

   I   in cost

   II in volume

   III in profits.

   (A) I

   (B) II

   (C) III

   (D) I, II and III

2. Wendy purchases smart phones at $2500 each and sells them for $6500 each. Her fixed costs are $100 000. How many smart phones will Wendy need to sell in order for her to break even?

   (A) 11

   (B) 15

   (C) 25

   (D) 40

3. George purchases accounting textbooks at $200 each and sells them for $450 each. His fixed costs are $40 000 and he wants to make a desired profit of $20 000. How many accounting textbooks will George need to sell in order to make the desired profit?

   (A) 133

   (B) 160

   (C) 200

   (D) 240

4. Prem manufactures Product S. The selling price is $50 and variable cost is $20 per unit. The fixed expenses for the month is $200 000. The contribution margin per unit is:

   (A) $20

   (B) $30

   (C) $50

   (D) $80

5. RRD Company manufactures preserved fruit. The company's projected total fixed cost for March is $150 000. Its unit selling price is $30 and contribution margin ratio is 20 per cent. What is the company's break-even sales revenue for March?

   (A) 25 000

   (B) 75 000

   (C) 750 000

   (D) 4 500 000

6. CAAI Company's unit variable cost is $30, total fixed cost is $42 000 and the contribution margin ratio is 20 per cent. What is the company's unit selling price?

   (A) $120.00

   (B) $37.50

   (C) $30.00

   (D) $6.00

Chapter 26

Capital budgeting techniques in investment decision-making

Businesses make decisions to spend lots of money (known as capital expenditures) on a daily basis. Common examples of expenditures are modernising of plant facilities, expanding operations or replacement of existing assets. Capital investment decisions are evaluated using discounted techniques. The process of making capital expenditure decisions is known as capital budgeting.

Capital budgeting is the process of generating, evaluating, selecting and following up on capital expenditures. Capital expenditures are expenditures incurred in obtaining, producing or enhancing assets (capital assets) that are expected to benefit (generate revenue) the firm for a period of time (usually longer than one year). These assets are tangible or intangible assets acquired for the purpose of providing a service to the business and not held for resale.

This chapter will review the skills for making useful capital investment decisions. The skills to be reviewed are known as capital expenditure appraisal. This appraisal is an evaluation of costs and benefits for a proposed investment in operating assets.

Objectives

At the end of this chapter you will be able to:

- understand the objectives of capital budgeting
- use the different methods to appraise various capital investment projects
- determine the advantages and disadvantages of each capital appraisal method
- assess the best-suited investment project based on the methods applied
- discuss the non-financial factors considered in making capital investment decisions.

Objectives of capital budgeting

Capital investment decisions play a significant part in the capital budgeting process, which is concerned with decision-making in areas such as determining:

- which specific investment projects the firm should accept
- the total amount of capital expenditure which the firm should undertake, and
- how projects should be financed.

Note: In making decisions, management must seek an optimum balance between risk and profitability because of the following effects:

1. A firm which invests in risky projects takes a chance that these projects may be unsuccessful.
2. The acceptance of risky projects lowers a firm's ability to survive in the future.

Therefore, the theory of capital budgeting reconciles a firm's goals of survival and profitability.

Minimum acceptable rate of return (hurdle rate, discount rate, cost of capital or cut-off rate)

Businesses have to ensure that all cash flows from investments are sufficient to cover the initial investments as well as providing a rate of return on investments that is in excess of the minimum acceptable return.

Initial investment of project

The initial investments of a project are all costs incurred in getting a project into a working condition. The following format can be used as a guideline in calculating the initial investment of a project:

- Initial investment = (cost of new project + installation cost) – (proceeds from sale or disposal of existing assets + taxes on sale of assets [if it is a tax saving])

Example

Ann Dass Incorporation buys a new machine for $2 000 000. Installation costs are $100 000, the existing machine has a book value of $150 000 and the firm is in the 25 per cent tax bracket. The company sells the existing asset for $150 000.

Required

1. Calculate the initial investment (indicate the tax effect and give reasons).
2. Assume that company sells the existing asset for $100 000:
   a. Calculate the initial investment.
   b. Compute the loss on sale.
   c. Calculate the tax savings.

Solution

1. Initial investment:

	$
Cost	2 000 000
Installation costs	100 000
Proceeds	(150 000)
Initial investment	1 950 000

There is no tax effect because the book value and the market value are the same.

2. Loss = Book value – proceeds = 150 000 – 100 000 = 50 000
   Tax savings = 50 000 × 25% = 12 500

	$
Initial investment:	
Cost	2 000 000
Installation costs	100 000
Proceeds	(100 000)
Taxes	(12 500)
Initial investment	1 987 500

Test Your Knowledge

KP buys new equipment for $1 500 000. Installation costs are $200 000, the existing equipment has a book value of $300 000 and the firm is in the 25 per cent tax bracket. The company sells the existing asset for $300 000.

Required: Calculate the initial investment.   **[6 marks]**

The effect of depreciation on initial investment

Depreciation is a non-monetary expense charged against the profits of a firm. It is a tax shield for capital budgeting decisions. The tax benefit is calculated as follows:

- Amount of depreciation deductible for tax purposes × tax rate

Example

Audrey Catering Company manufactures catering equipment. It is considering replacing an existing piece of equipment with more state-of-the art equipment. Audrey Catering Company gave the following information:

1. Existing equipment: this equipment was purchased 3 years ago for $300 000. The machine was depreciated using the straight line method with no residual value and a 5-year useful life. The machine can be sold on the market for its current value of $130 000.
2. The proposed equipment: this machine costs $360 000 and will depreciate over a 5-year period with no residual value. The installation cost of this new machine is $30 000.
3. The tax rate is 25 per cent.

Required

1. Calculate the book value of the existing equipment.
2. Calculate the profit or loss on the sale of the existing machine.
3. Compute the taxes on the profit to be paid from the sale.
4. Calculate the initial investment.

Solution

1. Book value of existing equipment:	$
Book value:	300 000
Accumulated depreciation (300 000 ÷ 5) × 3 years	(180 000)
Book value	120 000

2. Profit or loss on sale of the existing machine:	
Market value	130 000
Book value	(120 000)
Profit on sale	10 000

3. Taxes on profit:
   $10 000 × 25% = 2 500

4. Initial investment:	
Cost of new machine	360 000
Installation cost	30 000
Proceeds	(130 000)
Taxes	2 500
Initial investment	262 500

Evaluating capital investment proposals

Managers use several methods to evaluate capital budgeting decisions. Some methods involve predicting cash inflows and cash outflows of proposed investments, assessing the risks of and returns on flows and then choosing the investments to make. Future cash flows are restated in present value. This approach applies the time value of money. The process of restating future cash flows in present value is known as discounting.

In some companies, managers may apply evaluation methods that ignore present value. Managers use these methods to perform simple analyses of the financial feasibility of an investment's net cash flow. The formula for net cash flow is:
- Cash inflows – cash outflows

Common methods in this category are payback period and accounting rate of return.

Payback period (PBP) or payback time

An investment's payback period is the expected time period to recover the cash invested in a project. Companies desire a short payback period to increase return and reduce risk. The more quickly a company receives cash, the sooner it is available for other uses and the less time it is at risk of loss. A shorter payback period also improves the company's ability to respond to unanticipated changes and lowers its risk of having to keep an unprofitable investment.

Computing payback period is done with even cash flows or with uneven cash flows. The rule of thumb for both techniques for choice of a project is:
- Project that has the shorter payback period.

The reason for this is that project(s) with longer time period may be considered risky.

Key points to note

1. Payback ignores depreciation.
2. The payback period reflects the amount of time for the investment to generate enough cash flow to pay back the cash initially invested to purchase it.

Computing payback period with even cash flows

The payback period is expressed in years. Net cash inflow is the same every year. The formula for computing the payback period of an investment for even cash flows is:
- $\text{Payback period} = \dfrac{\text{Cost of investment}}{\text{Annual net cash flow}}$

Example

Franklyn intends to invest in a project that would have a 7-year life and require a $2 000 000 investment in equipment. At the end of the 7 years, the project would end and the equipment would have no salvage (scrap or trade-in) value. The project net cash flow for each year is $600 000. Franklyn's aim is to invest only in projects recovering initial outlays in less than 4 years.

Required

Compute the project's net present value. Advise Franklyn if the project is acceptable (include the reason for your choice).

Solution

$\text{Payback period} = \dfrac{\text{Cost of investment}}{\text{Annual net cash flow}}$

$2 000 000 ÷ 600 000 = 3.33 years

Franklyn should invest in the equipment because he will recover the initial investment in 3.33 years which is less than the 4 years.

Test Your Knowledge

Peter intends to invest in a project that would have a 5-year life and require a $1 000 000 investment in equipment. At the end of the 5 years, the project would end and the equipment would have no salvage value. The project net cash flow for each year is $300 000. Franklyn's aim is to invest only in projects recovering initial outlays in less than 3 years.

Required: Compute the project's net present value. Peter needs your advice on whether to accept or reject the project (include the reason for your suggestion).   **[8 marks]**

Computing payback period with uneven cash flows

Uneven cash flows refer to cash flows that are not all equal in amount. For this method, the payback period is computed using the cumulative total of net cash flows (which is the addition of each period's net cash flows). The format for the technique will look like this:

Period	Expected net cash flows $	Cumulative net cash flows $
Year 0	(xxxx)	(xxxx)
Year 1	xxxx	(xxxx)
Year 2	xxxx	(xxxx)
Payback period = 2 years		

Key points to note

Key points to note on the format are:

1. Year 0 refers to the period of initial investment in which the cash outflow occurs at the end of year 0 to acquire the asset.
2. At the end of year 1, the cumulative net cash flow is reduced because of the year's cash flow.
3. At the end of year 2, the investment is fully recovered.

Example		

Cheryl Joesph, a retiree, has been approached to invest $20 000. She is considering two investment projects as shown below:

Year	Investment A Annual cash flow $	Investment B Annual cash flow $
1	2 500	5 000
2	4 000	7 000
3	6 000	8 000
4	7 500	

Required
a. Compute the payback period for investment A.
b. Compute the payback period for investment B.
c. Advise Cheryl Joesph on which is the best investment to choose.

Solution

Year	Investment A		Investment B	
	Annual cash flow $	Cumulative cash flow $	Annual cash flow $	Cumulative cash flow $
0	(20 000)	(20 000)	(20 000)	(20 000)
1	+ 2 500	(17 500)	+ 5 000	(15 000)
2	+ 4 000	(13 500)	+ 7 000	(8 000)
3	+ 6 000	(7 500)	+ 8 000	(0)
4	+ 7 500			

Solution

a. The payback period for investment A is 4 years.

b. The payback period for investment B is 3 years.

c. Based on the payback period, Cheryl Joesph should choose investment B, which has a shorter payback period.

Test Your Knowledge

A machine cost $50 000. The table below shows forecast revenues and expenses for the next 4 years.

	Year	1	2	3	4
		$	$	$	$
Revenue		25 000	28 000	30 000	40 000
Machine running cost		4 800	5 400	6 000	7 500
Depreciation of machine		5 000	5 000	5 000	5 000
Interest on loan to buy the machine		3 300	3 000	2 800	2 400
Net profit on machine		11 900	14 600	16 200	25 100

Required: Compute the payback period for the machine.   **[10 marks]**

Advantages of payback method

The advantages of the payback method include the following:

1. The payback method is simple to use and understand.
2. The project with the shortest payback period is chosen because it reduces risk.
3. The method is easy to calculate.
4. It considers the timings of cash flows.
5. The method is useful for firms operating in markets that undergo fast change.

Disadvantages of payback method

The disadvantages of the payback method include the following:

1. The method ignores the time value of money.
2. It ignores longer-term profitability of projects (can encourage short-term thinking rather than long-term planning).
3. Ignores revenues and costs that occur after payback has been achieved.

Accounting rate of return

Accounting rate of return (ARR) (known as return on average investment) expresses a project's return on investment. It is also an indicator of profitability. ARR is the average annual net income from an investment expressed as a percentage of the average amount invested. The example below illustrates the concept of ARR.

Example

Skiffle Bunch purchased 10 G-pan steel pans for $200 000. The company uses the straight line method of depreciation for all G-pan steel pans. The useful life of these G-pan steel pans is 5 years and residual value is $10 000. The net income from these G-pan steel pans averages $20 000 per year.

To calculate the ARR:

Average investment = (Original cost + salvage value) ÷ 2

= ($200 000 + $10 000) ÷ 2 = $105 000

ARR = Average estimated income ÷ average investment

= $20 000 ÷ $105 000 × 100 = 19%

Rule of thumb

The factors that determine whether to accept or reject a project are given below:

Accept/invest	Reject/do not invest
• When the expected ARR exceeds the required rate of return.	• When the ARR is less than the required rate of return.

Example

Mr Thomas collected his pension of $500 000 and is considering two investment proposals which will produce profits over a 5-year period as follows:

Year	Estimated net profits per annum	
	Investment A $	Investment B $
1	7 000	5 000
2	8 000	4 000
3	5 000	8 000
4	6 000	6 000
5	7 500	2 000
Total	33 500	25 000

Required

Calculate the ARR and advise Mr Thomas on which investment to choose.

Solution

Workings:

Average profits per annum = Net profits ÷ number of years

Investment A
$33 500 ÷ 5 = $6 700

Investment B
$25 000 ÷ 5 = $5 000

ARR = Average profits ÷ average investment × 100

Investment A
$6 700 ÷ 250 000 × 100 = 2.68%

Investment B
5000 ÷ 250 000 × 100 = 2%

Based on the computations from ARR, we would advise that Mr Thomas choose investment A.

Test Your Knowledge

1. Evelyn Company is considering making a capital investment of $100 000 in additional machinery. The new machinery is expected to have a useful life of 5 years with $2 000 salvage value. Depreciation is computed by the straight line method. During the life of the investment, annual net income and cash inflows are expected to be $5 000 and $20 000, respectively. Calculate the accounting rate of return   **[8 marks]**

2. Deron Company is considering two new projects, each requiring a machine investment of $150 000. Each project will last for 3 years and produce the following profits.

Year	Project Y $	Project Z $
1	15 000	20 000
2	20 000	20 000
3	35 000	20 000
	70 000	60 000

The machine will have no salvage value at the end of its 3-year life. Deron Company uses straight life depreciation.
    a. Calculate the ARR for both projects.   **[10 marks]**
    b. Which project would you prefer and why?   **[3 marks]**

Advantages of accounting rate of return

The advantages of the accounting rate of return include the following:

1. It is simple to use and understand.
2. Takes into account the total earnings (measures profitability) of the project.
3. Considers the whole life of the project.
4. Easy to compare returns of different options.

Disadvantages of accounting rate of return

The disadvantages of the accounting rate of return include the following:

1. It ignores the time value of money.
2. Ignores the timing of the cash flow
3. Ignores the accrual concept of accounting
4. More difficult to calculate than payback.

Methods using time value of money

The two methods which help managers with capital budgeting decisions are net present value and internal rate of return (time-adjusted rate of return). Present and future values computations enable managers to measure or estimate the interest element of holding assets over time. The present value reveals the value of future assets today, whereas future values compute the value of present-day assets at a future date. Prepared present value tables or annuity tables are used to determine discounted values when making these calculations.

Net present value

In this method, the present value of all cash inflows is compared to the present value of all cash outflows that are associated with an investment project. The difference between the present values of cash flows and investment is called the net present value (NPV). Net present value determines whether or not the project is an acceptable investment. The approach used in the technique allows management of firms to evaluate the project's benefits and costs. These concepts will be reviewed, but first this chapter looks at the application approaches for even cash flows, uneven cash flows and the rule of the thumb for accepting or rejecting projects.

Salvage value, working capital and depreciation

Salvage value affects net present value analysis; in computing NPV, salvage values should be considered as an additional cash inflow and shown as such at the end of the final year of the asset's life, or as a reduction in the required investment.

In addition, some businesses may expand their working capital. Such needs should be treated as part of the initial investment in a project. Furthermore, projects requiring additional outlays for repairs and other additional operating costs should be treated as cash outflows. On the other hand, when a project is terminated, working capital released (example from the sale of inventory, receipt from receivables) should be treated as cash inflow.

NPV calculations do not include deductions for depreciation. They are based on inflows and outflows of cash and not on the accounting concepts of revenues and expenses. Depreciation is not a cash flow; it is a critical concept in computing net income for financial statements. It is a way of allocating the cost of a non-tangible asset to different periods.

Format (involving a variety of cash inflows and cash outflows)

	Year (s)	Amount of cash flows	Percentage factor	Present value of cash flows
Purchase of asset	Now	$(x)	1.000	$(x)
Working capital needed	Now	$(x)	1.000	$(x)
Overhaul (maintenance) of asset	indicate	(x)	Present value (see table)	(x)
Annual net cash inflows	1 – Number of years	X	Annuity (see table)	x
Salvage value of asset	End of the year	X	Present value (see table)	x
Working capital released	End of the year	X	Present value (see table)	X
Net present value				x

Example

Herry's company plans to buy a machine at a cost of $25 000. The machine will have savings in operating costs of $8 000 in its first year of use, $10 000 in its second year and $5 000 in its third year. The machine will then be sold at the end of year 4 for the sum of $6 000.

Herry's discount rate at 8 per cent is as follows:

Year	Discount factor
1	0.926
2	0.857
3	0.794

Required

Calculate the NPV of the investment.

Solution

Year	Inflow	Discount factor	Present value
1	8 000	0.926	7 408
2	10 000	0.857	8 570
3	5 000	0.794	3 970
4	6 000	0.794	4 764
Total discounted cash flows			24 712
Investment			(25 000)
Net present value			(288)

Format (involving even cash flows)

	Year (s)	Amount of cash flow	(x%) factor	Present value factor
Annual net cash inflow	1 – number of years	$ x	Annuity (see table)	$ x
Initial investment	Now	$(x)	1.000	($x)
Net present value				$x

The formula to compute NPV is:
* Net present value = Present value of discounted cash flows – amount invested

Example

Susie intends to invest in a project that would have a 7-year life and require a $2 000 000 investment in equipment. At the end of the 7 years, the project would end and the equipment would have no salvage value. The project net cash flow for each year is $600 000. Susie's cost of capital is 18 per cent.

Required

Compute the project's net present value. Advise Susie if the project is acceptable. (Give the reason for your choice.)

Solution

Items	Year(s)	Amount of cash flows $	18% factor	Present value of cash flows $
Cost of new equipment	Now	(2 000 000)	1.000	(2 000 000)
Net annual cash flow	1–7	600 000	3.812	2 287 200
Net present value				287 200

Susie should accept the project since it has a positive NPV of $287 200.

Test Your Knowledge

John is studying to invest in a project that would have a 10-year life and requires a $2 500 000 investment in machinery. At the end of 10 years, the project would end and the machinery would have no salvage value. The project net cash flow for each year is $500 000. John's cost of capital is 16%.

Required: Compute the project's net present value. Advise John if the project is acceptable. (Give a reason for your choice.) **[6 marks]**

Rule of thumb

The factors that determine whether to accept or reject a project are given below.

Accept project	Reject project
• When an asset's expected cash flows are discounted and yield a positive (greater) net present value.	• When an asset's expected cash flows are discounted and yield a negative (lower) net present value.
• When an asset's expected cash flows are discounted and equals zero.	

Key points to note

1. Use the annuity table when the cash flow is the same for each year.
2. To choose a preferred project, choose the one that yields the highest net present value.
3. Examples of cash outflows are initial investment (including installation costs), increased working capital needs, repairs and maintenance and incremental costs.
4. Examples of cash inflows are incremental revenues, reduction in costs salvage value, and release of working capital.

Advantages of net present value

The advantages of net present value include the following:

1. Considers the time value of money
2. Recognises income over the entire life of the project
3. Deals with risk by discounting future cash flow more heavily.

Disadvantages of net present value

The disadvantages of net present value include the following:

1. Difficulty in estimating the initial cost of the project and the time periods in which instalments must be paid back
2. Difficult to estimate accurately the net cash flow for each year of the project's life
3. Time-consuming to calculate
4. Based on an arbitrary interest rate
5. Difficult to understand.

Internal rate of return (IRR) or time-adjusted rate of return

Internal rate of return (IRR) is another technique used by a business to evaluate capital investments. The return can be defined as the interest yield promised by an investment project over its useful life. IRR equals the rate that yields an NPV of zero for an investment.

This technique is used to evaluate the risk of an investment (project) and assess the uncertainty of future cash flows. To do this, a predetermined hurdle rate is selected by management to compare and evaluate capital investment. Acceptance or rejection of projects will depend on the actual returns from the comparison of projects (to see if the result shows IRR higher or lower than the hurdle rate).

The firm computes the total present value of a project's net cash flows using the IRR as the discount rate and then subtracts the initial investment from this total present value to get a zero NPV. This chapter will now review the application approaches for even cash flows, uneven cash flows and the rule of thumb for accepting or rejecting projects.

Even cash flows

IRR for even cash flows can be computed in a two-step process. The steps are as follows:

1. Compute the present value factor for the investment project. The formula is as follows:

$$\text{Present value factor} = \frac{\text{Amount invested}}{\text{Net cash flows}}$$

2. Identify the discount rate (IRR) yielding the present value factor. The process is as follows:

   Search the interest table for a present value or annuity factor equal to the amount calculated in 1 above in the relevant year row. (The discount rate implies that the IRR is approximately (x%).)

Key points to note

When the present value factor is not exactly equal to the discount factor, carry out the following steps:

1. Search the interest table for upper and lower present value factors near to the present value factor.
2. Find the difference between the upper and lower present value factors identified in 1 above.
3. Determine the IRR by using the following formula:

$$\text{Discount rate of lower NPV} + \frac{\text{difference of rate of NPVs} \times \text{lower NPV}}{(\text{lower NPV} - \text{higher NPV})}$$

Format (involving even cash flows)

	Year(s)	Amount of cash flow	(x %) factor	Present value of cash flows
Annual cash flow	1 – number of years	$ x	Annuity (see table)	$
Initial investment	Now	($x)	1.000	($x)
Net present value				$x

Example

Karlisha Company is thinking of a project that would have a 6-year life and require $2 000 000 investment in equipment. At the end of 6 years, the project would terminate and the equipment would have no salvage value. The project would provide net income each year as follows:

	$	$
Sales		4 000 000
Less variable expenses		2 800 000
Contribution margin		1 200 000
Less fixed expenses:		
Out-of-pocket expenses	600 000	
Depreciation	300 000	
Total fixed expenses		900 000
Net income		300 000

Required

Compute the project's internal rate of return to one decimal place.

Solution

Net annual cash flow = Net income + depreciation

300 000 + 300 000 = $600 000

Factor of the internal rate of return = Investment required ÷ net annual cash inflow

$2 000 000 ÷ 600 000 = 3.333

Search for factor on annuity table for 6-year period.

18%		3.498	3.498
True factor		3.333	
22%			3.167
Difference		0.165	0.331

IRR = 18% + (0.165 ÷ 0.331 × 4%) = 18.2%

Test Your Knowledge

Jackie Company intends to invest in a project that would have a 5-year life and requires a $1 500 000 investment in a machine. At the end of the 5 years, the project would end and the machinery would have no salvage value. The net income each year is as follows: $400 000.

Compute the project's IRR to one decimal place.   **[6 marks]**

Uneven cash flows

When cash flows are uneven, a trial and error approach is used to compute the IRR. This is done by selecting any reasonable discount rate to compute the NPV.

Note: The NPV result must end in different signs (positive and negative) because using IRR, the NPV is zero and IRR lies between two discount rates. Assume that the amounts result in positive (negative), re-compute until the results end differently (positive and negative).

Key points to note

1. IRR is used to evaluate a project.
2. To accept or reject a project the rule of thumb given below should be followed.
3. Internal rate of return – hurdle rate.

Rule of thumb

The factors that determine whether to accept or reject a project are as follows:

Accept project	Reject project
• If IRR is higher (greater) than the hurdle rate.	• If IRR is lower (lesser) than the hurdle rate.
• If IRR is equal to zero.	

Advantages of internal rate of return

The advantages of internal rate of return are as follows:

1. Recognises the time value of money
2. Recognises income over the whole life of the project
3. Expressed as a percentage return, which is useful in ranking alternative projects
4. Emphasis is placed on liquidity.

Disadvantages of internal rate of return

The disadvantages of internal rate of return are as follows:

1. Assumes that earnings are re-invested at the IRR
2. Difficult to determine which of two suitable rates to adopt unless a computer is used
3. It gives an approximate rate of return only.

Summary of techniques

A summary of techniques reviewed in this chapter is given in Table 26.1.

Table 26.1 Summary of techniques reviewed

Technique	What is measured	Acceptance criterion
Payback	The period of time (in years and months) required to recover the initial investment and from the future net cash flows and residual value	The project with the shortest payback period (if it is lower than the firm's benchmark payback)
Accounting rate of return (ARR)	The percentage return of average future net profit over average capital expenditure (including any working capital and outlay)	The project with the highest rate (if it is above the firm's benchmark rate)
Net present value (NPV)	The difference between present value of future net cash flows and initial outlay	The project with the highest positive NPV
Discounted payback	The time (in years and months) required to recover the capital outlay from the present value of future net cash flows and residual value	The project with the shortest payback period (if it is lower than the firm's benchmark payback)
Internal rate of return (IRR)	The rate (%) that causes the initial outlay to be equal to the present value of future net cash flows OR The rate (%) that makes the NPV equal to zero	The project with highest rate (if it is above the firm's benchmark rate)

Non-financial (qualitative or non-quantitative) factors

Investment decisions are not only measured by financial factors, but also by non-financial factors generalised as environmental and social factors. Some non-financial/qualitative examples are:

- quality of output/process
- decrease in waste of resources and time
- decrease in production and delivery time
- increase in customer satisfaction
- better working conditions such as osha
- environmental concerns such as pollution
- corporate image.

MULTIPLE CHOICE QUESTIONS

1. Capital budgeting is the process of:
   - I generating and evaluating capital expenditures
   - II selecting and following up on revenue expenditures
   - III making capital expenditure decisions.

   (A) I

   (B) I and II

   (C) I and III

   (D) II and III

2. The elements used to compute the initial investment (capital outlay) for a project are the:
   - I cost of the new project
   - II installation cost
   - III disposal of existing assets.

   (A) I

   (B) II

   (C) III

   (D) I, II and III

3. Which of the following methods ignore the time value of money?
   - I payback period
   - II accounting rate of return (ARR)
   - III internal rate of return (IRR).

   (A) I

   (B) I and II

   (C) I and III

   (D) II and III

4. Which of the following methods ignore depreciation?
   - I payback period
   - II net present value (NPV)
   - III accounting rate of return (ARR).

   (A) I

   (B) I and II

   (C) I and III

   (D) II and III

5. Which of the following methods considers the time value of money?
   - I internal rate of return (IRR)
   - II accounting rate of return (ARR)
   - III net present value (NPV).

   (A) I

   (B) II

   (C) I and II

   (D) I and III

ANSWERS FOR MULTIPLE CHOICE QUESTIONS

UNIT 1: FINANCIAL ACCOUNTING

Module 1: Accounting Theory, Recording and Control Systems

CHAPTER 1
ACCOUNTING FUNDAMENTALS

1. D
2. A
3. C
4. A
5. C
6. D

CHAPTER 2
RECORDING ACCOUNTING INFORMATION

1. D
2. B
3. B
4. A
5. C
6. A
7. A

CHAPTER 3
ACCOUNTING AND ADMINISTRATIVE CONTROLS SYSTEM

1. D
2. A
3. C
4. A
5. B
6. D

Module 2: Preparation of Financial Statements

CHAPTER 4
FORMS OF BUSINESS ORGANISATIONS

1. C
2. C
3. D
4. A
5. B

CHAPTER 5
PREPARATION AND PRESENTATION OF STATEMENT OF COMPREHENSIVE INCOME (INCOME STATEMENT) AND THE STATEMENT OF RETAINED EARNINGS

1. B
2. B
3. D
4. C
5. B
6. A
7. A

CHAPTER 6
PREPARATION OF FINANCIAL STATEMENTS

1. A
2. A
3. D
4. D
5. C
6. C
7. D

CHAPTER 7
ACCOUNTING FOR PARTNERSHIPS

1. C
2. D
3. A
4. C
5. D
6. C
7. D

Module 3: Financial Reporting and Interpretation

CHAPTER 8
PREPARATION OF CASH FLOW STATEMENT (Indirect Method Only)

1. C
2. A
3. A
4. C
5. D

CHAPTER 9
FINANCIAL STATEMENT ANALYSIS: RATIOS

1. D
2. A
3. C
4. A
5. C

CHAPTER 10
NOTES, DISCLOSURES AND POST BALANCE SHEET EVENTS, RECEIVERSHIP AND LIQUIDATION

1. B
2. C
3. B
4. D
5. A
6. C
7. B
8. A

UNIT 2: COST AND MANAGEMENT ACCOUNTING

Module 1: Costing Principles

CHAPTER 11
INTRODUCTION TO COST AND MANAGEMENT ACCOUNTING

1. C
2. B
3. A
4. D
5. B

CHAPTER 12
MANUFACTURING ACCOUNTS PREPARATION

1. A
2. C
3. D
4. A
5. C

CHAPTER 13
COST CLASSIFICATION AND COST CURVES

1.	D	4.	A
2.	A	5.	D
3.	D	6.	C

CHAPTER 14
ELEMENTS OF COST: MATERIALS

1.	B	4.	B
2.	A	5.	C
3.	D		

CHAPTER 15
ELEMENTS OF COST: LABOUR

1.	C	4.	B
2.	A	5.	C
3.	D		

CHAPTER 16
ELEMENTS OF COST: OVERHEADS

1.	B	4.	C
2.	A	5.	D
3.	C	6.	A

CHAPTER 17
DECISION-MAKING

1.	A	4.	D
2.	B	5.	D
3.	A		

Module 2: Costing Systems

CHAPTER 18
TRADITIONAL COSTING VS. ACTIVITY BASED COSTING

1.	D	4.	D
2.	A	5.	C
3.	A		

CHAPTER 19
JOB COSTING

1.	B	4.	A
2.	B	5.	D
3.	C	6.	D

CHAPTER 20
PROCESS COSTING

1.	D	4.	C
2.	C	5.	D
3.	B		

CHAPTER 21
SERVICE SECTOR COSTING

1.	C	5.	A
2.	C	6.	B
3.	A	7.	B
4.	D		

CHAPTER 22
MARGINAL COSTING VS. ABSORPTION COSTING TECHNIQUES

1.	C	4.	C
2.	D	5.	D
3.	A		

Module 3: Planning and Decision-Making

CHAPTER 23
BUDGETING

1.	D	4.	D
2.	C	5.	A
3.	D	6.	B

CHAPTER 24
STANDARD COSTING AND VARIANCES

1.	C	4.	B
2.	D	5.	A
3.	D	6.	C

CHAPTER 25
COST VOLUME PROFIT (CVP) ANALYSIS

1.	D	4.	B
2.	C	5.	C
3.	D	6.	B

CHAPTER 26
CAPITAL BUDGETING TECHNIQUES IN INVESTMENT DECISION-MAKING

1.	C	4.	B
2.	D	5.	D
3.	B		

Index

A

ABC. *See* Activity based costing (ABC)
Abnormal gain, 172
Abnormal loss, 172
Absorption costing, marginal costing *vs.*, 188–191
Absorption rates, overhead, 145
Accounting cycle, 3
Accounting information, 2
Accounting rate of return (ARR), 238–239, 240
Accrual basis accounting
    cash basis accounting *vs.*, 3
Accruals, 14–15
Activity based costing (ABC), 162–163
    in service sector industries, 181
Activity ratios, 88
Adjusting entries
    expense account, closing off, 13
    inventories, 12
    revenue account, closing off, 13–14
Agreement
    partnership, 63–64
    security, 104
ARR. *See* Accounting rate of return (ARR)
Assets
    contingent, 100
    investment in partnership, 65–67
    non-current, purchase of, 21
    recording of, 20
Avoidable costs, 117

B

Balance sheet, 50, 112
    post events, standard accounting practice for, 101
Bank reconciliation statement, 55–56
Bankrupt, 104
Bankruptcy, causes for, 104
Basket price, 21
Bonuses, 66–67, 135–136
Bonus issue, of shares, 19
Break-even analysis, 224
Break-even graph, 226–227
Break-even point, 224
    formula to calculate, 224–225
Budget/budgeting, 195–204
    capital. *See* Capital budgeting
    cash, 202–203
    control, 195
    direct materials purchases, 200–202
    master, 197
    preparation of, 197–203
    process of, 195
    production, 199
    purpose/objectives of, 195
    sales, 198

    standards *vs.*, 207
    static *vs.* flexible, 212–214
Budget committee, 195–196
Buffer stock, 123
Business organisations, 33–35
    advantages and disadvantages of, 34
    government-run, characteristics of, 34
    non-profit, financial statements preparation for, 58
    private sector, 33–34

C

Capital budgeting, 233
    decisions, evaluation of, 236–240
    internal rate of return and, 244–246
    net present value and, 241–243
    objectives of, 233–235
Capital reserves, 20
Cash basis accounting
    accrual basis accounting *vs.*, 3
Cash budget, 202–203
Cash collection schedule, 198
Cash equivalents, 76
Cash flow statement, 76–78
    format for, 79–81
    limitations of, 77–78
    objective of, 76
    presentation of, 76–77
Commissions, 136
Comparability, accounting information, 7
Comprehensive income statement, 43–45, 58
Conceptual Framework, 6–8
    assumptions, 7
    constraints, 8
    principles of, 8
Consistency, accounting information, 7
Contingent assets, 100
Contingent liability, 100
Contribution margin technique, 225, 229
Cost accounting, 108
Cost accumulation, 182
Cost allocation, 182
Cost behaviour, 116
Cost behaviour analysis
    fixed costs and, 220
    variable costs and, 220
Cost curves, 118–120
Cost driver per unit, in service sector industries, 180–181
Cost of goods manufactured schedule, 113
Costs
    classification, 116–117
    and decision-making, 117
    defined, 116
    fixed, 220
    idle time, 129
    of inventories, 39–40
    inventory carrying, 123–124

inventory ordering, 123
labour. *See* Labour
materials, 122–127
mixed, 221
overheads, 139–145
overtime premium, 129–130
period, 116
planning/control and, 117
product, 116
traceable, 116
variable, 220
Cost volume profit (CVP) analysis, 220–230
income statement, 222
Current cost accounting, 97
CVP analysis. *See* Cost volume profit (CVP) analysis
CVP graph, 226–227

D

Day work methods, labour remuneration, 131
Decision-making, 148–154
and adding/dropping product/service/department, 152–153
costs and, 117
make-or-buy method, 150–151
qualitative factors and, 154
special orders and, 148–149
terms/characteristics critical in, 148
Deferrals, 14–15
Depreciation, calculation of, 13–14
Differential piece rate, 134–135
Direct allocation method, 139–140
Direct costs, 116
Direct labour, 129
overhead absorption rate, 159–161
Direct labour price standard, 210
Direct materials price standard, 208–209
Direct materials purchases budget, 200–202
Due Process, 4

E

Economic order quantity (EOQ), 123–125
computation of, 124
Equity, 17
owner's, statement of, 49
Equivalent units, 172
Expense account, closing off, 13
External auditors, internal auditors *vs.*, 29

F

Fair value measurement, 97
Fidelity bond, 26
FIFO (first-in, first-out) method, 173–176
Financial accounting, 108
management accounting *vs.*, 108
Financial analysis, 86–92
activity ratios, 88
liquidity ratios, 86
profitability ratios, 87
solvency ratios, 87–88
vertical *vs.* horizontal, 89–92
Financial reporting, users' needs for, 2
Financial statements. *See also* specific statements
analysis of. *See* Financial analysis
elements of, 7
formats within different industries, 112
general purpose, 2
from incomplete records, 51–54
for non-profit organisations, 58
preparation of, 4–5, 49–58
published, 102–103
Financing activities, cash flow statement, 77
Fixed costs, 116
and cost behaviour analysis, 220
Flat time/time rates, 131
Flexible budgets, static budgets *vs.*, 212–214
Fringe benefits, 129
labour, 130

G

Generally Accepted Accounting Principles (GAAP), 2, 26
General purpose financial statements, 2
Goodwill method, 66
Government-run business organisations, 34

H

Hazardous materials, 127
High day method, remuneration, 131
Horizontal financial analysis, vertical financial analysis *vs.*, 89–92

I

IASB (International Accounting Standards Board), 4
IASC (International Accounting Standards Committee), 4
ICAC. *See* Institute of Chartered Accountants of the Caribbean (ICAC)
Ideal standard, 212
Idle time cost, 129
Illiquid, 104
Incentives, 130
bonuses, 135–136
Income, determination of, 116–117
Income statement, 112
comprehensive, 43–45, 58
CVP analysis, 222
Indirect costs, 116
assignment of, 157–158
Indirect labour, 129
Inflation, 97
Insolvent firm, 104
Institute of Chartered Accountants of the Caribbean (ICAC)
members of, 4–5
Internal auditors *vs.* external auditors, 29

Internal control systems, 25–30
    limitations to, 29
    objectives of, 25
    principles of, 25–28
Internal rate of return (IRR), 244–246
Inventoriable costs, 116
Inventories, 12, 38–41
    costs of, 39–40
    purchasing cost of, 123
    valuation, 38, 39, 116–117
Inventory carrying costs, 123–124
Inventory ordering costs, 123
Investing activities, cash flow statement, 76
Investments
    assets, in partnership, 65–67
    initial, 233–235
    payback period, 236–238
IRR. *See* Internal rate of return (IRR)

J

Job costing, 165–168
    calculation of, 166–167
    in service sector industries, 181, 182

L

Labour, 129–136
    direct, 129
    fringe benefits, 130
    impact due to technology changes, 136
    indirect, 129
    remuneration, 131–136
Labour variances, 215
Liabilities
    contingent, 100
    recording of, 22
Limited liability company, partnership company sold to,
    72–73
Liquidity ratios, 86

M

Make-or-buy method, 150–151
Management accounting, 108
    in service sector industries, 180
    vs. financial accounting, 108
Manufacturing industries, 111
Manufacturing overheads, 157
Marginal costing *vs.* absorption costing, 188–191
Margin of safety, 228
Mark-up pricing, in service sector industries, 183–184
Master budget, 197
Materials
    hazardous, 127
    raw, 122–126
Material variances, 215
Measured day method, remuneration, 131
Members, organisation, 33
Merchandising industries, 111

Mixed costs, 116
    and cost behaviour analysis, 221

N

Net present value (NPV), 241–243
Net realisable value (NRV), 39
Non-cash transactions, from cash flow statement, 77
Non-profit organisations, financial statements
    preparation for, 58
Normal loss, 172
NPV. *See* Net present value (NPV)
NRV. *See* Net realisable value (NRV)

O

OAR. *See* Overhead absorption rate (OAR)
Objectives, accounting information, 6
Obligating event, 98
Operating activities, cash flow statement, 76
Over-absorption of overheads, 145, 168
Overhead absorption rate (OAR), 158–159
    calculation of, 161
    direct labour, 159–161
Overheads, 139–145
    analysis sheet, 158
    manufacturing, 157
    over-absorption of, 145, 168
    services departments. *See* Services departments
    under-absorption of, 145, 168
Overhead variances, 216
    fixed, 217
Overtime premium cost, 129–130
Owner's equity, statement of, 49

P

Pacioli, Luco, 2
Partners, 33
    admission in partnership company, 65–68
    retirement of, 69
Partnership Act (1890), 63
Partnership agreement, 63–64
Partnership company
    admission of partners in, 65–68
    agreement in, 63–64
    creation/formation of, 61–62
    dissolution of, 69–73
    investment of assets in, 65–67
    sale to limited liability company, 72–73
Payback period (PBP), 236–238
Period costs, 116
Piece rates method, 132–136
    differential, 134–135
    with guaranteed pay, 133–134
POHR. *See* Predetermined overhead rates (POHR)
Practical standard, 212
Predetermined overhead rates (POHR), 158–159
Private sector business organisations, 33–34
Process costing, 172

report, 172–176
    in service sector industries, 181, 184
Product costs, 116
Production budget, 199
Profitability ratios, 87
Profit graph, 227–228
Proprietor, 33
Provisions, 98–100
    recognising, circumstances for, 99–100
    usage of, 99
Purchasing cost of inventory, 123

Q

Qualitative characteristics, accounting information, 6–7

R

Ratios
    activity, 88
    calculations, 90
    liquidity, 86
    profitability, 87
    solvency, 87–88
Raw materials, 122–126
    recording steps, 122
Receivership process, 104–105
Reciprocal method, 141–142
Relevance, of accounting information, 6
Relevant range, 220
Reliability, of accounting information, 6–7
Remuneration, 130
    commission, 136
    day work methods, 131
    labour, 131–136
    piece rates method, 132–136
Repeated distribution method, 142–143
Reporting period, events after, 101
Reserves, 20
Retained earnings, 42
Revenue, 16, 37
    categories of, 37
Revenue account, closing off, 13–14
Revenue reserves, 20
Rights issue, of shares, 19

S

Sales budget, 198
Scrap value, 172
Secured creditor, 104
Security agreement, 104
Sensitivity/incremental analysis, 230
Sequential allocation method, 140–141
Service industries, 111
Services departments
    direct allocation method, 139–140
    reciprocal method, 141–142
    repeated distribution method, 142–143
    step-down method, 140–141

Service sector industries
    characteristics of, 180
    cost driver per unit, determination of, 180–181
    costing methods, 181–184
    difficulties associated with, 180–181
    management accounting in, 180
    mark-up pricing in, 183–184
    types of, 180
Shares, issuance of, 17–19
Small and medium-sized entities (SMEs), 4
SOCI. *See* Statement of comprehensive income (SOCI)
SOFP. *See* Statement of financial position (SOFP)
Solvency ratios, 89–90
Special orders, and decision-making, 148–149
Standard costing system, 207
    advantages/disadvantages of, 207
    setting, 208
Standard hours per unit, 210–211
Standards
    ideal, 212
    practical, 212
    vs. budgets, 207
Statement of cash flow. *See* Cash flow statement
Statement of comprehensive income (SOCI), 43–45, 58
Statement of financial position (SOFP), 50, 58, 112
Statement of owner's equity, 49
Step-down method, 140–141
Straight piece rate, 132–133

T

Target net income, 228–229
Total standard cost per unit, 211
Traceable costs, 116
Transactions
    recording, 11

U

Unavoidable costs, 117
Under-absorption of overheads, 145, 168
Understandability, accounting information, 7

V

Variable cost, 116
    and cost behaviour analysis, 220
Variance analysis, 214
Variances, 215
    accounting entries for, 217
    calculate, formulae to, 215–216
Vertical financial analysis *vs.* horizontal financial
    analysis, 89–92

W

Waste material, 127
Weighted average method, 172–173
Work-in-process (WIP), 165, 172
    calculation of, 166–167